ERIKA AND THE KING

ERIKA
AND THE
KING

By ERIKA LEUCHTAG

Coward-McCann, Inc.
New York

To the memory of Tribhuvana Rex,
King of Nepal

Contents

ONE

"O Jewel in the Lotus Flower!"

13

TWO

The Shrine of the Blue-Necked Narain

147

THREE

"The Flower Is Sweet and Beautiful"

205

FOUR

"A Light Shining from His Forehead"

247

Illustrations

Following page 128

King Tribhuvana in his coronation robes

The swimming pool in the royal palace

The first meeting between King Tribhuvana and his Prime Minister

King Tribhuvana as a "prisoner"

King Tribhuvana in his Durbar Hall

The "Shirt Ceremony" at Patan

The Buddhist temple of Bodhnath

The Maharaja Mohun Shamsher Yung Bahadur Rana, Prime Minister of Nepal

The Bura-Nilkanta (the blue-necked Lord Vishnu)

King Tribhuvana listening to the Indian Ambassador

At the wedding of Princess Bharati of Nepal

King Tribhuvana with Pandit Nehru

The cremation of King Tribhuvana

The author with a statuette of Maha Vishnu

THIS book is the fulfillment of a promise made eight years ago in a royal palace known as the Happy Cottage, in a Himalayan valley that the Nepalese call the Tank of Serpents. It was made to a king who was the incarnation of the Lord Vishnu, but who was as much a prisoner as the caged birds outside his bedroom windows. He had given me a bracelet. I have it still. It is a broad band of golden mesh, so flexible that it can be crushed or folded like silk. Twenty elliptical discs of thin gold are cunningly hooked to the mesh, and it is very heavy and very beautiful.

For days I wondered how I might repay him, not in the value of the gift, but in the spirit of its giving. Then I began to write a fairy story. I wrote on the coarse, cinnamon-colored paper of Nepal, using the typewriter which my mother had given me when I left Simla. I wrote in the early mornings, not long after dawn, at the hour when a little Nepalese girl would slip into my garden to pick marigolds for her prayer tray, thinking herself unseen.

When the story was finished I called it *The Young King and the Golden Bracelet*. It told of the King and myself, of his queens and his princesses. It told of his country and the Serpent who kept him a prisoner in the Happy Cottage. I wrote of the past and the present and the future, and what I wrote of the future was to come strangely true. Names I disguised by reversing the order of their spelling, but, when I read the story to him, the King's quick intelligence recognized them, and he cried out, "But that is I, Erika! And that is you!"

He asked if he might keep the story, and I placed it in his hand. I said, "It was written for you, but I promise you, one day the whole world will know your story."

E. L.

November, 1957

One

"O JEWEL IN THE LOTUS FLOWER!"

THE letter came from Katmandu and had been written on Christmas Eve, 1948. It was typed on fine, handmade paper and signed by a European doctor whom I had once met in Simla, and whose face I could now scarcely remember.

> DEAR MISS LEUCHTAG, [he wrote] I am writing to you officially (and in a hurry) to ask if you would be prepared to come here to give regular massage to a very highly placed lady. I suggested your name and I was asked to find out from you what your terms would be and for how long you would come. I am leaving this place on Monday so please write to my Calcutta address.

I was staying in Patiala as the guest of the Maharani and there I was content, I suppose, as content as it has ever been possible for me to be. In the beginning the letter was a faint disturbance only of that contentment. It was perhaps some days before curiosity changed to urgent compulsion. Katmandu, I knew, was the capital of Nepal, and Nepal was a Himalayan kingdom where the British recruited their Gurkhas, and where men climbed Everest. More than this I did not know. It was the initial curiosity that made me write to the doctor, asking for the name of his highly placed lady, asking him to tell me something about Katmandu. I wrote also to my mother in Simla, and her reply came to me like a little cloud of worry. Did I not realize, she said, that

Nepal was a forbidden land, its people and princes hostile to
foreigners, and that to reach it one had to *walk* across mountains seven thousand feet high? You shall not go, she said.
Do not go. . . . Everybody was to say this. Only the
Maharani of Patiala, a beautiful lovable woman, advised me
to go, perhaps because this freedom of choice that was mine
made her think sadly of her own imprisonment in purdah.
Meanwhile the doctor replied:

> The patient in question is Her Majesty the Senior
> Queen of Nepal. Katmandu is about 4,500 feet in a valley
> surrounded by the Himalayas. The nights are rather cool,
> but there are electric heaters in the rooms. I think it is
> in any case less cold than in Simla. There are, apart from
> about a dozen people belonging to the British Embassy, no
> Europeans in Nepal. I would suggest a salary of between
> 1,500 and 2,000 rupees a month, and you would get, of
> course, board and lodgings and first-class fare for yourself
> and your bearer. The matter is urgent. . . .

I was back in Simla when this letter came. There was snow
on the ground, heavy on the fir trees and banked along the
Mall. The distant mountains, beyond which lay Nepal, were
sometimes gray with snow, and sometimes breathlessly white.
Do not go, my friends were still saying. Mother came to me
with pictures she had torn from *The Illustrated Weekly of
India* and these showed an American ambassador lying exhausted in the grass on the mountain path to Nepal. If this
could happen to a man, she said, what would happen to me?
She appealed to Sherene Rustimjee for support, and this
gentle, compassionate Parsee, who was to be so good to me
in the future, also shook her head and said, "Erika, you must
not go."

But I had already accepted the invitation. I knew that I
had to go. There was suddenly in my mind the memory of a

children's story, one I had read long ago, or been told, the story of the *Sternthaler*.

There was once a beggar child, says this story, who stood by the roadside, in the sun and in the rain. She was poor, and she kept herself alive by selling matches. One day another poor child came to her and said, "I have no shoes and my feet are sore, please give me yours to wear." And the beggar child gave them. Then there came another child who said, "I am cold and I have no coat, please give me yours to wear." And the beggar child gave it. A third child asked for her dress, and this too was given. Now the beggar child had her shift only, and when she was asked for this by yet a fourth child she cried, "God help me, but I have nothing left to give!" She held up the skirt of the shift, and as she did so a golden shower of coins fell from heaven into it.

I felt that I was this beggar child and that what I had given to life was suddenly to be returned to me, not in coin but in happiness. To everyone who said, "Do not go!" I replied, "I must go!"

The doctor had informed Katmandu of my acceptance, and in the first week of February I received a letter from the Foreign Office in Nepal. It was typed in large letters on thick paper embossed in red with the arms of Nepal, the shield of Shiva, the crest of crossed kukri, the footprints of the Lord Buddha, the motto *Dulce et decorum est pro patria mori*. It was signed by the Director-General of Foreign Affairs, whose name was like a barbaric clash of cymbals—Major General Bijaya Shamsher Jung Bahadur Rana. In return for my "professional services in the household of His Majesty the King" I was offered a salary of 2,000 rupees a month, in addition to first-class traveling expenses and board and lodging.

I told him that I would need transport for myself, my servant Ghorki Ram, and my black and white spaniel bitch Peepchen. My servant, I said, was a meat-eating Hindu, and

I would be obliged if the Major General wrote this into our contract. I did not wish Ghorki to be starved by Hindus of more orthodox habits. For three weeks there was no reply to this letter stating my conditions, and one came only after I had reminded the Major General by telegram. He sent me a three-page letter containing ten clauses of agreement. Clause Four, I was happy to see, read: "I note that your servant is a Hindu bearer, unorthodox and meat-eating."

There was a Nepalese in Simla—Mr. Kathait, the manager of the Simla Bank, a small, diffident man with the smooth, still face of the Nepalese. He seemed pleased that I was to visit his country. He was the only person in Simla who could tell me anything about Nepal, but now, as I look back on it, I realize that he really told me nothing at all. His answers slid away from my questions and hid themselves behind his polite smile. When I asked him about the King and the King's two queens that smile appeared on his face with the abruptness of a slammed door. But he did agree that I should take a present for the Senior Queen, and when I asked him for letters of introduction to his friends in Katmandu he reluctantly produced one. This was to the Commander in Chief of the Nepalese Army, a man whose name, also, was like the opening crash of a military band—Major General Baber Shamsher Jung Bahadur Rana; and if, at that time, I was curious about the marked similarity between this name and that of the Director-General of Foreign Affairs, then the curiosity did not last long.

I was too busy. I had informed Katmandu that I would arrive at the border town of Raxaul on Thursday, March 3, and there was much I had to do. It was still bitterly cold in Simla, and I thought how colder still it must surely be crossing the Himalayas. So I went to the bazaar and bought long men's underpants for myself and Ghorki. I ordered for myself a khaki suit that looked like a battle dress, with slacks and a bush jacket with a hood. Wearing this, with my short-cropped hair, I looked like a man. So much like a man, in fact, that on the journey other bearers were to mock Ghorki, calling, "*Bai,* how old is your sahib?"

"My sahib," Ghorki would reply with indignation, "my sahib is a memsahib!"

Ghorki Ram had been my bearer for five years, since I had spirited him away from the service of a Punjabi raja whom I was treating. He was a hillman, a proud Rajput, a Kashatria of the same caste as warriors and princes, a tiny, bow-legged man in his fifties but with the strength and endurance of a man half his age. He was also an Anglophile and would be servant to no Indian below the rank of prince. He had a gentle face that glowed behind his white mustache, and I was very fond of him.

At the beginning of March we left Simla for Nepal. I was spiritually elated. I had the lightheaded feeling that all that was to happen to me had happened before and I had no reason to be afraid. What was to happen to me I did not know, yet each further step I took had a strange familiarity. My mother and my friends, however, parted from me as if they expected never to see me again.

Down from Simla to Kalka we drove, Ghorki Ram, Peep-chen and I, down from the melting snow to the heat of the foothill station where we took the night train for Ambala. It was a hot, bitter, uncomfortable journey across the Indian plains to the border, northeastward to the jungle of the Terai, passing little stations where the dry earth was stained by flower beds, where men with skins the color of old leather held up banyan leaves heaped with *dhal,* beseeching us to buy and eat. But we had brought our own food, enough for five days. Five days it would take, Mr. Kathait had said, and the itinerary sent to me by the Major General in Katmandu had confirmed this.

The heat twisted the yellow land into bizarre shapes, crippling the black-green clumps of trees, raising the white walls of a village into a glare that was almost audible. The heat was scarcely less at night, though there was nothing but an indigo darkness beyond the lurching windows of the train. We were always dusty, always dirty, and always tired, and at Muzaffarpur I was glad to move into the guard's car where a breeze took away some of the cruelty of the sun. We arrived at Raxaul, the border station, at noon on the third day of our journey, and because the narrow-gauge train northward to Amlekhganj would not leave until the following morning we had to find a resthouse. We found it at last, a white, slumbering building hiding in a pleasant garden. It was deserted. Ghorki and I walked about it, calling, until a little Nepalese boy broke from the shadows, the palms of his hands together below his face. He spoke no English and no Hindu, but chattered to us in singing, whispering Nepali until Ghorki made himself understood. He took us up a creaking staircase and showed us the bleak, sparsely furnished rooms in which we might spend the night.

I wanted a bath too, and this was harder to explain to the boy. I found the room myself, a bathroom like any bathroom in India, a tin tub, *lhota,* a drain in the corner. Cold water and hot water were brought to me, and these I poured over myself from the *lhota.* While I washed, a snake slipped cautiously from the mouth of the drain, swayed its cool, dark head at me in greeting, and withdrew.

It was hot that night. There were no electric fans in the resthouse. The air vibrated with the hum of mosquitoes, and Peepchen slept uneasily on her charpoy beside me. There was no netting over the bed, which had a dip in the center like a canyon. But the morning rewarded me with the beauty of the Terai, still, green waves of jungle flowing northward to an escarpment of blue hills. Beyond them was the snow line

of the high Himalayas, and higher still a mounting cumulus
of cool clouds. After the arid, empty skies of northern India a
cloud was a miracle.

The Nepalese railway station was a mile from the resthouse,
but it was still early and still cool when Ghorki, Peepchen
and I walked to it. It was a little station, crowded and loud
with noise, the singing, hissing lilt of Nepalese voices. Here,
for the first time, I really met the Nepalese, and instinctively
I loved them. They seemed to be dark faces bobbing on
a sea of white cotton, Mongolian faces with wide noses, high
cheekbones, and slanting eyes that readily answered my
smile. The men were all dressed alike, on their heads white
caps, like Gandhi caps and filmed with muslin. Their white
shirts flowed over crinkled, calf-holding jodhpurs. They wore
belts of colored cloth or dark leather through which, on the
left side, was thrust the wide crescent of a kukri. Each man
carried a black, unfolded umbrella, held upward against the
sun, or tucked beneath an arm, or stabbed into the earth.
Even some Gurkhas, returning home on leave, carried umbrellas.

I was the only European there, standing behind the little
rampart of my luggage, Peepchen at my feet. I aroused the
curiosity of a slender young Indian in smart Western clothes.
He came up to me, bowed politely, and said that he was the
representative of the United Press of India. "May I interview
you, madam?"

"Why?" was all I could ask.

"Because I see that you are going to Katmandu, madam.
This is most unusual for a European lady. Perhaps there is a
special reason?"

"Perhaps," I said. "Good morning." He smiled again and
took no offense, but he watched me with sad and curious
regret as I boarded the train.

Ghorki and I sat together as the carriage rattled, bumped

and swung through the Terai. It was as if we were traveling below the surface of the sea. Here, I knew, men came to hunt tiger and rhino, but we saw neither. No flower even broke the green with its color. It was a strong green, stronger than I had ever seen, opaque near the earth and in the shadows, translucent where the top branches snatched at the sky. I leaned from the window, my fingers grasping the leathery leaves, feeling them tearing in my hand.

We arrived in Amlekhganj at noon. Thirty miles through the jungle, that was the beginning, the end and all of the Nepalese Railway. Now there would be no more trains, and I was not sorry. Now there was a road, and a dusty station wagon waiting, its chauffeur a white-capped Nepalese who sang as he drove. We climbed higher and higher with each whip-bend of the road, into air which, sharper and sweeter than that in the jungle below, seemed sprinkled with minute fragments of sunlight. In the bleak corrugations of the sandstone hills there was an occasional grove of meditative trees, but for the most part the land rose in smooth, naked folds toward the mountains. Streams leap-frogged the boulders down into the valleys, or paused in dark pools, and there I saw pilgrims crouched, their shaven heads lifted to watch us pass, their saffron robes kilted, their begging gourds slung behind them, and their open umbrellas throwing purple shadows on the earth.

We crossed a gorge with no slackening of speed, over a bridge of slats that speeded our passing with a musical *ting-tong-ting-tong*. The dust of our wheels hung over villages of meager cane huts, or white-walled houses with gables that curled superciliously. There were shrines by the roadway, dark niches in the green rock, and the eroded images within them were smeared with scarlet and yellow, their feet sprinkled with flower petals.

There was a time when the road ran for a quarter of a mile

through a tunnel, a long, cool, echoing cave dripping with water. From this we emerged suddenly into the sunlight and turned to the right as the road swung itself out into the air, clinging to the cliff face by fragile tendons of rope and wood.

The road ended at Bhimpedi. The world seemed to end there too, at the foot of a wall of rock. Here was the first great barrier of the Himalayas, here must men walk to enter the valleys of Nepal. At the foot of the rock wall the town was scattered along the dry bed of a stream. It was not a town, a village rather, and the sun throbbed on its white walls. Where the plaster had crumbled away the pink brick beneath seemed to be bleeding. The narrow streets were blackened by shadows. Little shrines, guarded by fantastic stone beasts, were further protected by gilded roofs on which fluttered paper and silken pennants. A silversmith sat cross-legged in his corner shop, his little hammer beating echoes against the mountains, and the sun gleaming upon his knees as brightly as upon his metalware. I felt a great surge of happiness.

We were expected. Where our car halted there was a chattering group of porters—chests, arms, and bowlegs naked, thin wisps of mustache hanging below the corners of their mouths, and their slant-eyes studying me without emotion. Standing before them was the headman, smart in Nepalese cap, flounced shirt, crumpled jodhpurs and a black European jacket. He was a man with a grave face and a great sense of his own dignity which, his manner implied, was merely a projection of his country's dignity. He bowed, and in the greeting was something far more humble than anything of the kind I had known in India. He put the palms of his hands together below his face and bent his back until his forehead almost touched the ground, the kukri in his sash making a brave, dipping swing to the rear. He spoke to me in hesitant English, the consonants hissing pleasantly, and he told me that it was his honor to take me over the mountains to Thankot in the valley of Katmandu. That is, he would do so if I would be good enough to get into the *dandi* that awaited me. He indicated it with a sweep of his hand.

It was a sedan chair, luxurious and old, standing in the dust as if it had been abandoned there long ago by a great raja. It was upholstered with purple velvet, and although this was frayed and faded the *dandi* was obviously reserved for honored guests. I was suitably impressed. Great poles were thrust through hoops on either side, and by them waited eight bearers, their crooked legs and sinewy arms jutting from swirls of soiled cotton. Behind this purple glory was another *dandi* for Ghorki, cruder and without upholstering. And behind that was a smaller *dandi* still, for Peepchen.

But I did not wish to be carried. I felt as if I could leap those mountains. I love to walk, and after four days in the cramped heat of trains I wanted to walk. I shook my head to the headman and set out up the path, with Peepchen scurrying ahead of me. The path began leisurely as it crossed the white stones in the river bed, but then it leaped upward suddenly. I walked no more than a few yards before my heart began to thump, and Peepchen lay down and looked at me reproachfully from between her forepaws.

The headman said nothing. He turned to the porters and waved his stick. The *dandi* was lowered and I climbed onto its purple cushions. I was swung into the air with a throaty cry of "*Narain-ah!*" from the porters. Peepchen was lifted into her little chair and there she sat with head down and eyes silently weeping in the maudlin fashion of spaniels, until I called to her and she came running, leaping up to me to travel to Katmandu on my lap.

We climbed to the sky, and when the path was steep the bearers cried passionately upon God, "*Narain-ah!*" and I saw the sweat running down the deep grooves in the backs of their necks. The headman walked proudly beside my *dandi*, waving his stick to give the porters that strength which God might not feel disposed to grant them.

That day we climbed two thousand feet to the resthouse at Sirsaghari, on a path that wound upward in four great loops. The earth fell away from us on one side and rose steeply on the other. Sometimes the clouds were high above us, sometimes below in the valleys, thin, fading puffs of wool. We passed travelers going to Bhimpedi, pilgrims with their feet stained gray by the dust, or men and women carried on the backs of porters, their legs dangling over the edges of conical reed baskets, their faces impassive, or at least impassive until I smiled at them. Then they smiled back, as people always will. Once we were passed by two postmen, coming over the mountains from Katmandu, running rhythmically and smoothly together. They wore anklets of tiny bells, and I was then ignorant and innocent enough to find this custom charming.

I was like a child, like a favored child sitting on faded purple velvet, being carried toward the sky by men who found their strength by calling aloud the name of God. I was as excited as a child by each fresh miracle of rock, earth and sky, by the yellow and blue flowers spilled along the banks of the streams. Each time my heart was moved I called out, "Ghorki, *dekko!*" and turned back to see his patient, answering smile.

In the late afternoon we reached Sirsaghari, where it clung to a mountaintop more than seven thousand feet above sea level. It was known as a fort, but I saw no walls, no battlements, only a village, white where the sun fell and mauve where shadows gathered. There was a small bazaar in which red brass glowed, and the woodwork along the lintels and eaves of the houses writhed with allegorical carvings. We stayed the night in the guesthouse, and I poured cool water

over myself from my *lhota* and was refreshed. Ghorki and I
dined together, although in India one does not eat with one's
servants. But Ghorki was my friend and we had traveled
together over the roof of the world. So we dined together on
fried chicken. I went out onto the veranda to watch night
filling the wrinkled valleys.

The next morning, very early, we went on, climbing still,
and now the climb was hard, and there was great feeling in
the voices of the porters, hissing through clenched teeth. The
path rose and fell. The feet of the porters slipped against the
stones, or kicked them in little avalanches down the mountain. At last we came down into the Chitlong Valley, high in
the sky still, where paddy fields glittered like black mirror
glass along the terraces. We halted by a small stream that was
thick with young water cress, and we lunched on chupatties
and curry, and the porters sucked gratefully at the cigarettes
I gave them. They crouched on their flat feet as they made
tea, and they smiled at me for the first time.

I looked on to where the path still climbed toward the
Chandragiri Pass, a pencil line of red rising, perpendicularly
almost. It was past noon before we reached it. The red earth
was wet clay, thick and slippery. The porters sighed, bent
their backs until they seemed to be kissing their knees. Still
the headman strode boldly, black coat flapping, stick swinging.

Now the mist was thick, and the black arms of wild apple
trees reached out of it toward us. Where the sun shone, great
butterflies of incredible beauty were posed over the ice-blue
rhododendrons. There were forget-me-nots thick in streamside
clusters, and yellow flowers in mustard stains across the earth.

Two hours after noon we reached the top of Chandragiri
Pass, and there I looked down into a green valley, a smooth
floor fifteen hundred feet below. I cried, *"Bandkaro!* Stop!"
and leaped from the *dandi*.

"Nepal!" said the headman, as if this cupped emerald were all there was to this country.

I had and have seen nothing so beautiful. The mountain wall to the north was white-ridged, separated from the earth by a long band of amethyst, so that the peaks hung between earth and sky. Three rivers ran across the valley floor, changing in color from melted butter to dark blue as each lazy loop caught or avoided the sun. The fields, spaced by groves of black trees, were brilliantly green and crossed by gray roads like pencil lines faintly drawn. There were paddy fields pricked by young rice, and great patches of burning mustard flowers.

Again I was like a child, clapping my hands, running from porter to porter with questions they did not understand but which they acknowledged with the tolerant smiles of men who understand that life is mostly work, and that pleasure must come from the things that are free.

There were cities in the valley, three cities close together like a cluster of jewels, winking with gold and white in the sun. I saw red tiles and the fingers of golden spires. From porter to porter I went, pointing to the greatest glow of gold, asking, "Is that the King's palace?"

They smiled at me, but did not understand.

"Ghorki!" I cried, "Dekko! Do you think that is His Majesty's palace?"

He smiled tolerantly, too, and he said, he the Rajput whose ancestors had once brought the sword to this valley and burned its cities, "Madam, how can I possibly know?"

I stared down at the valley for a long time. This was Nag Hrad, the Tank of Serpents. I was to hear many stories of its origin. That it was once a great turquoise lake has no doubt been proved geologically, and by what great physical change it was drained has no doubt been proved too, but the stories I later heard were not geological but magical.

They say that once the valley of Katmandu was indeed a great lake, full of fish and snakes. Then, over the snow mountains from China came the giant Manjusuri with his two wives. They sat on the hills and looked down on the lake. Manjusuri took his sword and struck the hills, and the water drained away through the cleft he made. Garuda, the bird-god and messenger of Vishnu, slew the snakes that remained. As the waters drained away, the Lord Buddha watched and saw a great lotus of incredible beauty rest gently on the green earth that was left.

Some stories say that it was not Manjusuri who released the waters but Krishna, the incarnation of Vishnu, and he broke the mountains with a great thunderbolt that later assumed the shape of the elephant-god Ganesa. But the change in principals does not alter the wonderful imagery of the legend, nor affect the belief that when men came to the valley after the waters had gone they built a city about a house made from the wood of a single tree. This house was called Kasthmandap, and the city became Katmandu.

I walked most of the way down the mountain to the town of Thankot at its foot, although the descent is steeper than the climb on the other side. I let myself down by clutching at the great branches of the rhododendrons, where green orchids were woven among the dark leaves. And now fir trees marched up from the valley and filled the air with their scent. I was happy to walk, and Peepchen was happy to run, her nose trailing this strange earth, and the porters stared at her as if they had never seen a dog like her, which was indeed true.

Thus in this way did I come over the Himalayas to the valley of Katmandu and the palace of King Tribhuvana.

THERE was a car waiting in Thankot, a great American car many years old, with an open hood and with gray dust on its fenders, and a Nepalese official standing beside it. A little silver badge was pinned to his cap, and as he bowed, with palms pressed together below his face, I saw that it was not really a badge but a tiny silver frame containing the photograph of a round-faced man with pince-nez and hooped mustache. "Memsahib," said the official, "will you please enter the car?"

So we got in, Ghorki, Peepchen and I, while the official sat with the driver, and our luggage was piled in another car. We drove along a gray, stony road to Katmandu. As the schedule prepared by General Bijaya had stipulated, we had arrived in Thankot before sunset, but now shadows were running out along the ground from the groves of trees, darkening the meadows that looked so much like English parklands. We passed through a little town where rich black earth was thick with growing vegetables, and the official turned his head to tell me that this was Thim, kitchen garden of Katmandu, and that each tiny section of land grew enough to support six families. The city ahead of us, which had been white and red, golden and glittering from the top of the pass, was now splashed by great blue shadows, and the glow of the gold was like a fire quickly dying. We drove over an ugly bridge of iron girders into the streets, and my mind was suddenly bewildered by dark, carved wood, by pagoda roofs, by white plaster and red brick, by immobile cataracts of mauve-pink blossoms that tumbled over high walls.

The car stopped at a gateway, on the corner of a gray dusty road darkened by tall trees. What was left of daylight fell in the garden beyond the gate, on flowers and a green lawn. This, said my Nepalese, was Tripureswar Number One, this was the guesthouse where I was to stay.

A man came out of a little lodge at the gate and saluted me. He was dressed untidily in a khaki uniform and white puttees, black belt, and red turban. He was my bodyguard, the Nepalese told me, and I was impressed.

I went up the garden path, mounted a few shallow steps into the main room. It was bare—a table, two chairs and no more. It looked miserable and impersonal, and it instantly depressed me. There was a young man waiting in the dusk. He was dressed in white and his head was shaven, and on his feet were canvas shoes. Although I did not know it then, this —the white dress, shaven head and cloth shoes—was how the Nepalese mourned their dead, and the young man was grieving for his mother. He greeted me devoutly, bending his back until his spine was parallel to the floor, raising his hands together with palms toward his face, and beckoning me forward with them as he stepped backward.

It was strange to me, and yet it was not strange. There was this feeling that I had seen this before, that what I would do I had already done before. I put my hands together and lowered my head.

He smiled faintly as he straightened his body. He said that he was Lala Ram, the son of Mani Ram, keeper of the guesthouses, and would I like to see the rest of my home? He showed me all, the living room, the dining room, the bedrooms. All were bare, all empty of warmth and feeling, but the windows of the bedroom opened like doors onto the garden, and I flung them back to let in the evening scent of the flowers. I knew that I was going to be happy there.

I saw the servants' quarters and the kitchen beyond the garden, and there was a little group waiting in the dusk— cook, bearer, sweeper, gardener, laundryman, dark faces smiling above the white of their shirts.

I wanted tea, and it was brought, not very elegant, perhaps, but good tea, and good milk, and crisp English crackers which, I reminded myself, had been brought over the Himalayas as I had, to the sad calling of Narain's name. Ghorki sat with me, both of us cross-legged in that great room, and when Mani Ram's son came again, still devoutly bowing, I asked if it were not possible for me to have more furniture, a wardrobe, perhaps, for my clothes were European and must hang, and they could not be folded and placed in chests like saris. The furniture would come, promised Lala Ram, and so it did come, almost before Ghorki and I had finished our tea.

So that evening, while the excited music of tiny bells came across the air from the center of the city, I played interior decorator and made those bare rooms into a home. I never travel without taking some of the little possessions which a woman of forty has gathered in her life and made a part of her nature, her feelings and her thoughts. I had brought bright Indian shawls, and tablecloths, and I made a home from them in Tripureswar Number One. I had no vases, but I asked the *khansamah* to bring me soup plates from his kitchen, and these I filled with the heads of flowers, marigolds, sweet peas, and gentle forget-me-nots. The cook watched me and smiled his delight when the color of the flowers put warmth into the room.

And then I wrote to Mother. Every day I was to write to her, because she worried about me. The night beyond the shadows of my garden was full of sound. Those bells ringing, many, many of them. Not the heavy, sonorous note of European bells, but a thin, hysterical jingle that rose and fell and ceased suddenly at the boom of a great gun. Then there was silence. Ghorki came to me. It was curfew, he said, the servants had told him. Every night at ten the cannon sounded and no Nepalese dared stir from his house until the morning gun gave him permission.

I rose early in the morning, bathed, and walked from my bedroom to the garden. A fine bird, erect in dignity, shining black but with a flowing tail of spotless white, walked away from me slowly, and at the sound of the cannon the valley air was once more full of the music of bells.

As I sat at breakfast I saw a stranger in the garden, standing on the pathway between the lodge and the gatepost, and waiting there politely. He was a short man in a Nepalese suit, a dark Nepalese cap tilted over his intelligent face. He was a middle-aged man, and a little paunch was outthrust below his belt. Ghorki came to me with a visiting card. It said *Siddhimani A. Dixit, M.B.*

"He is the royal physician, madam."

Dr. Siddhimani came in, not an impressive man, but gentle and humble in his manner, and he sat on my sofa, his hands flipping out the skirts of his old European coat. His English was good, and he was openly pleased when I congratulated him upon it. He said that he had been trained in Calcutta.

"What can I do for you, Doctor Sahib?"

"Madam, what can I do for *you?* I am here to help you."

So I asked him what was expected of me, when I would be called to give treatment to the Senior Queen, and although I wanted to ask him what she was like I suddenly remembered Mr. Kathait, and something held my tongue. He smiled a little, and he said that for this day I would not be needed, but on the next day, at four-thirty in the afternoon, he would call for me and take me to Singha Durbar for an audience with the Prime Minister.

"The Prime Minister?"

"His Royal Highness the Maharaja Mohun Shamsher Jung Bahadur Rana," said Dr. Siddhimani, as if he were reciting, and I was too surprised to realize that here was one more permutation of the name possessed by the Foreign Minister and Mr. Kathait's friend the Commander in Chief. I could think only that among all the things I had packed in Simla, the new clothes I had brought, there was nothing that I could wear for a formal presentation to a maharaja, no hat, no gloves.

I said, "Doctor Sahib! I wasn't told it would be like this. I have nothing fitting to wear. I cannot go."

He raised his eyebrows and then studied the tips of his fingers. "Madam," he said gravely, "you *must* go. It is the Prime Minister's order." He did not say so, but the inference was plainly that the absence of hat and gloves was not a sufficient reason for disobeying the Prime Minister.

"I shall call for you," said Dr. Siddhimani, and softly he departed.

By four-thirty the next day I was dressed as fittingly as possible. I wore a green woolen frock with long sleeves and a high neck, and I placed a beaver fur cape over my shoulders. I matched all this somehow with my jewels, but I knew that it was wrong. Dr. Siddhimani arrived punctually, a slightly wistful figure in the back of an old-fashioned open car. The chauffeur was in Nepalese dress except for a shiny-peaked cap. We drove for five minutes through a cloud of dust until, suddenly, we were in front of what seemed at first to be the prototype for the Palace of Versailles.

"Singha Durbar, madam," said Dr. Siddhimani, "the official residence of the Prime Minister."

I said, "If this is how his Prime Minister lives, what can the King's palace be like?"

But for some reason the doctor did not reply.

A great building rose out of the earth, four stories high, colonnaded in Italian style, white where it was not tinted rose by the sun. Reflected in the still waters of a lake, it seemed to be standing on its own image. In the center of the lake was a large allegorical fountain, stone nymphs with classical European profiles, wrestling with the obstinacy of their marble horses. One does not see everything at once, the eye is not a camera and can catch impressions only. My impression was of

a white magnificence painted on the blue sky beyond it. It
was strangely silent and deserted.

We left the car at the foot of a staircase made from pink,
almost mauve, marble. My bodyguard stayed with the chauffeur. I have a lopsided memory of an anteroom filled with
mirrors that distorted my reflection, a fountain playing softly
in the middle of a hall, great paintings of tigers snarling in
lush jungles. Stairways again then, leading deeper into the
palace, and the echo of our footfalls hurrying away from us
down long corridors. At the top of the staircase bowing servants showed us into another room. We had been there scarcely
a few minutes before the door opened and we were bowed
into an adjoining chamber. I looked at my watch. It was five
o'clock, the hour of the audience.

There, in that room, the sun fell in geometrical patterns
through the high windows and across golden and crimson
carpets, breaking over furniture that looked as if it had come
from some aristocratic Victorian drawing room, rich in velvet, in golden and silver woodwork. The doctor and I stood
alone and silently for a few minutes, while from the walls we
were watched fiercely by the portraits of arrogant generals.

The doors at the far end of the room swung back, and we
saw the sun again in the far room, slanting bars glittering
with tiny motes. A little, elderly man came toward us, and I
heard the bowing rustle of Dr. Siddhimani's coat.

This was the Maharaja, His Highness Mohun Shamsher
Jung Bahadur Rana, and the grand name lost all its effect on
me because he looked like Theodore Roosevelt. His face was
pale, the startlingly light color of a Rajput, and was bisected
by the curving hoops of a white mustache. The pince-nez on
his nose gave him a bland, genial expression, but it was a
deceptive one. The eyes behind the lenses were black and
emotionless. I felt that I had seen his face before, and this

time the feeling was not supernatural. I *had* seen it before. A photograph in a tiny silver frame, worn on the cap of the official who had brought me from Thankot.

The Prime Minister wore a long frock coat, once known, I believe, as a Prince Albert, with shining silk lapels and a fresh red flower in the buttonhole. His shirt was white, the creases of his jodhpurs might have been molded from snow. But none of this held my eyes for long. In the center of his round black cap there gleamed an enormous diamond. Like the glow of headlights from an approaching car it blinded me to everything else, and I was hardly conscious of the group of young officers that followed him.

In the short journey to Singha Durbar, Dr. Siddhimani had nervously warned me that His Highness was an orthodox Hindu, strict in protocol, and hated to shake hands with Europeans, believing that therein lay defilement. I accordingly bowed over my hands and said, "*Namashkar,* Your Highness."

But he came toward me with his hands outstretched, taking mine and guiding me to a sofa, and there he sat beside me on the red velvet and gold brocade, his black coat flipped out and the fingers of one hand gently brushing his mustache.

The young officers stood before us in a half-moon of khaki and polished leather, and I heard the soft fall of Dr. Siddhimani's feet as he tiptoed away into the background.

The conversation was stilted. Had my journey been comfortable? Yes, Your Highness. Had I enjoyed the country? It was beautiful, Your Highness. Had I not been tired by the long climb over the mountains? I said, "Your Highness, I wasn't carrying the *dandi.*"

He looked at me carefully, and then a slow smile lifted the pale cheeks, tilted the great mustache. He turned his head momentarily to the officers behind us, as if giving them per-

mission to smile too. Suddenly aware of them, he introduced
me to them, his good English slipping through names that
refused to take hold on my mind, except that all of them
seemed to end with "Jung Bahadur Rana." Finally one did
touch my memory.

"Madam—my son, General Bijaya Shamsher Jung Bahadur
Rana."

A young man bent forward and shook my hand, a young
man with broad, athletic shoulders. His dark hair curled out
from beneath his cap, and a pencil-thin mustache along his
upper lip straightened with his smile.

I said, "Your Highness' son? This is General Bijaya the
Foreign Minister who wrote to me?" The Prime Minister said
that this was so, and I raised my hands. "But he's so young,
and a general! He must be very brilliant."

The smile halted on the young man's lips as if he had forgotten it. The Prime Minister stared at me. He seemed to be
searching beyond my words for my thoughts, but what he
found there, or thought he found there, must have satisfied
him, for at last he said, "In Nepal we marry while we are
very young, madam, and thus our children are also born
while we are young." It seemed to be no explanation for the
young man's early rise in his profession, but obviously it was
all the explanation I was going to be given. And then, quite
unexpectedly, the Prime Minister said, "How old do you
think I am, madam?" He brushed his mustache in the unmis-
takable gesture of a man expecting a compliment.

I smiled. "How can I guess, Your Highness, with that
diamond dazzling me? If you took it off I might be able to
tell."

One of the older officers stiffened his back, but the Prime
Minister bowed his head gently and removed the cap and
placed it on his plump little knee.

I said, "Your Highness might perhaps be fifty-five?"

A smile lifted the mustache with pleasure. "No, madam, I am almost sixty-four."

"*Shabash*, Your Highness," I said. "Well done!"

He turned to his son, Bijaya. "I should like to see this lady again."

He offered me a cigarette. I smoked and I was at ease, yet at the same time I was aware that I was answering the questions with a schoolgirl naïveté, and the more naïve my answers the better pleased he seemed. At last he stood up, turning to General Bijaya and saying once more, "I should like to meet this lady again." His cap was on his head now, the diamond glowing, his hand extended. "Good-bye, madam, I hope you enjoy your stay in Nepal."

His hand brushed his mustache in two quick movements, and then he was gone through the far doors, his white legs moving quickly beneath the black flare of his coat and the uniforms of his officers closing about him. The doors shut on them all and only then did I realize that the Maharaja had not once mentioned the Senior Queen or my purpose in coming to Nepal. Dr. Siddhimani was at my side. "Madam, we must go. We must hurry. There is more."

Down the marble staircase we went to the car, where chauffeur and bodyguard sat in the sun and the white palace and the white clouds were still reflected serenely in the lake.

"Madam," said Dr. Siddhimani, "now I must take you to Naran Hity Durbar." He saw my expression. "It is the palace of the King. Now you have audience with His Majesty."

"Doctor Sahib!" I cried, almost in anger. "I knew nothing of this either. I cannot go as I am. Let me go home, at least for a moment so I may powder my nose and collect a present I've brought for the Queen."

"It is possible," said Dr. Siddhimani, but he seemed unhappy about it, and he looked at his watch like the White Rabbit.

IT IS nearly nine years since I first saw King Tribhuvana, and sometimes the time seems that long, and
sometimes it is yesterday only, and I can hear the pigeons in
the royal gardens. I can hear a harsh rustling, like a sheet
shaken, as the rooks rise from the trees at dusk. That is how
it was every evening. When the lights were lit in the gardens,
pale globes hanging in the darkness of the trees, those black
birds swept up, circled the palace, and flew away to the
mountains. The scent of flowers was always very heavy in the
evenings.

Such things are so much a part of me now that it is hard
to realize that for most of my life they did not exist, and that
when Doctor Siddhimani and I set out again from Tripureswar the King, his queens, his princesses and his palace were
nothing to me. I knew only his name—perhaps Doctor Siddhimani had told me, or Mr. Kathait, I do not remember.
I knew his name (or part of it, for in full it stretched over
twenty words and more). He was His Majesty the Maharajadhiraja Tribhuvana Bir Bikram Sah Deva, King of Nepal
and the incarnation of Lord Vishnu the Preserver. Tribhuvana, I learned, means he who dwells in the three worlds,
material and spiritual, of human existence.

A few paces from my guesthouse, where the dirt road
began to run alongside the grass of the *maidan,* I had already
seen a statue of him, a white stone figure beneath an ugly
Western cupola, a monument that looked as if it had origi-
nally intended to emulate the Albert Memorial but had early
abandoned the attempt. It was conventional and characterless,
and it might have represented this man or that. There was
nothing about it that was striking, except perhaps the plume.
This rose from the top of his skull-fitting helmet and fell
backward, like a fountain caught in the wind. Even in stone
there was something breath-taking about it.

That was all I knew of the King that late afternoon when the doctor and I left Tripureswar again and drove past the Thuni Kel. This was the *maidan*, a great grass parade ground, a green floor that rolled smooth and flat for most of the way and then rose to what seemed like an earthwork, crowned with tall bamboo, taller than I had ever seen. In the center of the *maidan* was a huge banyan tree, its branches bending over to shelter a stone rostrum beneath. At each corner of this platform was a statue of a Gurkha rifleman, head and slouched hat lifted to the sky. In the dusk white egrets were perched, motionless, on the banyan branches.

But perhaps I saw none of these things clearly that evening, and only think I did, since they were to become commonplace later. The main city of Katmandu lay away to our left, to the west. I could hear the excited jangle of its tiny bells. I saw the white of its walls, the dull, burning crimson of its roofs, and gold glittering on temple eaves and spires. We passed serenely calm buildings behind rectangular tanks of green-scummed water, white buildings that were Western in design, yet oriental in mood. They seemed deserted to me, as if the mind that had created them had failed to find a use for them beyond their empty, mauve-shadowed beauty. But Doctor Siddhimani was murmuring beside me, identifying each with wistful pride—the Bir Hospital, the College of Katmandu . . .

Now the car turned into a long drive, between two black obelisks covered with white stucco like sugar icing. There were soldiers at this gate, in khaki, black caps and white puttees, like my bodyguard. They did not stop us, scarcely removing their backs from the gate as they waved us through. The car drove on, following the bend of the trees, until it skirted the front of the royal palace. It was magnificent, but not as magnificent as Singha Durbar, and no lake reflected the image of its splendid Corinthian columns. Yet the white of it against the blue sky was unnerving.

"Naran Hity Durbar," said Doctor Siddhimani, a little primly, "the Palace of Narain's Well. It has one thousand rooms, but His Majesty does not live in it. It's for official purposes only."

We did not stop, but circled the palace, passing a square white building, fronted by columns, crowned by a fine pediment in which was a flaming golden sun. It looked like a small palace on its own, with pert little bushes growing on a lawn before it, and I was not to know then that it was a cinema. We stopped at last by an ordinary, unhappy door in a white wall, and the doctor, still consulting his watch like the White Rabbit, hurried me through to a small anteroom, and there we waited. We waited twenty minutes in this bare, uninteresting chamber that had no more charm than a railway restroom.

At last a soldier came, his face impassive, bending his head over his hands, and saying nothing.

"Come, madam!" The doctor was away again, beckoning me through a door into a little courtyard where leaves were dark against the high walls and a fountain sang to itself in the middle of the flagstones. Through this courtyard and through another door into a great garden. It was dusk, and I could see little clearly. The lamps, which seemed to be hanging from the branches of the trees, were throwing their reflections into a lake, among the flat leaves and great blossoms of lotus. Across the crazy paving before us a tortoise moved slowly, jerking the burden of its shell, its horny head swinging. Doctor Siddhimani stepped by it carefully and walked a pace ahead of me, talking quickly, the way people will when they are nervous. I did not hear what he was saying. The beauty of the gardens, the strong scent of flowers, the throaty bubble of a pigeon in the trees to my right were having an odd effect on me. I began to feel lightheaded. The palace grounds were an unexpected mixture of fairyland and an English suburban garden. With the hanging lamps, the tortoise, the lotus pool and the exotic flowers there were also hammocks on the lawn and ridiculous little dwarfs and mushrooms made of plaster. I was chattering like a girl as we crossed the lake by a wooden bridge, and I almost collided with the doctor when he stopped suddenly, his back bowing over his hands, and his voice hissing back to me.

"Madam, *we are approaching His Majesty!*"

I looked ahead and I said, "*That* is the King?"

"It is His Majesty, madam," said Doctor Siddhimani, bowing lower.

There was a little tea pavilion of gray stone at the end of the path, white columns supporting its angled roof, and it shone with light against the dark trees like a violet lantern. On the steps stood a slender, faery figure, Nepalese cap tilted forward over dark hair, one foot forward and broad shoulders drawn back in a faintly defensive pose. I do not know what I had expected. Perhaps someone old, like the Prime Minister, pince-nez and a hooped mustache, and a cloud of generals in attendance. Yet here was a young man who personified the handsome princes of Indian mythology, tall, erect and regal. All the light of the pavilion seemed to gather behind him, the better to throw him into relief. I ran forward to greet him, leaving the doctor still bent over his hands.

"Your Majesty, *namashkar!* I greet the Divine in you! I thought you would be an old man, but you are young and beautiful!"

His face was in shadow, and I could not see if he smiled, but there was an amused delight in his voice. "*Namashkar!*" he said, and half turned his head to speak to someone behind him. "She speaks Nepali!"

He took my hand firmly and led me into the pavilion, and the perfume of attar of roses was strong about him. He did not release my hand, but held it as he paused in the doorway,

halting me also. It was a small room, a marble floor covered
with soft rugs, furniture of Western design but draped with
brocaded cloths. The lamps, concealed in the walls, filled the
room with a luminous, watered light.

Five women were waiting, dark flowers in gold-bordered
saris that glittered with sequins. Their faces were pale, their
dark eyes large and soft. Jewels were clustered at the lobes
of their ears. Their arms, unlike those of Indian women I had
known, were hidden to the wrist by the long sleeves of their
cholis. They wore flowers in their thick hair, and the sheen
of it was blue.

I heard the King's soft, high-pitched voice singing each
name.

"Her Majesty the Senior Queen Kanti Raja Lalshi. . . ."

"Her Majesty the Junior Queen Ishwari Raja Lakshmi. . . .

"Their Royal Highnesses, my daughters Nalini, Vijaya, and
Bharati."

And he released my hand. From each to the other I went,
bowing over my hands. "Your Majesty, *namashkar*. . . .
Your Majesty, *namashkar*. . . . Your Royal Highnesses,
namashkar." None answered me, but each watched me softly
with a sad curiosity.

Then there was silence in which the King, too, watched
me, his shoulders drawn back again in that defensive pose,
and I began to gabble nonsense. Doctor Siddhimani retired
to a corner, or left the pavilion altogether, I do not remember. I faced the queens and I spoke to the Senior Queen.
"Your Majesty perhaps speaks English?" and I received no
reply. I turned to the Junior Queen. "Your Majesty speaks
English?" There was no reply. To each of the princesses, to
each still, lovely face I said, "Your Royal Highness speaks
English?" Only from the girl called Bharati, the last to whom
I spoke, did I get a reply. "Yes!" So faint, and so high a voice,

it was almost certainly involuntary, as if she could stand the strain of silence no longer.

"Please, madam," said the King, "will you sit down?"

We sat together on the sofa, he on the right, his legs apart and the long, finely manicured fingers of one hand extended along his right thigh. He was a tall man, with the unconscious grace that many tall men have. He wore no jewels beyond a thick band of gold on one finger. His legs were slender in white jodhpurs, and he wore a beige Nepalese shirt taped at the throat, a beige European waistcoat and jacket. His face was pale, pale as a Rajput's, and paler still, I think, with a film of powder. His nose was firm and straight, his brows plucked to two dark crescents above eyes that were inexpressibly sad. Never, in all the months I was to know him, were those eyes to be anything but sad, even when his lips smiled. His hair was thick, brushed forward in a wing that almost obscured his forehead, and held there by the tilt of his white Nepalese cap.

So there we sat, and in silence again, and King, queens and princesses stared at me, not in rude curiosity but with what seemed so like unhappy alarm that a ridiculous thought entered my mind: *Nothing like this has happened to them before, and they are wondering why you have come.*

Then the silence was broken, but I can remember little of what was said, except that it was only pleasantries, the noises which our tongues make at first meetings while our minds absorb the shock or pleasure of the occasion. It did not seem strange to me then, not then at that precise moment, that there was no talk of the world outside Katmandu, of India across the Himalayas. The King asked about my journey, my impressions of his country, questions which the Prime Minister had also asked, but he put them automatically, almost, with none of the Maharaja's sharpness of tone. It was as if he did not care to hear the answers. His sad, reflective eyes

watched the movements of my hands and my body. They
looked at my necklace, with its three strands of pearls, emeralds and rubies. He looked at the rings on my hands, and he
looked at my hatless, cropped hair. And when he looked at
my hair my eyes turned instinctively to the thick, lustrous
hair of his wives and daughters.

I offered my little present to the Senior Queen. I had
bought it in Simla and was ashamed of its poverty. In Simla,
in winter, the bazaar is mostly closed, and there is little of
worth that one can buy. But I had found two slender flower
vases of silver, and these I had wrapped as tastefully as I
could. They had been in my hands all this while, and now I
offered them to the Senior Queen. She and the others had
been sitting motionless on the chairs that faced the sofa. Now
I drew her into the conversation. Her eyes shone as she unwrapped the present. She held the vases up for the King to
see and turned to show them to the others. The King watched
gently.

There was a great difference between the two queens, and
I would not have believed, even had I known it then, that
they were sisters. Their clothes, their jewels, the styles of
their hair, were identical but seemed only to accentuate the
difference between them. The Senior Queen was short, with a
round face and shining birdlike eyes. Her hair, though
dressed in the same fashion as her sister's, was fluffed about
her face, making an indistinct frame. The Junior Queen was
tall and slim, with a beautiful figure subtly flattered by her
sari. The expression of her eyes was detached and dreamlike.

The vases were passed from hand to hand among the princesses, and the King touched them once with his fingers and
then turned his head sharply toward me.

"Will you tell me what you will need for treating Her
Majesty, madam?"

I said that I would need a table, and I handed him a drawing of it that I had brought.

He took it without looking at it. "It will be made."

I said that I would need a mattress, a pillow, towels and olive oil.

"They will be ready tomorrow."

He stood up. The air in the little pavilion was hot and close, intoxicating with perfume.

"Please," said the King, placing the palms of his hands together, "may we go now?"

Doctor Siddhimani was at my side, hurrying me away, through the garden again, past the plaster mushrooms and the red-capped dwarfs, the black water of the lake and the green lotus leaves. Along the path the shrubs were crowded close to the stones, not shrubs growing freely, but shorn and tailored to mannered shapes. In relief, on each of them, had been cut the letter T.

I brought my hands close to my face. I could smell the scent of roses.

IN THE car, returning to Tripureswar, Doctor Siddhimani cleared his throat several times before he remarked diffidently that a doctor would have to be present when I gave treatment to the Senior Queen. I said that I could not agree to this, that it was my custom to work alone. He shook his head worriedly and pushed the tips of his fingers together. He made a confused attempt to explain something to me and then abruptly abandoned the explanation, saying that what he had said was not a suggestion but an order, and an order from His Highness the Prime Minister. At the time I was too angry and too determined to have my own way to wonder why such an order did not properly come from the

King. Doctor Siddhimani pleaded, but I would not agree. He looked very worried when the car left me at the guesthouse and took him away to his home in Dilly Bazaar, speeding to be there before the curfew gun.

But I had my way. I was never told what the Prime Minister said when the doctor carried my refusal to him. Perhaps he shrugged his shoulders, deciding that no harm could come from a silly European woman who was too ignorant and too stupid to know that of course all his sons were generals from the second of their birth. When I went to the palace the next evening Doctor Siddhimani was not there.

With one exception, all my visits to the palace were to be in the evening, and that one exception was not to be by invitation. The royal family loved the evening and the night. They came alive, as it were, with the lighting of the lamps in the gardens and the departure of the rooks for the mountains. In the beginning I took this to be the affectation of an idle family and saw nothing deeper in it. But to the King night was a protection. He drew it about himself and hid in it, just as he drew the wing of his hair over his forehead as if to hide his face.

The car called for me at six. The heat of the day was cooling, and from the *maidan* came the thick, sweet scent of mown grass. That morning I had watched a group of peasant women cutting it, crouching on flattened feet, their saris kilted and their steel kukris swinging.

The chauffeur of the car was a little, brown-faced Newar with high cheekbones and black button eyes. I sat in the back with Peepchen and Ghorki, my bodyguard in front. And this was how it was to be every time I went to the palace—chauffeur, bodyguard, Ghorki and Peepchen. I could not leave Peepchen alone at the guesthouse, but when I reached the palace I sent her home by road with Ghorki. The chauffeur and the bodyguard pulled their hats over their eyes and went to sleep in the car, waiting for me.

I was not taken to the tea pavilion that second evening, but, greeted by a lady in waiting in a whispering sari, I was led beyond it to the door of the private palace. This was a large door of translucent glass on which was etched the letter T. Against the wall, by the door, there stood a motorcycle, beige in color and glittering with chrome.

Through the door I stepped into a heady atmosphere of sandalwood and incense, so overpoweringly intense that my mind momentarily lost its balance. Yet I might have walked into the hall of an English country house, except that the floor was marble, white and black, and covered with rich rugs. Sofa and chairs were Western. Beside me was a hatstand covered with topcoats, mackintoshes, and tweed caps. In the corner, walking sticks and umbrellas, fishing rods and golf clubs sprouted from a tangle of sports shoes and roller skates. Beyond me a staircase reached upward in one elegant curve. Sunlight broke through small windows that were shaped like arrowheads, and all tightly closed.

The King was waiting at the foot of the stairway, shoulders back and foot outstretched, the expression of his face withdrawn behind that wing of hair. The queens were beside him, their hands clasped gently together at their waists, and each wore a white flower in her hair above the right ear.

The greetings and devout *namashkars* over, the King turned on his heel and passed through a door in the right-hand corner of the hall. His queens followed him and I came last. We walked along a little corridor that turned this way and that, skirted a little patio into which the sun was spilling a rich red-gold, and finally entered a bathroom of so pale a blue that it might have been at the bottom of a Mediterranean grotto. This, the King said, was the Senior Queen's bathroom, this was where she would receive my treatment, where the equipment I had asked for was awaiting my inspection. He stood back, his hand outstretched suddenly, like a child, asking approval of what he had prepared.

It was a large room, its door screened by a plastic curtain. Plastic was strange to me in 1949 and not something I had expected to find in Nepal. The bath was large, with glass panels that could be pulled forward so that water might not splash the thick rugs on the floor. There was a divan, and beside it a low table on which stood a vase of towering flowers. If they had any perfume it was lost in the thick competition of row upon row of lotions, salts, soaps and cosmetics that filled the cabinets on the wall. Against the wall was a squat, mundane safe for the Queen's jewels.

Between the bath and the divan was the massage table that had been made for me overnight, high and moving smoothly on casters. The King was pleased when I said that it was more than adequate. He took a golden cigarette case from his pocket, opened it, and offered it to me. All the movements of his hands had an effortless grace, and, although obviously natural, they seemed as practiced as the delicately beautiful *mudras* of an Indian dancer. The cigarettes were American, Lucky Strikes. He smoked deeply, with the urgent intensity of an emotional man, taking the smoke far into his lungs and allowing it to linger there.

The queens had said nothing, but stood together, with hands clasped still, their dark eyes watching me. As I raised my cigarette to my lips the King saw the ring on my finger, smiled suddenly with pleasure, and took my hand. It was a silver band with three elephants in relief, a thing of little value and, despite its Eastern motif, of French origin. I took it from my finger and showed it to him. He put it on his own finger, holding his hand before his face, turning to his queens with one eyebrow lifted, his lips making a gentle sound of approval, "*Ah!*" Had it not been of silver I would have given the ring to him, but I had been long enough in the East to know that gold only is the gift for a king.

He returned the ring to me and stepped back, with head to one side, as if to study me even better. He was wearing Nepalese clothes again, white jodhpurs, a light European jacket, and a beautiful shirt of poplin. In the stronger light of this room he looked older than when I had seen him in the tea pavilion the nght before. I knew that he must perhaps be forty, but the youthfulness of his handsome face was only just beginning to thicken along the line of his jaws. Only by his eyes was his age betrayed.

The smoke of the American cigarettes was soon very thick. I found the heat and the stifling perfume unbearable. I pointed to the window, high on the wall and, of course, tightly closed. "Your Majesty," I said, "I must open the window."

He looked at it quickly, his expression darkening, as if I were proposing a deliberate breach of his personal privacy, and then he nodded. I raised myself on my toes, lifting a leg to reach higher and unlatch the window. The air that came in was scarcely cooler than that already in the bath-room, and it brought the sweet night scent of the garden. Turning, I saw him staring at me curiously again. He said, dispassionately and without offense, "You have beautiful legs, madam."

I laughed. "If I have, Your Majesty, it comes from danc-ing."

His face brightened. "You can dance, madam? Can you teach me?"

That the King could not dance surprised me, this king who smoked Lucky Strikes, whose motorcycle leaned against his palace wall, and who had the natural grace of a splendid animal.

"You cannot dance?"

For a moment he did not answer me. Then he said, "There has been no one to teach me. Will you?"

"With great pleasure, Your Majesty."

"*Ah!*" he said. Again that faint sound, the lift of the voice which I was to come to know as his only expression of pleasure and which, by change of intonation, could also express disgust. He turned his head sharply to his queens as if to invite them to share his happiness. They smiled at me.

"When, madam?"

"Now, if you wish."

"Then, come!" He swept aside the plastic curtain and walked back toward the hall, past the little courtyard where, on a low shelf, I saw perhaps two dozen pairs of shoes, old-fashioned shoes like slippers, with cord soles and uppers of bright green, yellow and scarlet velvet. When we reached the hall a portable phonograph was brought, ordered by some subtle lift of the eyebrow or hand that escaped me, for I had not even seen a lady in waiting. It was a good phonograph, and records were brought with it. The King, whose movements and expression had now lost some of their languid reserve, watched me as I turned disc after disc. They were all new but, to my taste, bad—fast, cacophonic American swing, music without melody and without the floating rhythm needed for ballroom dancing. The King watched without comment as I discarded them one by one until, at last, I found one by Victor Sylvester, "Peg o' My Heart," a lovely melody. I knew that this was the record by which to teach him to dance, for Sylvester's music not only touches the heart with its sweet sentimentality but also moves in the limbs and creates a responsive rhythm. I held it up. "This will do."

He took it from me. "Sylvester," he said. "I have a book

of instructions written by him." He looked regretfully at the swing records I had rejected. "He is good?"

"He is very good."

We were alone, and at that moment I did not wonder what had become of the queens and why they had not followed us to the hall. "Shall we begin, Your Majesty?"

He had never danced a step before, never held a woman in the slow, sensual movements of the ballroom dance. I held out my arms. I said that I would show him what to do. For all the grace of his carriage, the soft, catlike spring of his walk, he was suddenly wooden. A European man might perhaps have smiled, covered his embarrassment with laughter. This king stood with arms out, gravely intent.

"You must put your hand here, Your Majesty, on my spine. Press so that I may feel it, so I can lean on it. Keep your elbow up. See, my head must look over your shoulder and your knees touch mine. . . ."

We played that slow fox trot again and again, and I saw that it was useless. I looked at the rugs on the floor, and I broke away from him, rolled them up and tossed them into a corner. It was still no good. I looked down at the thick crepe soles of the black shoes he was wearing. "You cannot dance in those. Take them off, and we'll try our bare feet."

We took off our shoes and placed them by the wall. I showed him how to feel my feet so that they might guide his own steps, and thus we danced, for an hour, for two hours, or it may have been more, while the sun set and the curfew gun boomed far away unheard, and the lights were lit in the hall.

The evening ended abruptly. He broke away from me and lifted the needle from the record. He put his hands together before his face. "Madam, may I go, please?"

I was driven back to Tripureswar with a clouded mind,

a mind full of an evening that had begun in a bathroom and ended with the music of Victor Sylvester, a king's shoeless feet following mine about a marble floor. I had an insane desire to laugh at this odd way of giving treatment to a Nepalese queen. Then suddenly I was filled with a great sadness and could think of no reason for it.

At a crossroad the car halted and a policeman came to us out of the moonlight, bending his broad-cheeked face and black pillbox hat to look into the car. The chauffeur chattered to him, and the bodyguard, stirring reluctantly from sleep, grumbled too, until the policeman saluted me sharply and let us proceed.

When the car had driven away to the city, and the bodyguard had walked stiffly to his lodge, I went up the pathway to the guesthouse. White roses were livid splashes in the darkness, and the scent of the flowers was so rich that I wondered if all Nepal, from the palace to the mountain pathways, were not some perfumed dream. Ghorki was crouched on his heels by the doorway, his head nodding over his tiny body, and in front of him was Peepchen, asleep on her charpoy. Between the two of them was a great love, and they would never go to bed until I returned home.

There was a full moon that night. I could see it from my windows. It hung over the indigo escarpment of the far mountains.

I WENT to the palace again the next evening to begin my treatment of the Senior Queen, and to dance again with the King. Thus it was day after day, and thus began my devotion to the royal family, to the palace they called the Happy Cottage, and to the whole of Nepal. The car came for me when the valley air was cooling, and the sunset was red on the temple spires, and the egrets had begun to settle in the great banyan tree. My life fell easily into a daily routine.

Each morning I awoke early, early enough to see the little Nepalese girl stealing marigolds from my garden and arranging them on her *puja* tray. Along the dusty road in front of Tripureswar, shortly after dawn, there rolled a convoy of lumber trucks, heading for the mountains. Apart from the old-fashioned palace cars, and the latest models owned by the Ranas, these trucks were the only motor vehicles I saw in Nepal.

After breakfast, brought to me by Ghorki, I walked around the *maidan*. It was never deserted. The sun had scarcely risen before there were platoons of young boys there, marching and drilling, shouted at by hoarse Gurkha sergeants. When they had gone, a dozen peasant women with their slouch hats came to cut the grass, and they drilled until noon. In the afternoon a herd of brown and white cows flowed gently across the grass, cropping what the kukris had not shorn.

From the *maidan* I walked along the bank of the sacred Bhagmati, sacred because when its waters have breached the Himalayas they flow into the Ganges. I saw peasant women washing their hair, their ankles and feet tattooed with serpents and peacocks, the color of their skins a warm copper. Their controlled movements as they washed were slow and symbolic, a dance without music, and, when they had finished, they threw back that blue-black hair with one graceful sweep and lowered their bodies, nose clasped, until the holy water covered them. Their hair hung loose and unbraided until the sun dried it, and then they tied it back in a bun, placing against it a yellow flower, or scarlet, or white. They carried their burdens away on their backs, supporting them with a band of cloth across their foreheads, and on top of each would be great armfuls of rhododendron blossoms that they had gathered.

The Nepalese, men and women, fascinated me. They had a purity and a simplicity which the impact of the West has too often obscured in India. I began to recognize their faces and determine their origin—Tibetans whose women wore pleated kilts and large metal plaques on their braided hair, little Sherpas from the hills, Gurkhas coming from the western mountains to seek enlistment, and industrious Newars whose valley this had been long before the Rajputs and the Gurkhas conquered it.

Providence has given me a musical ear which enables me to learn languages quickly. Within a few days I acquired some Nepali and could understand, in part, what the royal family said to each other in their modest, whispering voices. And, because I understood, I wanted all to know that I understood, so I spoke my few phrases of Nepali. Yet the result was not as I expected. The King's face darkened, and thereafter, when he spoke in Nepali in my presence to his wives, or to his daughters, it was so softly and so gently that I could not hear.

All Nepalese men I saw, passing along the dusty road in front of my guesthouse, or in the alleyways of the bazaar, were dressed alike. First the white shirt, tied by tapes at the waist and throat, and reaching to the knee over baggy jodhpurs. Over the shirt a waistcoat, and over the waistcoat a jacket, sometimes European in style and cut away sharply at the hips, and sometimes as long as an Indian *achkan*. The shirt was belted with cotton or leather, through which was thrust a kukri. Even the women carried kukris.

All day the music of the bells never ceased, ringing from the eaves and spires of the five thousand temples in the valley, and often there was the sardonic braying of horns, the throbbing of drums. Three times a day the curfew gun, a green and ancient cannon, sounded on the *maidan,* the white ball of its smoke bouncing across the grass. It sounded at five in the morning, at noon, and at ten in the evening. It was a strict curfew and once the evening gun was fired there was silence. My way home from the palace at night passed several police sentries. They stood on circular stone plinths beneath deckled red umbrellas, their puttees white, their khaki black-belted, their pillbox hats pushed forward over snub noses. For the first few evenings they stopped my car by standing in front of it with arms outstretched, coming forward to look at me suspiciously. After a few evenings of being stopped this way I devised a method of dealing with them. Ordering the chauffeur to continue driving, I lowered the window and shouted at the top of my voice, *"Maharajad-hiraja kar Naran Hity Durbar!"*

Literally this means "Palace of the King of Kings by the Well of God," and it seemed to satisfy them.

There were five guesthouses in Tripureswar, and among my neighbors, to my surprise, I discovered an American. He left Nepal a few days after my arrival, and I scarcely came to know him. His name was Charles Baskerville ("Like the hound, Miss Lauchtag!"), a middle-aged, blond man, with that overgrown schoolboy look that some middle-aged Americans have. He was an artist, and I never knew him well enough to ask or understand why an American artist should come to Katmandu. Although he told me that the Prime Minister had commissioned him to paint official portraits, this somehow did not seem a logical explanation.

In the few conversations I had with him he was preoccupied by some inner bewilderment. He was painting a portrait of the King, he said, the sittings taking place on the veranda at Naran Hity Durbar (he was not allowed inside). What bothered Mr. Baskerville was that throughout the sittings the King said nothing, not even in answer to the artist's pleasantries. "There he sits, Miss Erika, and doesn't say a blessed word, but just stares at my shoes!"

They were fine shoes if your taste runs in that direction. They were a new style then, without laces or straps. At the time Baskerville told me the story I was puzzled, too, and could not understand why the King should sit so silently, staring at a pair of shoes. Baskerville had gone before I discovered the explanation. The King was intensely interested in all things new and Western. Baskerville's shoes were something he had never seen before, and something he instantly wanted. But because he was forbidden to speak to Europeans without the permission of the Prime Minister, he could stare at the shoes only and hope that Baskerville was intelligent enough to divine the reason and tell him where they might be obtained.

I had few visitors at Tripureswar Number One. Baskerville once or twice until he packed up his paints and easel and went away to India. Doctor Siddhimani came sometimes to take a glass of lime juice, to sit politely on my sofa and ask me if all was going well with me. And Doctor Debabrata Das Gupta also came.

Doctor Das Gupta lived at Tripureswar Number Five, and he too was a physician to the royal family, although he was officially in charge of the Bir Hospital. He was a Bengali and a poor man, his clothes as shabby as his spirit and heart were rich. He should, by logic, have been well-to-do and comfortable, but the poor of Nepal were very poor, and the doctor treated many of them for nothing. The rich, the very rich Rana aristocracy believed that it was a privilege for any doctor to treat them, and that the presentation of an account for such treatment would be more criminal than impertinent.

He was a middle-sized man with a big head and light hair brushed stiffly back from his calm, resigned face. He had been trained in Rome and, I am sure, dreamed of Italy each night. He would come into my garden, calling pleasantly, *"Buon giorno, Signorina!"* He lived in his sparsely furnished home with his Indian wife, Mara, and three children—rolling, laughing, riotous little bundles that tumbled among the dust and the grass at the feet of the brown cow that always grazed in the Das Gupta garden.

The doctor came to mean a great deal to the King and to me in later days, but in those early weeks he was only a sad and gentle man anxious to help me. Almost immediately I arrived in Katmandu I was ill with dysentery, and only someone who has had this filthy and degrading affliction can know how miserable it made me. It was caused, perhaps, by the water, and although I boiled all the water I used this was of no help. The sacred water of that valley had touched every vegetable before it reached my table. Baskerville, who had suffered too, gave me some tablets before he left, but they made no difference to me. I appealed to Doctor Das Gupta. His face crumpled with concern, and he prepared a black powder for me that stained my mouth and teeth but which gave me some relief, though I continued to suffer all through my stay.

I never saw the Prime Minister again, except on official occasions, until the week of my leaving. He did not, however, forget me. Every day I received a tin of fifty cigarettes from Singha Durbar. Sometimes a bearer would come up my pathway, carrying a shallow basket of fruit, mangoes and oranges in flaming color.

It is perhaps a key to my attitude of mind during my stay in Katmandu that food meant nothing to me. I was cut off from the world beyond. I had no newspaper. I had no radio. Each day I received a letter from Mother, and each day I wrote to her; that was the only contact I had with India. I had quickly lost myself in this faery country, in this mys-

terious royal family, in their whispering palace. Yet I did
not feel lost. Never had I been so aware of myself, physically
and spiritually. Thus food meant nothing to me. Alcohol,
that I needed, and cigarettes, not so much to stimulate my
emotions as to control the emotional tension I began to feel
about and within me. I ate what was placed before me, and
since my *khansamah* was a wise cook and knew that all Europeans are mad enough to season their food after it has been
cooked, he put no salt at all into what he made. It was not
until I returned to India five months later that I realized I
had lived all that time without salt.

The *khansamah*, in any case, believed in taking the least
trouble. Once, it must have been the first day after my arrival, I agreed with his suggestion that it would be nice to
have an orange omelette for dessert after lunch. An orange
omelette I had every day after that, made from tiny bantam's
eggs and red-skinned mandarins. The cook came to me that
first morning after breakfast to ask what I would like for
lunch, and, when I said that it did not matter, he said that
perhaps a chicken would be acceptable. Yes, I said, a chicken.
Two hours later I saw a coolie walking into the garden, and
on his back a reed basket from which peeped the red-combed
head of a very live chicken.

"*Khansamah!*" I called. "You are not going to kill that?"

"Yes, memsahib. Kill chicken!"

"No!" I said, and the chicken lived, was liberated in my
garden, and repaid me by laying an egg.

The next morning the *khansamah* suggested a duck, and to
this, too, I said yes. But when the duck was brought in the
coolie's basket, quacking, yellow-beaked, I could not have it
killed. So it was liberated with my chicken and laid its grateful egg. After that it was a live goose to be reprieved, and
so on every day until the garden was alive with poultry and
the *khansamah* very much out of humor.

I ate very little and grew thin. Ghorki Ram looked at me speculatively one day and said, "Madam, do you know what you look like? You look only eyes and teeth. Your eyes have got so big that there is nothing left."

I had lived long enough to know that when the heart and the mind and the spirit are sustained the body requires little. This is how it must have been with the old Christian ascetics who lived on nothing but a handful of corn and a cup of water. Perhaps this is how it was with the sadhus, the holy beggars I saw in Katmandu Bazaar, gaunt, hollow-cheeked men wearing nothing but loincloths, and sometimes scarcely that. They sat at street corners, among the bicycles, the wandering goats and cows, their bodies covered with gray ash, their foreheads daubed with holy marks in orange, red, or white, or biscuit. It was through their eyes that you saw their strength. Perhaps that was what Ghorki Ram saw.

From the beginning, from that first evening when the King and I danced, something happened to me, and my emotions became a confused mixture of elation and fear. When the car left me at the palace I stepped into a world that was mysterious, fantastic, and, in some inexplicable way, frightening. There was no harsh note in the palace or in the lives of the royal family, yet fear and sadness were the undertones. But for the music of the phonograph when we danced, it was a palace without noise. What sounds I did hear were soft and gentle. No bells, no voices calling, no footsteps. King, queens and princesses would appear suddenly. The ladies in waiting were scarcely noticeable, coming and going soundlessly in the swirls of their saris. The King was the only man in his palace.

If he or his queens wanted an attendant they would softly clap their hands, halting the movement, almost, before the palms met. A lady in waiting would materialize from the wall or the sunlight, her lustrous head bent low over her hands.

She would not appear before the King, but to the rear of him, and he never looked at her. He scarcely spoke to her. What he wanted would be understood before he asked. If he wished to speak to one of his queens he would say "Ah?" so gently and so softly. How either of them knew that she was the one he desired, I do not know. Perhaps, in his understanding and theirs, they were both so fused into one being that it did not matter.

When I had given the Senior Queen her treatment in her bathroom and left her there, I would often wait in the garden for the King to come for his dancing lesson. I waited by the sundial he had designed, or by the pool he had planned, the rich flower beds that had been planted to his direction. I would wait five minutes, I would wait an hour, two hours, I never knew how long it might be, and when the King came he never explained the delay. I waited, watching the leathery, heart-shaped leaves of the lotus. The pigeons cooed in a bubbling river above me. At dusk the lights came on among the trees, and the rooks rose up in a great cawing cloud, and very often, at this precise moment, the King was suddenly there, standing among the trees or at the top of the steps, his hands together. "Madam?"

Then we would begin our dancing lesson. He was learning quickly. He had the superb, suspended grace of the angelfish that swam in the blue-green water of the tanks above the portico. His eyes never left me when we were together. They stared, not impertinently, not rudely, but with a sad concentration. I often saw the same expression in the eyes of the queens, and I searched my mind for a definition of it. When the answer came it was almost as a shock. It was the same thought that had come to me in the tea pavilion on the first evening. *He is wondering why you are really here.*

Even when I was alone in the garden, waiting, I felt that I was not unobserved. I knew that behind each tight window, through the locked leaves of the shrubs perhaps, I was being watched, not unkindly, not with hostility, but with this unhappy doubt.

We talked as we danced, but what we said was often so inconsequential that I would have forgotten the words had not that ever present tension in the air given them a meaning beyond what was intended.

Once he touched the lobes of my ears and smiled. "They are pierced, and so are mine. Are you a Hindu then?" And I could not tell from his voice or his smile whether he meant the question seriously, whether he knew so little of the world.

In the beginning I asked few questions, and when I did his answers were often so bitter that I was ashamed of the question.

"Your Majesty, do you read much?"

"I read, madam. It is my hobby. I have only hobbies."

One morning, over Katmandu I saw the rainbows, not one, not two, nor yet three, but five, forming a great arch from rim to rim. The memory of it was still in my mind when I went to the palace, and I told the King about it, saying, "I could stay in so beautiful a country forever."

He released me abruptly, and there was a long pause before he spoke. "Madam, if you had been here for forty-two years you would tire of the country."

He danced no more that evening, but placed his hands together and said, "Madam, may I go now, please?"

After the first week he was curious about the treatment I was giving the Senior Queen. He asked me for details, listening to my replies gravely, questioning the value of the treatment, and then he was silent for some while. He looked up at me and said, "You must give me treatment, then."

He had the figure of an athlete. I said, "You, Your Majesty? You do not need my treatment."

He drew up his head. "You do not understand. It is necessary for me to be fit. You will give me treatment."

When I called the next evening he was waiting for me in
the Senior Queen's bathroom. He was smoking, holding the
cigarette between the third and fourth fingers of his right
hand, not touching it with his lips, but drawing the smoke
through his clenched fist and inhaling deeply. Later I understood that he always smoked this way when he felt at ease
and happy. He stood erect by the treatment table, wearing a
bottle-green dressing gown, with his initial, that flowing T,
embroidered in white on the pocket. He had tied a light silk
scarf about his long throat. He was not wearing the Nepalese
cap, and his eyes were darkened by the forward sweep of
that protective wing of hair.

He took off the dressing gown. Beneath it he wore black
and white bathing trunks, and his body was as superbly
muscled and as graceful as that of the dancing deity Nata
Raja. About his hips, and dipping down toward his loins,
was a broad belt of thin golden mesh, fastened in the center
by a clip mouthed with a great emerald. Around the biceps
of his right arm writhed a golden snake, its head a milky
moonstone. From his throat hung amulets, strung to threads
of gold and emeralds.

From neck to ankle he was tattooed, twisting, cunning
convolutions of blue lace on his pale skin. The intricate patterns combined on his chest, thighs and shoulders to form
ferns, flowers and the outstretched beauty of peacock's
feathers.

FROM the beginning, from that first evening in the
tea pavilion, I think I sensed that something was
terribly wrong, not only with this pale-skinned king but
with his people, among whom, I discovered, he was scarcely

more than a name and a statue on the *maidan*. It was a restless feeling, and it contributed to my emotional tension in
the palace, yet I could not bluntly speak of it to him. It
was he who gave me the opportunity, within two weeks of
my arrival.

We had danced, and we were walking alone in the garden.
The rooks were gone, the lamps were lit, and the tortoises,
whom I had nicknamed John and Betty, were lurching
wearily to the undergrowth beyond the lake. We stopped
by the water and he put his hand into his pocket, withdrew
it and placed something in my hand. He said, "It is a present
for you, Miss Erika."

It was the bracelet, cunningly and beautifully wrought
of the same golden mesh I had seen about his waist. He gave
it to me with such simple affection that I could find nothing
to say and could only *namashkar* humbly, touching his feet
in the devout custom of his people. He raised me and, still
holding my hand, walked with me along the lake. He had,
perhaps intentionally, broken one of the barriers that he
had built about himself, and I began to speak of the things
that were disturbing me.

"Your Majesty, I don't understand many things. There is
something wrong with this country. I don't know what it is
but I feel it."

Doubt and suspicion made his voice harsh. "How do you
know?"

"I cannot explain it, but there are small things. This bodyguard who lives at my gate. He has not been put there to
protect me, but to watch me. Why?"

"I did not order it," he said.

"There is something else. I have never seen so many poor
people as I have seen here, so many diseased and maimed."

"Is this so?" he asked sadly.

"Don't you know, Your Majesty? Is there nothing to be done for them?"

"There is nothing I can do," he said, his voice cold again.

I learned the truth slowly, some of it from the King in the weeks that followed, but most of it long after I had left Nepal, and if I tell the story fully here it is because the sequence of my story demands it. In those days I knew nothing about the history of Nepal, but the longer I stayed in Katmandu the more terrible the picture that took shape, little pieces of colored stone coming together to form the mosaic. My initial feeling about the bodyguard soon made sense, for I was before long so enraptured by the gentleness and kindness of the Nepalese that the thought of needing protection from them was absurd.

The old Prime Minister, who, when I met him, had seemed to me to be little more than a charming and archaic figure, now began to appear faintly sinister, if only because of his omnipresence.

I noticed this first when I went to the Nepalese Post Office. There were two post offices in Katmandu, one Indian and one Nepalese. I learned that to post my letters to Mother at the Nepalese office would mean an unconscionable delay, so I took them to the Indian Post Office. But her letters for me arrived at the Nepalese office. Early in my stay I went there to tell the Postmaster that he might expect letters for me daily. The office was a derelict little house crouched in a scrubby garden. Inside was a dark room, a floor of uneven stone, a wall pigeonholed for letters, a row of clerks at their desks, and, beyond, the Postmaster's room. I went to him and said, "*Namashkar*, Postmaster. May I please collect my letters from you every morning? They are from my *mua-ji* in Simla who worries about me."

"Madam, of course," he said, and bowed. On his cap I saw the same little picture frame I had seen on the cap of the official who met me at Thankot, and in it the same portrait of the Prime Minister, with hooped mustache and pince-nez.

"Master-ji," I said, "why do you wear the Maharaja's picture in your hat?"

"Because we are very proud of His Highness, madam."

"But does no one wear the King's picture?"

He did not answer. He smiled, just as Mr. Kathait had smiled.

I had brought with me Mr. Kathait's letter of introduction to General Baber Shamsher Jung Bahadur Rana, Commander in Chief of the Army, and I asked Doctor Siddhimani where the General might be found. I was told that he could be seen every morning, riding on the *maidan* at eight o'clock, and there, the next morning, I found him. He was a fine man, bold in carriage if stoutish, his face fierce with a bristling mustache. I *namashkared* him when he passed, and at this unexpected greeting from a European he halted his horse, saluting. "Good morning, madam. What are you doing in Katmandu?"

I told him, and I handed him the letter from Mr. Kathait. He passed it to his aide, without looking at it, saluted again, and rode on. Each morning after that, as I took my walk about the square, he halted, saluted and spoke to me politely. But it is not this that makes me remember him.

He came on a fine bay horse. His sons, grandsons, equerries, and aides rode behind him, and behind them an escort of tall lancers with fluttering pennants of red and white. At the beginning of the exercise the cavalcade walked their horses about the square. Very grand they were, the well-groomed horses stepping prettily, bridle chains ringing, pennants snapping. On the far side of the *maidan* was a little temple of red earth and gold, and when the riders had walked twice about the square they dismounted and went inside to say their *pujas*. Then they came out and put their horses to

the trot, passing twice more about the *maidan*. By this time
little groups of peasants and artisans, old and young, were
gathering at the edge of the grass, holding scraps of paper
in their hands.

Now the horses began to canter, hoofs thudding, and the
waiting Nepalese broke into a stumbling run, trying to keep
up with the horsemen, waving their pieces of paper. Now
and then the General's principal aide might bend over and
take one of the papers, pushing it into his pocket. Most of
them he ignored. Every morning it was like this, and only
when the horses began to canter were the Nepalese allowed to
offer up their petitions against this or that injustice, their
appeals for this or that mercy. Only the strongest of men can
keep pace with a cantering horse, and in this way, I suppose,
the number of petitions to be dealt with was kept to a mini-
mum.

Sometimes, past my guesthouse at noon, soft-footed elephants would pass, and riding in their gay howdahs would
be little boys and girls, their eyebrows plucked, their mouths
painted, and jewels glittering in their ears or hair. They
wore European clothes, adult in style and strangely old-
fashioned. They looked like Edwardian dolls. I asked Doctor
Das Gupta who they were, and he replied that they were
Rana princes and princesses, and very rich.

"Doctor Sahib," I said, "are there no rich in this country
but the Ranas?" He shrugged his shoulders unhappily.

Nepal belonged to the Ranas and not to King Tribhuvana
or his people, that much was soon plain to me. How this had
come about I did not then know, but in the atmosphere of
the valley I felt a macabre mixture of the sacred and the
profane.

Since the days when Manjusuri breached the mountains
and drained the Tank of Serpents, Nepal has been a holy

land and a land of blood. Twenty-five hundred years ago the
last Buddha was born in Nepal, and a little more than a
century ago the Ranas took the country and made it theirs
with great slaughter.

Two main peoples lived in Nepal for many hundreds of
years, separated by mountain walls: the Gurkhas to the west,
and the Newars in the valley of Katmandu to the east. The
Gurkhas were warriors, but the Newars were craftsmen of
great skill and artistry who created the three kingdoms of
Katmandu, Patan and Bhadgaon, kingdoms that were really
but cities and so close together that an arrow might be shot
from one to the others. Late in the eighteenth century the
Newars were conquered by the Gurkhas, led by their Rajput
king, Prithwi Narain Sah, the incarnation of Vishnu. He
burned and slaughtered and made all Nepal a kingdom for
himself and his sons. But within a century of his conquest
his descendants were prisoners in their palaces, gibbering in
madness or dying in debauchery. The man who had done this
was a Rajput noble, Jung Bahadur Rana, whose ancestors had
come eastward with Prithwi Narain Sah.

The king in his day was Rajendra, a man mad and sane
by turns and much tormented by the infidelity and intrigues
of his wife. One day he called Jung Bahadur to him, put a
musket in his hand, and told him to kill his own uncle,
Mathabar Singh, the Prime Minister. This Jung Bahadur did,
and he made himself Prime Minister. Rajendra's queen, who
had been intriguing with Mathabar Singh, was angry and
called all the royalist nobles to the quadrangle of the Kot
Palace, there to decide how to be rid of Jung Bahadur. But
he surrounded the palace with three regiments, and when
the afternoon was over there was not a royalist noble left
alive, and the blood, running from the gates of the Kot
Palace, sent King Rajendra too deep into madness for re-

covery. Jung Bahadur Rana made himself hereditary Prime Minister, and he and the men of his family became the only power in Nepal.

Within five years he was the honored guest of Queen Victoria, sitting with her in the Opera House in London and sweetly comparing the singers to nightingales. Within ten years he had lent Gurkhas to suppress the military mutiny in Bengal and secured for himself the sympathy and support of the British. Rana succeeded Rana as Prime Minister, the title passing from brother to brother, or from father to sons when brothers became extinct. There grew up a complex dynasty, legitimate and illegitimate, that graded itself in precedence and privilege. There were A, B, and C Ranas, the A Ranas being the sons and daughters of the Prime Minister and his senior consort, the B Ranas the children of his second Maharani, and the C Ranas the children of his concubines. There was no aristocracy but Ranas. Only an A Rana could become Prime Minister, the others finding their fortunes in military or civil affairs. The Prime Minister held his position until death. Only one ever resigned, having made more than thirty million pounds by investments in Indian industry. Beyond power, the Ranas were interested in whisky, in women, and in hunting the tiger and rhinoceros in the Terai. Their people were serfs, forbidden to wear Western clothes, to ride in vehicles. The Ranas lived in great palaces within Katmandu and filled the rooms with pianos from Europe, billiard tables, Greek statuary. They married their daughters to Indians, and their sons also, drawing greater wealth in dowries. They built no roads except those from palace to palace, over which they might drive their Rolls-Royces.

Yet they lived in fear. They allowed no welfare work, lest it create dangerous public gatherings. They were suspicious of mass prayers in the temples for the same reason. When the Bikku Amritananda, the finest Buddhist monk

Nepal has produced, preached and spoke along the highways, the Prime Minister (he of the hooped mustache and pince-nez) ordered him to cease. The Bikku would not obey, asking what else was there for a Buddhist monk to do but to give comfort to those who needed it? So his monastery was closed and its monks were banished.

When I went to Katmandu I often saw the dark, ugly jail within the city and thought little of it beyond the natural spasm of distaste one feels when seeing such places. It was the King who told me there were five hundred political prisoners there, many of them chained, many of them having been imprisoned for ten, or fifteen, or twenty years. So it would be wrong to suggest that there was no active opposition to the Ranas. There was a Nepalese Congress Party, working in India, supported by disaffected Ranas. As later events proved, there was also an underground movement within the country, but for the most part the ordinary Nepalese were, like my Postmaster, I suppose, loyal to the Ranas as a weak wife is loyal to the husband who beats her daily.

The fiction that the King was the titular head of the country was thinly observed. Foreign decorations and honors, sent by convention from other nations, were in fact pinned to the already overburdened chest of the Prime Minister. The throne was maintained only because, to the Nepalese, the King was a deity. His titles were hollow, having no substance. The King was *Mahipati*, Lord of the Land. He was *Narpati*, Lord of Men. He was *Deva*, a god who could be and was often publicly worshiped. But he was also a prisoner of the Ranas, and the ceremony was a pantomime they performed when it pleased them. King succeeded king following the death of Rajendra, and king after king was coaxed into vice or driven into madness until, in 1911, a boy of five, Tribhuvana Bir Bikram Sah Deva, came to the throne, the ninth in line from

Prithwi Narain Sah. When he was twelve the Ranas found
brides for him in India, the sisters Kanti and Ishwari, each
younger than he. Before he was fourteen these girls had borne
him children.

From Tribhuvana I learned few of these details. What he
did tell me about himself, about the Ranas and his country,
came haltingly, and only as his early distrust of my presence
faded. When I understood I could not blame him for that
distrust. Never before had he been allowed to talk to a European alone, never had a European been allowed within his
private palace unescorted by a Rana. So when I came it was
natural that he should think me a spy for the Ranas. This
doubt did not wholly pass until my last few days, after we
had planned so much, and then he cried, "Erika, I cannot
understand why I have been given this incredible luck!"

Yet he did tell me much. One day I spoke of the postmen
I had seen on my way to the valley, the half-naked, brown
men, with bells ringing on their anklets and on the bamboo
poles in which they carried their messages. I said how charmed
I had been by the sight and the sound of them. He smiled
and took my hand, tolerantly, as with an innocent child.

"Do you know why these *dak* runners are belled, Erika?
So that men may hear them and know they are running. If
the bells are silent this must be reported by whoever notices
it. Then the postmen are punished. They are tied together,
trussed like poultry, their arms behind their backs and their
legs bent to their wrists. Ropes are tied across their mouths to
gag them. They are left in the sun on rough rocks for a day,
or two days, perhaps more, until they are bleeding and swol-
len. Then, perhaps, they may be rolled down the mountain-
side."

"It is not possible!" I said.

"Such things are possible, Erika. Not long before you came

here, a man was executed in Katmandu because he listened to Gandhi on the radio."

I put my hands over my ears and said that I would listen to no more. Then I said, "But surely men cannot be executed without the King's seal. Why do you not refuse?"

"There is a royal seal," he said ironically. "And it is locked in the Prime Minister's desk at Singha Durbar, so that I may not lose it."

Imprisoning Tribhuvana within his Happy Cottage was not enough for the Ranas. They built about him a more subtle cage of slander. By lies they destroyed any instinctive sympathy or curiosity that foreigners might feel. To the people of the British Embassy he was a name, a nonentity, a pale figure in a white sharkskin uniform, standing at his throne for official durbars, saying only what had been written for him, and then hurrying away to enjoy the private vices which the Ranas, with winks and shrugging shoulders, said were his only interest. He meant so little to the few Europeans in Katmandu that a woman at the British Embassy could say to me, "The King? Oh yes, a handsome brute, isn't he?" Travelers to Nepal, Westerners who came and who left to write books of what they had seen, wrote what they had been told about the King, what the Ranas told them. Thus it was believed beyond the Himalayas that Tribhuvana was dissolute, a man who passed his time with drunkenness, lechery and opium, a man with the physique and spirit of a weak girl. Such a picture fitted the tradition of the debauched oriental raja, just as the Ranas fitted the picture of the strong grand vizier, and this was how they wanted it. It was easy for the British and for the Indians to believe this, so long as the Ranas sent their baskets of fruit, held tennis parties, drank tea, and ordered done what needed to be done.

Chance, the Prime Minister's conviction that I was a friv-

olous and stupid woman, made me the first European to discover the truth. The debauchee was in fact a muscular man
who had learned judo in his youth, who could ride two horses
at the gallop with one foot on each, who could play most
sports superlatively well. The drunkard was in fact a man
who would do no more than touch his lips with spirits in
courtesy, because by alcohol the Ranas had destroyed his father and grandfather. The lecher of the lies was in fact a man
with respect and love for his wives and a belief that all Western women were immoral. As for taking opium, his only
drug was cigarettes.

He was proud of his fine body and jealous of its strength,
not in masculine vanity, but because this was one thing he
had preserved from the Ranas. As the days passed I saw him
as a man ready and waiting, a desperate man and a bitter
man, yet keeping despair and bitterness in patient check.
Every day the reality of his imprisonment was impressed
upon him. If he wished to drive his car beyond the grounds
of Naran Hity Durbar he could do so only after asking the
Prime Minister's permission, and only then in the company
of an armed Rana officer. Every Thursday he was summoned
to Singha Durbar and kept waiting there, for an hour, for
two hours, until the Maharaja was ready to discuss those mat-
ters which needed discussion. Sometimes he would begin to
speak to me of the Nepal outside Naran Hity and then
abruptly break off the conversation, as if he had remembered
that the soldiers at the gates of his palace were there to keep
him in, not others out.

This country, Nepal, the Cherished of God, which his
ancestors had conquered, was almost completely unknown to
him. Far more real were the department-store catalogues
which he had delivered to him from India, France, England,
Japan and America, and from which he learned much of the
outside world. He would endure the Happy Cottage for

days or weeks and then, unable to stand it any longer, humbly ask permission to drive his car through Katmandu. With a Rana general beside him, he drove quickly, but with great skill. Once I saw his beige Mercury on the Judha Road, and in the evening I asked him why he went abroad without a protective escort, a squadron of lancers such as followed General Baber. Was it not dangerous?

"Erika," he said, "who would wish to kill *me*?"

But he was not as safe as that, and once he had been very afraid. He told me about it much later. He gave no details, but I deduced that it had happened some years before my coming, when there had been a minor revolt of disgruntled C Ranas in which the Prime Minister believed the King to be implicated. All day he and his sons waited alone in Naran Hity Durbar, expecting to be shot at any moment.

"We all told the same lie," he said, "and they let us live."

For a long time I wondered how a man, imprisoned since birth, his letters censored, his every movement scrutinized, could have learned so much about the outside world, particularly the economic and political structure of Western democracy. He could not have learned of this from the mail-order catalogues which were the only books the Ranas allowed him to receive. Nor could it have formed part of his education, which, as he said, was given "by a poor Nepalese." When I finally asked him for an explanation he smiled, like a schoolboy remembering a particularly successful hoax.

Years before, in the time of the current Prime Minister's predecessor, the King had twice been allowed to visit India. Political necessity made it essential for him to be shown beyond the Himalayas. It was a moment's freedom, a freedom very much on leash, and therefore no release at all, unless you believe that when a caged animal puts its head between the bars it has secured a measure of liberty. The King went to Delhi and to Calcutta surrounded by Rana generals, and he saw little over their shoulders and heard nothing against the sound of their voices. India, official India that is, saw little of him either and perhaps did not care, for the governments of nations deal with cynical realities, and the reality of Nepal was that the Ranas controlled it.

Tribhuvana was not a fool, even in his youth. Before he left for India he went alone into the gardens of Naran Hity, night after night, returning with stones he had gathered. With these he filled two trunks, and he locked them. In India he removed the stones and filled the trunks with books, books on economics, on the political and social history of the West. How he obtained such books, watched all the while by the Ranas, he would not tell me.

He had returned from India, too, with the belief that he had found a friend. From childhood onward, from the death of his father, from the time the great skullcap of gold had been placed on his head at his coronation, he had been surrounded by women—by his mother, by his father's concubines, by his own wives, daughters, and ladies in waiting. His sons were taken from him while they were still boys, educated by the Ranas and married to Rana princesses. He saw no men except those who came to him from the Ranas. And then he had gone to India and there met a man who was not Indian or Nepalese, who was not a creature of the Ranas, and who was perhaps, because of his position, the only other kind of man the King was likely to meet. This was Boris, the manager of the hotel. He sat all afternoon with the King, talking to him, while the bored Rana escort nodded sleepily at the window. The King never forgot Boris.

"He was my friend," he said. "He was my only friend."

And I knew then how those books had perhaps been obtained.

From India the King also brought back a view of European women which, when I first encountered it, nakedly, was like a blow in the face. Yet, remembering the type of Western women in Delhi and Calcutta whom the Ranas would probably have put in his way, I had to admit that his narrow view was at least justified by his experience. To him all European women were harlots and without that skill of intellect and charm that makes an Eastern courtesan an artist in her profession. He considered European women to be vulgar, immoral and promiscuous. Once, when he referred briefly to an Englishwoman whom he had met in India, I asked him what she was like. I was less concerned with her than with him, for when a man attempts to describe a woman he has met he often tells you far more about himself.

He smiled. "She wore a wide skirt, and above it she wore two roses. When I asked her the name of the perfume she was using she said 'Sweet Cocktail,' and I believe that was all she ever said to me."

If we respect the knowledge that comes to us we should act upon it. Slowly I began to believe that it was not just an accident that I had met this man Tribhuvana. I began to understand a little of the odd prescience I had experienced when the letter came to me in Simla. I had come to a land where the Prime Minister's gold crown was worth two hundred thousand pounds and a laborer's daily wage was only twopence-ha'penny; where I could walk up from the funeral ghats on the riverbank and narrowly avoid being run over by a Cadillac; where an imprisoned god-king read mail-order catalogues and dreamed of a constitutional monarchy. And I knew that I could not leave Nepal without helping him.

What I could do, I did not know. That knowledge was to come later, much later. Meanwhile my life was spent in the evenings, in the transported atmosphere of the royal gardens, a phonograph playing records by Victor Sylvester, and a shoeless incarnation of God gravely learning the fox trot, the one-step, the waltz and the tango.

ALMOST every morning, when the drill sergeants on the *maidan* were still shouting to little mountain boys who wished to become Gurkha warriors, a bearer trotted up my pathway with a cinnamon-colored note from the palace. *Miss Erika please come today at five p.m.* Sometimes no note came at all until the evening, when I was dressed to leave, and this might say: *Miss Erika please do not come to the palace today so come at six p.m. tomorrow.* No reason was ever given for anything that happened at the palace. All day I would wait with nerves and emotions tight, and if a visit was postponed the collapse of the tension was worse than the enduring of it.

The notes were all signed by Sardar Pushparaj. He was an elderly, melancholy Nepalese from the offices at Singha Durbar, and he was in charge of the King's secretariat. Such work was of no official importance, no more than the clerking of the King's solitary private life, the writing of letters to Europe and India and America, ordering jewelry, cameras, electrical fixtures, clothes. Sardar Pushparaj was a Rana man, of course, and of course a copy of every letter he wrote, a report of every conversation he had or heard at the Happy Cottage, was placed before the Maharaja at Singha Durbar. The King knew this, yet he had a tolerant affection for the old man.

Sardar Pushparaj was not unlikable. His skin was parchment-colored, his mustache white. He looked like a dried lemon, and beneath his sad, resigned features there smoldered a hesitant charm. Despite his primary obligations to the Ranas, which he undoubtedly observed, he was loyal to the royal family, and long after, when the world turned upside down, he remained in the service of the Senior Queen.

So, almost every day I went to the Happy Cottage in the

cool evenings, and almost every day I learned more of these pale prisoners, and each time I loved them more. I gave the Senior Queen her treatment with great care, for her white skin bruised easily. Sometimes I treated the King, too, for although his body was strong and superbly made it was wasting now, as a tiger's magnificence will waste when caged.

When the treatment was over for the evening, the King and I danced on the black and white marble of the hall, for two, three, and sometimes four hours. Soon, too, I began to give lessons to the queens and the princesses. I have never known more modest people than these two gentle women to whom the King was married. I saw them as projections of his thoughts and his feelings. Among all three of them there was an oddly sensitive understanding, a mutual experience of all sensations. The King made no distinction between the sisters, and if, in his spontaneous generosity, he gave one a present for some pleasure she had given him, then he gave the other an identical present. They were not two women to him, but one, Lakshmi, his consort. His children, also, looked upon both queens as one parent, calling each *Mua-ji*—Mother— whether she was in fact or not. And it seemed to me that neither queen showed a preference for her own children against her sister's.

Yet to my eye there was a difference between the King's wives, and I called them by pet names that marked the difference. The Senior Queen I called Birdy, because of her bright eyes. The Junior Queen was Dreamy because of that sad, contemplative look in her face. Within a few days the King was referring to them by these names. Dreamy had beautiful hands, long, slender and waxlike, so beautiful that when I greeted her I would *namashkar* and kiss them. After some days she began to hold them out to me when we met.

The King also made no distinction in favor and treatment between his daughters. They, too, dressed alike, in the same materials, the same colors. They wore the same jewelry, the same hair-caught flower, and when he smiled to one the smile rested on her momentarily only, before it moved to embrace all three impartially. Nalini, Vijaya, Bharati—tall, slender and pale. They were like lilies that have grown in the shade. Their faces were carefully powdered, their brows exquisite, lipstick and mascara applied discreetly. Each morning their hair was dressed in identical styles, in heavy, rolled curls. Their English was not as good as the King's. They had been taught by Sardar Pushparaj. Their voices were pitched on a high note, yet whispered, and there were times when I longed for one of them to open her throat and lungs and try the full strength of both. Once, in desperation, I caught Vijaya about the waist, lifted her light body from the floor and thumped it down suddenly. She squealed, and I cried triumphantly, "Hah, I see you have a voice after all!"

The soft rustle of their voices, the heady perfume they always wore, once had an extraordinary effect on Peepchen. The spaniel got away from Ghorki when I arrived at the palace one evening, and she ran on ahead of me through the gardens to the pool. Animals are peculiarly sensitive to muted sound and strong scent. In the garden the three princesses gathered about Peepchen, talking quickly. Poor Peepchen, overwhelmed by the whispering voices and the perfume, ran madly in circles until she finally fell into the lake.

There was a fourth princess, Triloki, whom I never met in Katmandu. Long before I came she had been married and sent away to India. It was many days before I was able to differentiate the three I did know, but slowly their distinctive characteristics became known to me. Nalini was perhaps the loveliest of all, with eyes like a young doe's. She was also the least intelligent and had the dreaminess of her mother, the Junior Queen. Her voice, the gentlest of the three, would linger on unfinished sentences, as if the effort of completing them was not worth it. But she was the best dancer. Vijaya was very slim. Sometimes it seemed to me that she was wasting away. But of all three I liked Bharati most, although I tried to be as impartial as the King. Bharati had the strongest character, the strongest will to be an individual, an instinctive need to act and think for herself which she kept in check dutifully for most of the time. I think Bharati understood something of what I felt in the Happy Cottage. Among all the rich and extravagant presents I received from the royal family, I cherish one simple gift from Bharati, given to me impulsively one day. It is an arm bangle of pale blue plastic, the sort of thing Indian women will wear on their arms and a thing of no value in itself. When I told her that I never would part with it she put her arms about my shoulders quickly.

In the presence of Tribhuvana the princesses would never speak, unless drawn into the conversation by him. They would sit apart, sometimes silently, sometimes talking among themselves so softly that I scarcely heard the sound. Whatever I asked them (and I asked much I should not have asked) I always received the same answer, "*Ma lai taha cha-in-na*. I do not know." When I came in the evening and found them alone in the garden, I would say, "Is *Bua-ji*, is your father inside?" and they would answer, "I do not know."

I would ask, "Is *Bua-ji* reading? Are we going to dance this evening?"

"We do not know."

They knew. But not-knowing was one of the bars of the cage the King built about his family for his and their protection. Sometimes, when her sisters could not hear, Bharati would take my hand, bring her beautiful face close to mine, and very softly answer my questions. This was a great manifestation of her love.

The princesses would ask no questions, though sometimes their curiosity would be very evident in their great eyes. My clothes, I knew, fascinated them, yet all they would do would be to lean forward and touch a ring, a handbag, a dress, and say, "That is nice." They had the King's horror of untidiness and uncleanliness. As I sat talking to him, and smoking, a wisp of ash might fall to my skirt, and Malini, or Vijaya, or Bharati would lean forward and softly, gently, with puckered lips, blow it away.

When we met in the evenings I would sometimes pluck flowers from the gardens, carnations perhaps, or velvet-skinned pansies as large as the palm of my hand. I gave them to the princesses, and often to the queens, and they put them in their hair, wearing them until they withered or until I brought them fresh ones. If, when I came, I saw that the King had no flower in his lapel, I picked one and put it there.

At night when I left, passing through the glass door, through the gardens to where my car waited at the foot of the steps, I received a present. It was more often given to me by the King, but sometimes by the queens. When I asked the queens from whom the present came, they would say, "From Narain."

The presents were fabulous or frivolous. One evening it might be a single, giant carnation, the next a watch, a simple notebook, or a diamond clip, a bracelet, or underwear, silk stockings, a golden fountain pen, a cigarette case, a cigarette lighter. When I received the lighter I said, "But, Your Majesty, I have one. You asked to see it yesterday."

"You change your clothes frequently," he said. "Why not change your cigarette lighter also?"

There seemed no end to the things he possessed, to the things he could produce at a moment's notice, brought to him by a lady in waiting, or by one of his queens in response to his lifted eyebrow. All of them, whether it was a pair of nylons or a book on ballet, he had ordered from his mail-order catalogues, and the thought of it sometimes brought me close to tears.

For a long time he continued to call me "Madam," a form of address so cold, and so much in contradiction to the warmth of affection with which they all surrounded me, that I longed to ask them to call me by my name. But I could not find the opportunity until he, himself, made it possible.

In addition to the garden, to the dancing in the hall, we began to use a room upstairs. We went up the marble staircase in procession, the King first, often in one of the beautifully tailored Western suits which he had made for him in India, and leading me by the hand; then came the queens and the princesses. The walls of the staircase were hung with Chinese paintings, soft, watery landscapes, with tiny boats held poised on gentle ripples and boatmen with poles upraised. Each painting had a plate on the frame, declaring it to be a gift from Chiang Kai-shek, and I wondered, and never discovered, why they had reached the Happy Cottage and not been taken by Singha Durbar.

At its head the staircase led to a gallery from which we went through a door into a long, narrow room. It was, but for the scent of sandalwood and roses, and for the inevitable arrowhead windows tightly closed, a room such as might be found in a rich Western house. In one corner was a cocktail bar with high stools, in another a right-angled sofa and a low coffee table. There was another wall sofa and a table in a third corner. There was a long dining table, elliptical and covered with black glass. One end of it was fastened to the wall, and nobody could sit there. The tables were covered with tall vases of flowers, burning with color like torches.

On the first evening I was taken there the King asked me if I would like a drink. Until this evening I had been

offered no food and drink during my visits, and I had begun
to think that these faery folk existed without the needs of
normal people. He opened a green wooden cabinet on the
far wall. Its shelves were full of every spirit and liqueur that
a wine merchant might be able to name. His hand on the
door, the King turned and said with gentle mockery, "You
know that there is Prohibition in my country?" I said that
I did. "Well, then, I think we should open King of Kings."

He poured the whisky into a great cut-glass beaker and
handed it to me. I gave it back to him to drink, and he
smiled, barely touched his lips with it, and returned it. I
never saw him drink more than this.

We sat there that evening, the King and I on the wall
sofa, the queens beside us, and the princesses like a gathering
of flowers on a great cushion, whispering among themselves.
The phonograph was brought and placed on a table, and
sometimes we danced, sometimes we listened to the music, the
King with his arm about my waist, and the queens happy
in his happiness.

One evening, as we sat there, the King said, "Madam, do
you know my name?"

"I do. It is His Majesty the Maharajadhiraja Tribhuvana
Bir Bikram Sah Deva."

He was delighted. *"Shabash!"* He stood up, lifted his head
away from me, thinking, and then said, "Madam, you are a
friend of the family now. I would like you to have my visiting card."

He glanced at the Junior Queen, and she rose with a delighted smile, rustled through the door, and returned shortly
with a golden *mohur,* a thick, yellow coin as large as a silver
dollar. The King held it in the air between finger and
thumb and turned it so that the light gleamed on it. He
read the characters about its edge, softly, his voice an odd
mixture of pride and bitterness.

"Svasti Shri Girirajachara Chudmani Nara-Narayanetyad
Vividh Virudavali Virajmana Monnonata Prajjovala-Nepal-
Tara Maharajadhiraja Shri Shri Tribhubanarurani Rana Jang
Bahadur Shamsher Jang Devanam Sada-Samara Vijavinam.
Madam, my card!"

He placed it in my open hand.

"I make you an honorary member of the Royal Family of
Nepal."

And I touched his feet in *namashkar*.

The next day I brought him my own visiting card, white
pasteboard with my name engraved, and on it I wrote, "For
gold I give paper. I will prove—sooner or later—that I am
loyal to you, dearest H.M." I asked that he call me Erika.

There was little I could give him, little I had brought
with me from India, and less to be bought in the Katmandu
bazaar. One day I took him a rose from my garden and said
that I wished it were more. He said, "Erika, a dry leaf from
you would be better than a diamond."

We began to spend much of the evening in this room upstairs. We danced there, and sometimes we ate there. I never
became used to the royal family's languid indifference to
time. I was always punctual in attendance, knowing that if
I were five minutes late only, the King would disapprove.
Yet he would himself often be two hours late for his dancing
lesson, without explanation, without apology. He never once
mentioned the time of day. The watches he wore on his wrist,
a different one each day and never the same one twice, were
an ornament, and I never saw him consult them. Why should
he? Where had he to go, and what had he to do?

I learned that he awoke each morning at nine and drank
the tea brought him by a lady in waiting. Very slowly and
very elaborately he dressed, assisted always by one of his
queens. At eleven-thirty he ate a light meal which lasted him
until midnight sometimes. In the evening he would order

food to be brought, and the queens, the princesses and I would eat while he stood silently at the door watching, his body held gracefully immobile, his face shadowed by his hair. Sometimes, with no explanation he would leave us, going away in a mood of melancholy, and returning in a contrasting humor of boyish high spirits, having purged his sadness by solitude. He came silently always. If my back was to the door I knew that he had come, not by any sound but by some extrasensory awareness. I would turn my head and there he would be, in white Nepalese clothes, or beige, or green, his favorite color, having changed his dress with his mood. He would be smiling in pleasant enjoyment of his silent arrival.

One evening the tea wagon was brought to the cocktail bar by a lady in waiting whom I had never seen before. She was a Nepalese, darker-skinned than the queens or the princesses, but indescribably beautiful. She was tall and slender and graceful, and her saris were always richly embroidered and of the finest materials, as fine as the queens'. Her dark hair was rich, and not drawn back tightly from the forehead as is the way of Nepalese women, but brought forward in two waves, one above each eye, and then backward and upward to form a crown. Her neck was long, her arms slender, and they moved gracefully as she passed the fragile cups of pale tea, the plates of ridiculous English sandwiches. I could not understand her. She was so unlike the other ladies in waiting who always smiled at me, giggling, their faces dimpling when I gave them nicknames like Muffle, Ball and Whiney. This lovely creature would not look at me. I tried to smile at her, to greet her, but I got no response.

Much later, when I was alone with the King, I said, "That was a beautiful woman. Does she belong to Your Majesty?"

He was surprised. "How could you know?"

I said, "A thing like that is not difficult for a woman. But why will she not smile at me, or answer me?"

"It is my order," he said briefly.

But this girl, whose name was Sala, and whom I called Sadface, became very much mine. I persuaded the King to give permission for her to join our dancing lessons. She was like a frightened animal as I tried to teach her, clutching at me with her beautiful fingers, burying her face in my shoulder. It was obvious that the royal family thought of her as more than a lady in waiting, and much later I discovered that it had been the queens who had brought her to the Happy Cottage, hoping that she might be able to give to the King some consolation which they, even in their great love, were unable to give.

When I learned of this I had no conventional reaction. Within that palace I was like a taut violin string, and I vibrated in sympathy with the emotions about me. I began to sense the King's pleasure or displeasure before they were manifested, just as I sensed his presence before a sound was made, and I began to understand some of that extraordinary telepathy that passed between him and his queens and his daughters.

Life in the palace, transported though it was, was not without its ludicrous situations, to me at least. Every door was locked and kept locked. Every door, even the bathrooms. When the King bathed he unlocked his bathroom, locked it behind him, emerged, and locked it again. When we went upstairs to the cocktail bar in the evenings there was always a pause while this door, too, was unlocked. I could not have moved alone about the palace, even had I had the intention, for twenty paces would have brought me to a locked door. The King, the queens and the princesses all carried about their waists a little bunch of golden keys, and each key was stamped with the letter T.

After two or three hours in the evening I would feel the pressing need of a key to the door of one very ordinary but

essential room. The need soon passed from the ridiculous to
the critical, and when I could bear the situation no longer
I would whisper hoarsely, "Bharati—*the key!*" Smiling she
would detach the key from its ring and, still smiling, replace
it when I returned.

Locked doors and closed windows, unexplained delays and
the fiction of "not knowing" were all of psychological importance to the King. One would think that a prisoner would
develop a pathological hatred of locks and secrecy, but the
truth is more subtle. Shut in from the world by the Ranas,
he preserved some of his individuality by shutting out life
from himself. Every aspect of his nature, too, was another
locked door, each enigmatic smile and each melancholy look
of his eyes another key turning.

I tried, not always successfully, to do those things that gave
him pleasure. With my hair I failed. I knew he admired rich,
lustrous, black hair. I had come over the Himalayas with my
hair cropped short in the style of the twenties, but even short
hair needs attention now and then and I sent Ghorki down
into the bazaar to find me a barber. The man he brought was
a little Hindu whose usual customers were male Nepalese,
and I think he looked on my hair as a new and exciting challenge. His own instruments were dirty, and I made him use
my scissors and comb. He was a busy little man who seemed
to believe that the best testimonial to his work lay in the
amount of hair he cut off. Every week he came, and every
week I cried "*Bandkaro!* Not so much!" But he clipped away
happily, and my short hair grew shorter and shorter.

The King said nothing.

Before sunset in the evenings, while we waited for the
King, the princesses and I sat on the hammocks in the garden,
Bharati and Nalini on either side of me, and sometimes Vijaya
at our feet. Or perhaps we would sit on the bench above the
lotus pool, and sometimes I would know that the King had

come and would turn to find him standing there, relaxed and smiling. The latest moment he chose to come would be dusk, just as the lights came on and the rooks rose, and I knew that he picked this moment for its dramatic effect, and I did not blame him.

While we waited the tortoises lumbered about the rich grass, crunching mangoes, or seeking shelter for the night. I knew that they were not just pets to make movement in a garden where the air was sometimes so still that the flowers looked like wax. I had seen enough images of Lakshmi in the rock-hewn shrines. A calm goddess with downcast eyes, wide-hipped, slender-waisted, great-breasted, her delicate feet resting on the shell of a tortoise.

It was the day after I christened those sad beasts John and Betty (inaccurately determining their sex, by the way) that Nalini asked me whether I would like to hold one, holding it up to me herself. I shook my head in horror, and she placed it on the ground, and all three girls regarded me in grave speculation. When I was not looking Vijaya picked up one of the animals and placed it in my lap, and there I sat, ridiculously patting it, while the princesses put their hands over their mouths, as close to hysterical amusement as I ever saw them. For the rest of the evening, as if ashamed of this breach of deportment, they were more silent than usual.

Perhaps to pass the time in the long hours we waited for the King, I began to teach them embroidery in the style I had learned from my grandmother. I taught them to sing German *lieder,* too, and for the first time they raised their voices above a whisper. I began German lessons, and because we had no textbooks I took my examples from the things about us in the garden, pointing to one of the silly plaster dwarfs and mushrooms. "Bharati, *was ist das?*" And she would say *"Das ist ein Zwerg"* or *"Das ist ein Pilz."*

And I knew we were being watched. Behind one of the

closed windows, from the little balcony outside the King's
bedroom, hidden by the caged birds or the angelfish in their
tanks, the King watched us until he chose his own moment
to arrive.

Now and then I saw the King outside Naran Hity Durbar,
at those official functions where the Ranas considered it politic for him to make an appearance. There was, for example,
a sports festival on the *maidan*. In khaki uniform and peaked
cap, from the center of which shone a great diamond that had
once belonged to Napoleon, he sat on the rostrum beneath
the banyan tree. Sitting to his right were his three sons,
Crown Prince Mahendra and the young men Himalaya and
Bashundera. They were sad pictures in smart tunics, breeches
and Sam Brownes, the legs apart dejectedly and their heads
bent. The King's face, head lifted, was emotionless, and about
him and his sons the Rana generals gathered in brilliant
colors.

Although the *maidan* was close to my guesthouse, my car
took me there for the festival, parking close to the great
American Buicks and Cadillacs in which sat the Rana women,
glorious in white and scarlet, blue and gold, purple, green and
silver, their throats, wrists, ears, nostrils and hair glittering
with jewels. They watched the sports through black binocu-
lars. I joined the queens and princesses in their car.

It was an entrancing festival. Gurkha bagpipers in scarlet
coats and green breeches marched up and down, up and
down. Nepalese girls and boys went through a breathless and
wondrous display of gymnastics. Beyond the banyan tree the
ladies from the British Embassy, in flowered frocks and wide
hats, clapped politely.

When it was over I drove on to the palace. The King was
like a boy released from school that evening, laughing as I
mimicked for him the overgracious hand-waving of the British Ambassador's stately wife.

"She is like Mount Everest," I said. "We will call her that."
And ever after we did.

Having seen his sons for the first time that day I was curious about them, and I spoke of them. He would not talk about them, beyond saying that they lived away from him, in palaces of their own within the grounds of Naran Hity Durbar, or elsewhere, and then he spoke of something else, and I was left to wonder.

One day, however, I met one of Prince Bashundera's children. I came to the palace and found Dreamy standing by the pool, where the shadows fell across it, and in her arms was what first seemed to me to be a doll. It was a beautiful girl of perhaps three, no older. Dreamy smiled and placed the child on the ground between us. "This is Princess Ketaki, Erika."

She was beautiful, her tiny, oval face framed with the dark hair of her grandfather, her cheeks powdered, and in the lobe of each ear was a huge yellow diamond. She watched me cautiously until I dropped to my knees and called "Mickey Mouse!"—for all Nepalese and Indian children, with their wide, innocent eyes, are Mickey Mouse to me. She hesitated and then put out her arms and ran to me.

She was often in the gardens when I came after that, and she would call to me excitedly, "Erika-ji!" I taught her to dance, a few first ballet steps, and on the first day she was able to lift her little body onto her toes and turn it gracefully.

When I discovered that she had no dolls I was depressed, and I felt that in some way she had been robbed. I made a rag doll for her from scraps I had at the guesthouse. But a doll should be dressed, and while I had material for such dresses too, I had no machine to make them on. So I went to the bazaar in my car, stopping by a shop where a tailor sat cross-legged in the shadows. I asked him if I might use his machine, and, without surprise, he said with the courtesy of all Indian storekeepers, "Madam, the shop is yours."

So I sat there all morning in the cool shop, my foot working the treadle, my fingers pushing the material beneath the throbbing needle, and children and beggars, and cows and goats gathered outside to watch.

That evening the King was waiting for me, and I think this was the first time he had ever done this. He was excited. With scarcely an acknowledgment of my *namashkar* he said, "Erika, what were you doing in that tailor's shop this morning?"

"Your Majesty, how on earth could you have known?"

"I know," he said. "Now tell me what you were doing."

I let him have his mystery, remembering those sudden, desperate drives he took in his car through the bazaar, and I said, "I was making this for Mickey Mouse!"—producing the doll from under my arm.

He spread out his hands with delight. He laughed and was then suddenly sad. He took my hand and walked with me in the gardens, silent for a long while.

Once, when I was telling him of the little Rana princesses riding on their elephants, dressed in their quaintly old-fashioned clothes, I said that I would design and make a dress for Ketaki such as European children of her age wore. Gravely he asked me to describe it, and I sketched it quickly on paper—a little smock with short sleeves and a Peter Pan collar. He looked at it and he studied it carefully, and then he put it back into my hand, saying coldly, "It is not necessary."

The next evening there was Ketaki waiting for me by the pool, her hand held by her grandmother. She called "Erika-ji!" and ran to me. She was wearing a little smock with short sleeves and a Peter Pan collar.

Out from behind a shrub came the King, enjoying his surprise.

I should have known that there was nothing he had not bought at one time or another as he read through his mail-order catalogues. The world they could not enter was not strange to either him or his queens. Queens and princesses always dressed in fashion, for there is a fashion in saris that changes subtly but as arbitrarily as Western styles. The fundamental basis of the sari, the most flattering of all women's clothes, has remained unaltered for centuries, Indian women having long ago discovered that no other form of dress can grace them so well. Yet its mood changes. For a time saris will have broad borders, then only thin piping. Sometimes the choli, the blouse worn beneath the sari, leaves the waist naked, then again it covers it. The contrasting colors, between sari and choli, vary rhythmically, at one time a green sari with yellow choli, then yellow with blue, ivory with scarlet, so that season by season Indian women work wonderful permutations of color and style from these two simple garments.

The queens and princesses followed these fashions as dutifully as the women of India, with one exception—their cholis were always long-sleeved, and they never exposed the slender beauty of their arms, even in the high heat of the summer. I asked Bharati why this was so, and she said, "It is a royal *hokhum*, it is *Bua-ji's* order."

"Why?" I asked the King. "Don't you like to see a woman's arms bare?"

"Yes," he said, "but not among my own family."

Like most Western women I admired the sari without believing that I had the grace or figure to wear it. My fulsome admiration of the queens' clothes was always accepted with gentle smiles of pleasure. One evening I came to the palace and found them and the princesses waiting for me in the hall, and on this occasion all were dressed differently. It was some festive day, but what I did not discover, yet their happiness and excitement for once broke through their reserve and lightened their voices. When I clapped my hands and cried, "*Shabash!*" at their appearance, they turned slowly so that I might admire the beautiful, fragile material the better. They were like magical fountains of color, showered with sequins. Then they took my arms, like girls, saying, "Erika, we have one for you too!"

In the Senior Queen's bathroom, on the divan, they had laid out for me a pink, filmy sari, and a turquoise choli with a high waist and short sleeves, and they dressed me in it, chattering excitedly, standing back with hands clasped when the end of the sari had been draped over my short hair to frame my face. The King came, and we all bowed before him, like a bank of flowers suddenly moved by the wind. "Well done!" he cried.

He insisted that I should wear the sari more often, that one should be made for me. Soundlessly, almost, he asked for a tape measure, and Birdy brought it. He measured me carefully, noting the figures on paper, and when he had finished he said, "Tomorrow evening you will see."

The next evening, in his emerald-green bathroom, on the ground floor close by the hall, he and his wives and his daughters were waiting for me. There were two saris and two cholis, a brown, gold-bordered sari, and another the color of heather —known botanically as *erica*. I chose the second—my color— and with it an ivory choli embroidered in gold, and I drew the palu over my ugly hair and went upstairs to the King, *namashkaring*.

We danced until late in the evening, and when it was time for me to leave, when the King put his hands together and said, "May I go now, please?" he brought me a little suitcase

in which I could put my Western clothes. Home I drove, in
my erica sari, my head shrouded in the palu, and I walked
up the guesthouse pathway to where Ghorki sat waiting on
the step with Peepchen, his eyes wide with astonishment.

Away in Singha Durbar where the Ranas governed I had
not been forgotten. Daily the Prime Minister's presents of
cigarettes arrived, and I had sense enough now, sufficient
awareness of the situation and my potential danger, to thank
him with letters of diplomatic politeness and flattery. Now
that I knew more about him and his regime I could not look
at him, on the *maidan* for the sports festival, or at official
durbars, without a mixture of revulsion and anger. I do not
know whether it was I or the King who nicknamed the
Maharaja "Goebbels." Probably it was I, since I more than
once drew a comparison between the "Ranarchy" of Nepal
and Hitler's Germany. Certainly, from then on, he was
"Goebbels."

His son Bijaya, however, I genuinely liked. I respected his
sharp, inquisitive mind and his chivalrous nature. I had not
been long in Tripureswar before Mani Ram, the guesthouse
keeper, came to me, saying that by the express order of His
Highness General Bijaya (Mani Ram almost bent his forehead
to the floor when uttering the name) he was asking whether
I had everything I desired. I said that I had everything,
except something to drink in the evening.

"There is Prohibition in Nepal, madam," said Mani Ram.
I said that I knew this, but he had asked. He went away
worriedly, but that evening a bottle of brandy and a bottle
of whisky were delivered to me with the "compliments of
Major General Bijaya Shamsher Jung Bahadur Rana, Director-General of Foreign Affairs." Below this was a characteristic note in Bijaya's sprawling, Western handwriting, asking

me to accept his "modest gift." More brandy and more whisky were sent to me at frequent intervals, more often than I needed.

If such a gesture showed the instinctive warmth of Bijaya, I soon discovered the iron beneath. Doctor Siddhimani called one morning and for a while sat silently drinking the *nimbu pani* I gave him, and when he had found the courage, or the words, he began to explain that Singha Durbar desired a monthly report from me, giving details of the Queen's health, the treatment she was receiving, and also details of whatever treatment I might be giving the King and other members of the royal family. Should my time at the palace be passed in any other way, perhaps I would inform Singha Durbar of this also.

I angrily refused. I said that it was not my custom, not professional etiquette to do such a thing.

"Madam," said the doctor, "this is the Prime Minister's order."

"I understand that, Doctor Sahib, but it makes no difference."

Within the hour, almost, I was summoned to Singha Durbar, the car calling for me and an officer sitting by the driver. In the large office on the first floor of the palace, a room of dark brown wood and deep leather chairs, like an old-fashioned smoking room, Bijaya was waiting behind his desk. His face was cold, the pencil line of his thin mustache straightened by his compressed lips. He did not come out from behind the desk to greet me, but briskly indicated a chair and seated himself. He listened impatiently to my obstinate refusal to submit the reports he desired. Then he put his hands heavily on the desk. "Madam, understand that the royal family of Nepal is not covered by your ethical standards. I order you to submit the reports we have asked for!"

I returned to the guesthouse angry and depressed that I

should be made part of the intelligence system that spied on the King. I typed the report on the machine that Mother had given me, and, to add to my frustration, it refused to work properly. The keys missed spaces, and the final result looked as if it were stuttering in sympathy with my anger. By heading it *Strictly Confidential* I retained part of my self-respect.

I felt compelled to tell the King what had happened. He smiled and moved his shoulders imperceptibly. After so long and so much persecution by the Ranas this one thing could not surprise or anger him. He took my hand and patted it consolingly.

March ended with the Nepalese New Year. Through the squares and streets at dusk passed long processions, singing and chanting, pulling great wooden cars that were sacred to Matsyendra, the protector of Nepal, strung with ribands and garlanded with flowers. The air throbbed with drums or vibrated with the reedy calling of flutes. At intervals there would be the blare of a bugle, or a frenzied crescendo of bronze bells. There was no rhythm or melody in the music. I heard the high, quavering voices as I sat in my garden, waiting for the car to take me to the palace, and all the sounds came in great shock waves. As I drove past the *maidan* I looked down the Judha Road and saw the distant crowds, the bobbing torches throwing ruddy shadows on white walls.

All the royal family were waiting for me in the cocktail room—King, queens, princesses. The women had presents in their hands, wrapped in paper that glittered with silver and golden threads. They gathered about me and thrust them into my hands, a golden fountain pen, a cigarette holder of coral and gold, a key ring with a silver *mohur* attached. They brought me money, Nepalese notes that bore portraits of the King, his profile in pale, watered blue, a great bird-of-paradise plume in his helmet. On the reverse side of the notes a tiger emerged regally from the jungle. I returned the notes

to them, asking them to sign them, and this they did, with the
fountain pen they had given me.

I flung my arms about the queens and the princesses, and
the King put out his own arms and said, "Well, why not me
too?" And we embraced, to the right and to the left.

"Come," he said, "this is a day for my servants too, and
I must show you." So we went down from the cocktail room,
all of us, and Sadface too, wearing in her hair the letter T in
diamonds. We went along corridors, through doors that were
locked and unlocked with golden keys, until in a courtyard
I was shown a great table laid with flowers and fruit, with
chairs set about it, and all of it oddly and unexpectedly European in appearance. This was where the ladies in waiting were
to celebrate the New Year, and when we had looked at it
and I had admired it we went back to the cocktail room,
where we danced.

Before I left, long before I left, the King placed another
present in my hand, a small parcel beautifully tied with colored ribbons, lapping and overlapping each other in rainbow
hues. Attached to it was one of the great, cool carnations
from the garden. I could not open it, it looked so beautiful,
and it rested on the table before me for the rest of the evening. Each time I looked at it, and from it to the King, I put
my hands together and said "*Bohut namashkar*, Your Majesty." I do not think he had ever winked in his life, but his
expression then was as close as he was ever likely to get.

Even when I got home I could not open the present. Ghorki
received me sleepily, and Peepchen snuffled about my feet
until she crept into her charpoy. Ghorki took off my shoes,
I undressed, and still the present lay on my dressing table, the
scent of the carnation filling the room. At last I was too
curious. I took away the flower and untied the ribbons. Beneath the wrapping I found yet more ribbons and more
paper. These I removed, and found more, and still more, until

at the end was revealed an ordinary cigarette tin, light and empty with the seal broken.

I took off the lid. There was nothing inside but a note in the King's handwriting:

"April the First, you little fool!"

ONE recalls a country best in memories of people one knew there, as if they and the land were incomplete without each other. Nepal was to me, first and always, the royal family. It could scarcely be otherwise. Because I loved them I loved their country, and by the end of my stay there I had perhaps seen more of the valley of Katmandu, and been closer to its warmth, its smells and its color than the King had been in all his life. I would tell him where I had been, and he would listen as if I were telling him something that was strange to him, as I believe it sometimes was.

There can be no more holy land in the world than Nepal, for it is the heart of the two great religions, Hinduism and Buddhism, their temples breaching the timbered hills and towering over the narrow streets. The history of the country and its religious mythologies are inextricable, fantasy supplements fact, and the story of Manjusuri seems more reasonable than a geological accident.

The mornings, the afternoons of each day were my own. I ordered the car and, with my bodyguard sitting in front with the chauffeur and Ghorki, Peepchen in the back with me, I traveled. Yet I did not know what I should see. There were no official guides, there was no guidebook. There was, as a startled clerk in the Foreign Office once told me, Percival Landor's two-volume book on the country, but this had been published many years ago, and the clerk made it clear that though there *had been* a book on Nepal (since that was what I had asked) it was not possible to find a copy in the country.

My bodyguard, in crumpled khaki and tarnished brass, was of little help and scarcely understood my words anyway. Bad-temperedly, he resented being taken away from his afternoon's sleep. Whenever possible, and only when I did not use the car, I tried to escape him and walk on my own, and how he explained this to Singha Durbar I neither knew nor cared.

I rose early each morning, at six o'clock when Ghorki came with my tea. Then I would smoke a cigarette, exercise myself, and walk into the garden to pick fresh flowers for my soup plates. The gardener would be waiting for me, with a rose in his hand. This became his invariable custom after the first day, when I rewarded the gesture with a half-rupee. The rose he gave me each morning was rich and almost blown, a small explosion of pink, or red, white or yellow. This was not because the *mhali* was jealous of his flowers and had no wish to bring me anything but one already dying. It is an Indian custom that when a rose is given it should not be the crisp, dewy bud that would be a European's gift, but a flower full-blown, and perhaps there is a philosophy to be found in this.

Without fail each morning the valley delighted me, the emerald meadows, the sky reflected in the still paddy fields, the foothills stretched with soft rugs of green timber, and beyond them, separated by that band of amethyst haze, the snow peaks—northeastward the Everest range, northwest-ward and hardly discernible the spine of Anapurna. The air in Katmandu was as clear as the streams that raced madly down from the passes to swell the yellow Bhagmati, and always, always, there were towering clouds in the sky, turning the bowl of it into blue and white porcelain.

The Nepalese believe that every grain of soil in their land is holy, each twig, stone and leaf a divine manifestation. Bud-dhist, Hindu and Tibetan temples are sprinkled liberally among the trees, cities and villages, slender spires and pump-kin cupolas. At sunrise I saw them sparking one by one, like newly lit fires. All day their bells rang, and all day the roads were full of men and women walking to and from them.

The natural fertility of the valley earth is reflected again and again in the *lingam* and the *yoni*, the symbols of coition, unintelligible at first, but startlingly obvious once their meaning is known. The masculine *lingam*, emblem of Shiva the Destroyer (and not unparadoxically of Life), juts abruptly from the female *yoni* or lotus. This blunt combination, which has a holy rather than priapic significance, is found everywhere, in stone, in bronze, in brass, in iron, in gold, in crystal and in painted wood. It is the most primitive of all life symbols and perhaps antedates Hinduism. I found it by temple steps, by roadways and also obscured beneath butter-colored orchids. I saw it through the doorways of simple houses, surrounded by oblations of flowers, of rice and water, and in the end I scarcely noticed it.

I enjoyed the pleasures of this valley slowly; time was mine, I had no need to hurry. I was charmed by the gable ends of the temple roofs, curling superciliously from the russet tiles, and I believed that the cart had come before the horse, that some influence had come down from China centuries before and persuaded the Newar architects to design their roofs like pagodas. In fact, Kubla Khan, warring through Nepal, saw these uptilted gable ends, admired them, and took the style back to China. Or so the Nepalese say.

From my windows each morning, looking beyond the little stone Buddha who kept evil from my house, I saw the pink-brick, white-plastered houses thickening in number until they joined the main city of Katmandu. I watched the pilgrims passing dusty-footed, cooking pots on their backs, staves in their hands, and behind them long miles of traveling that stretched to the far southern tip of the India peninsula, to Ceylon and Japan. Sometimes, but rarely, I saw Buddhist nuns, with shaven heads and in orange robes. Except for the

soft, plump faces and slender hands of the young women,
they looked no different from their brother monks. Between
the old men and the old women there was no difference at all.

I would walk down from Tripureswar to the Bhagmati
river, where it curled past terraces of low, two-storied houses,
where the ashes of the dead floated down from the burning
ghats at Pashupattinath, and where, one morning, I saw an
elderly Nepalese wading in melancholy thought, his jodhpurs
rolled above his knees, the water lapping on his thin calves,
and his head bent beneath a great black umbrella. All day the
river was busy, with women washing clothes or cleaning the
vegetables that floated about them in baskets like a red and
green carpet, with children splashing in play, with the carcass
of a dead goat held in the shallows, with humpbacked cows
that almost seemed aware of their sacred immunity. And the
river moved on through the valley, to drop down the mountain wall, to join the Ganges and the Jumna, holy for centuries since the day when their waters touched the heels of the
infant Krishna.

I went often to Katmandu, to the old bazaar, northwest-
ward from the modern ugly Judha Road with its square,
spiritless houses and its drunken telephone poles. In the beginning I went by car, and before I could alight chauffeur
and bodyguard leaped from their seats, holding back the
crowds with long canes. The Nepalese pressed about me, to
stare not at me but at Peepchen. It was obvious that they had
seen nothing like her before. The dogs of Nepal are mostly
pariahs, mangy and yellow, kicked and despised. They repro-
duce themselves with a peculiar desperation. Perhaps this is
justified by the two occasions in the year when they live well.
These are during the autumn festivals of Diwali and Durga
Puja. The second day of Diwali is *Kukoor Tewar,* "Dog's
Day." Then the Nepalese garland them with flowers, feed
them on specially prepared meat and rice.

The dogs' second day of delight, during Durga Puja, is less charming. On the eighth day of the festival herds of water buffaloes are driven to the great square of Kot, decorated with flowers, their horns and hoofs painted scarlet. There, where the great Jung Bahadur butchered the Queen's followers, the buffaloes are sacrificially slaughtered. That is when the *pi*-dogs bloat themselves on the blood that runs in the gutters.

I stared and shopped in the Katmandu bazaar, but mostly I stared. The great Middle Bazaar lies westward from the *maidan*, at the end of the Judha Road, and to get to it I drove by a tall white column, two hundred feet high and known as Bhim Sen's Folly. It was built centuries ago by a prime minister who wished to perpetuate his name and memory. He emphasized the point by leaping from its summit astride his horse, and, according to the story, survived, which is more than his horse did. Today the Folly's slender shadow traces the sun's daily passage across the grass of the *maidan*.

I never knew what I might find on my way to the Middle Bazaar—a Nepalese on a bicycle wobbling past a crouching camel, an ancient Rolls-Royce immobilized in an alleyway by a sleeping cow, a scabrous sadhu sitting beneath the wall of a Rana palace, the blossoms that spilled over its lip dropping petals into his begging bowl. There were bicycle shops in the bazaar square, hung with tires and inner tubes like entrails. What European goods there were to be bought were cheap and worthless, yet once I saw three cakes of Maja toilet soap, Spanish and among the best there is, wrapped in black tissue paper with Goya's Maja crudely reproduced on the label. I bought them and took them delightedly to the palace for the King and the queens. They set the soap proudly in the cabinets in their bathrooms, and it was still there when I left Katmandu.

The bazaar is a great square with a hundred alleys about

its periphery, like the fringe on a brilliantly colored carpet.
It is hedged with old houses, bricks crumbling beneath the
plaster, wooden eaves and gables of ancient, purple wood. The
wood, I saw, was carved with passionate figures locked in an
eternal orgasm. The shops where I lingered were open, black
gaps in the pink and white walls, with merchants sitting out
of the sun, cross-legged behind saffron mounds of rice, escarp-
ments of green and red peppers, quarries of tiny brown eggs,
walls of oranges, bananas and aubergines. In some shops there
were long lines of glass jars, filled with sticky English sweets.
Ducks, geese, goats and sacred cows walked unmolested about
the money-changers' tables in the center of the square. The
changers were grave and dignified old men, with high-
cheeked Mongolian faces, their fingers constantly dismantling
and rebuilding their little pillars of silver and copper coins.

Soon nobody stared at me in the bazaar, and soon everybody knew that I was Miss Erika who lived at Tripureswar
Number One. If I bought something and found myself without money, and promised to return and pay, before I reached
home the merchant or his clerk would be waiting at Tripureswar, with hand outstretched.

I saw shops that seemed to be immobile waterfalls of cloth,
cottons, woolens, homespuns of coarse yellow or brilliant
prints. I saw shops that sprouted with tall bamboo canes, each
carrying coils of the bright red, blue, white and green bangles
that Hindu women love to wear on their arms. There were
shops selling the plaits of black cotton, woven with scraps of
cyclamen and electric blue cotton, which Nepalese women
braid into their hair. All day the sun threw a thousand reflections onto the brass and copper pans and pots.

Yet I bought little, some antiques, some minute *lingam*
and *yoni*, arguing with the merchant and insisting on real
antiques and not the trash he wished to sell me. For the most
part I was content to wander, drunk with the color of the

banya shops, the bowls of liquid butter, the big mounds of white radishes, the comic columns of Western topees outside a hatter's, the smell of sickly perfume, of overripe fruit, of excrement, of cooking food, of men and animals.

I had a camera with me and had been wise enough to obtain Bijaya's permission to use it. It was not a good camera, and when the King said that I might photograph the royal gardens I took it to show him. He laughed at it, for he was a fanatical photographer, and he gave me an expensive Kodak and told me to throw my own away. He would not let me photograph him or the queens and his daughters. Their pictures he preferred to take himself, and he was jealous of the efforts of anyone else.

So I took my camera into the bazaar, and one day I climbed the stairs of a corner house, seeking a window where I might best catch the whole teeming view below. I had no time to focus the camera before the room was filled with excited, hysterical Nepalese, men and women, screaming at me, driving me from the house into the street. It took me many rupees to placate them, and them many days of sweeping, scrubbing, and whitewashing to cleanse their house of my defiling presence.

But it is one thing to take photographs in a city like Katmandu, and quite another to find someone to develop the films. I searched for days and at last, on Judha Road, found "The Grand Studio." The adjective was hopeful rather than descriptive. It was an ugly, square building, whitewashed and in the depressing contemporary style that was creeping across Katmandu. It stood back from the road behind a parched strip of grass, and it could be entered by a small flight of steps. I visited it three or four times and always found it empty. Its showroom was full of portraits of the Ranas, A, B, C and D. And, pushed away in a corner, a little, miserable photograph of the King and his sons.

On my fourth visit I found someone who could speak moderate English, a Nepalese leaning against the wall outside the studio. He told me that if I climbed the stairs outside the building I would probably find the proprietor above. Up I went, to an exhibition room, and there a worried old Nepalese said, without too much surprise at finding a short-cropped memsahib in his office, that yes, he would print my pictures. I asked him why he had no portraits of the King displayed in his showroom alongside those of the Maharaja, and with this question his English failed him and he just smiled. I asked him again, and again, and in no good humor he said that if I wished to buy a photograph of His Majesty I might find one in his files next door. This was a room full of half-completed oil paintings, all being copied from photographs, and all, of course, portraits of the Ranas.

But the workmanship of "The Grand Studio," however magnificent its owner's aspirations, was poor, and I searched until I found another photographer. This one called his establishment "The New Studio," and, while it looked as old as the first, at least it was cleaner and its work was done with some speed and efficiency.

Before the Judha Road reaches the Middle Bazaar it leads to the Durbar Square, where stands the old Durbar Hall of the Kings, and where all the beauty and the horror of Nepal's spiritual existence mingle symbolically in strident colors. None of the buildings is less than four hundred years old, but I was most moved by the royal temple of Taleju, five-storied, with gilded pagoda roofs. Its shrine is dedicated to Tulaja Devi, protectress of the Royal House, who must be propitiated by the beheading of goats. Taleju, I was told, is opened once only every year, when the royal women come to it in procession. No man may enter it, although Prithwi Narain, Tribhuvana's conquering ancestor, once did and offered a human sacrifice there. Tulaja Devi visited him in his dreams and admonished him, and she afflicted him with a plague of lice. There have been no human sacrifices since.

But the deserted beauty of Taleju, its tinkling bells of bronze, its lonely galleries, would, each time I visited it, be driven from my mind by the golden Hanuman Dhoka, the monkey-god gate. There sat Hanuman himself, on a pedestal, with an umbrella thrust into the nape of his neck, and guarded by two silently roaring lions of green stones. His leering face was so smeared by scarlet paint and native butter that it was scarcely recognizable as human or animal. His knees and feet were black with flies clustering on the blood of sacrificial goats.

But if he was revolting when first seen, he was gentle compared with the image in the center of the Durbar Square. This was "The Great Black," Mahakala the Beneficent but Terrible, the Nepalese aspect of Shiva the Swallower of Ages. He was hideous, and when I first saw him my arms and hands began to tremble, and I was pushed this way and that by the crowds moving across the square. They, the Nepalese who stared into my face, surreptitiously fingered the material of my clothes, perhaps saw no terror in this image, or perhaps did and rationalized it. He was forty feet high, orange, red and black stone, a monstrous creation that seemed to move in his own shadow. He had six arms, one holding the trident that symbolizes the three worlds of earth, air and ether. Another hand clutched a torch, another seemed to be thudding in agony against his breast. His white-edged eyes protruded from his ugly face, his mouth leered in a clown's scarlet grin, his body bellied over his crossed legs. He wore a necklace made from the skulls of his devotees, and beneath his foot he crushed the demon Ignorance.

All day at the base of the image sat a Brahmin priest, kirtled in white cotton, his head bare, and patiently passing from hand to hand a long string of beads.

I would turn from the hypnotic horror of Mahakala to the pipal tree at the far corner of the square and refresh my mind with the gentleness of it. On its branches white egrets were perched, as they perched in the banyan on the *maidan*. But the Durbar Square to me meant the Court of Silence at the back of the Durbar Hall, beyond the gate where the crimson-robed Hanuman sat. When first I found this place and saw the gilded herons at its entrance, I was entranced. I pressed close to the gate and stared through its fretwork to the still courtyard, its flagstones crowded with stone dragons, griffons, and curly-maned lions. All about the court rose gallery after gallery of wood carved intricately and lovingly, shadowing latticed windows, climbing by pagoda eaves to the final triumph of golden spires. I had been told that in the apartments behind the windows once lived aged and distant members of the royal family. Perhaps this was still the case, but I saw no men and women there. On the day I discovered the Court of Silence I opened its gates to walk through and was immediately met by a withered old Nepalese who waved his arms at me, pushed at my shoulders with his twisted hands. But I coaxed him and begged him and bribed him, and finally he let me stand for a moment alone in the courtyard, looking upward to the peaceful square of sky and cloud above the spires.

The gods of Nepal, animal-headed or human, repeated themselves above every lintel and at every corner of Katmandu. Men and women turned from their shopping, their laughing, their arguing, to offer *pujas*. There was Garuda, the bird-god, with his collar of snakes and his beautiful wings folded behind him. Nepalese women squatted at his feet, their hair blue-black and flaming with a single flower, their legs crossed, their knees stretching the white cotton of their saris. They bowed their heads and put their palms together over the offerings they had brought—raffia trays of marigolds, rice, herbs, and jars of *ghee* or milk.

Ganesa, benign and elephant-headed, is the protector of children, and I saw his image set into the plaster walls, or carved into the woodwork of doorways. He is the god of learning and success, and pregnant women, with labor almost upon them, walked awkwardly to his image and sprinkled his feet with petals. Where his trunk and domed forehead jutted from the walls there hung bronze bells, and little girls brought their tiny brothers and sisters to him, holding them up so that the pudgy hands might stroke the worn trunk, ring the bell and summon Ganesa to listen. When they saw me watching them great flowers of laughter would bloom on their faces.

I drove from Katmandu to its ancient sister cities of Patan and Bhadgaon, wherein the Newars had flourished until Prithwi Narain overcame them by guile or the sword. To the Nepalese of the valley, mostly Newars, Patan is still their capital, built seventeen centuries ago of brick, plaster, stone, bronze and gold. It is a dead city now, alive only in its petrified history, in the harsh, declamatory sound of its temple bells. The Buddhists hold it in particular reverence, for here, three hundred years before the birth of Christ, came Asoka, Emperor of India, convert to Buddhism, making a pilgrimage to the birthland of the Bodhisattva. He built four great stupas that square the city, four tumuli that were once milk-white and are now red with naked brick and green with climbing grass. Upon each stand golden spires.

Gongs and cymbals, chanting and the blast of bugles sounded all the hours I spent in Patan, the noise dying away across the dry grass fields that surrounded the city. Narrow alleys spread like a sun's ray from the central square of Patan, breaking across smaller squares where temples stand, leaping from bronze gateway to golden gateway, where I saw saffron merchants sitting, and so thick was the dust upon them that they looked as if they had been molded from it. But I came

back again and again to Asoka's lonely stupas, to stare at the
spire in each center which, to the Hindus, is another manifestation of the phallic *lingam*, and, to Buddhists, is the sacred
flame of the "One Sole and Supreme God, First Cause of All,
Creator and Preserver of the Universe."

If Patan is the Dead City, Bhadgaon is Golden, and it was
its bright spires that I had seen from the top of Chandragiri
Pass. I drove to Bhadgaon one morning early, passing the
great rectangular lake called Siddha Pokri, built two hundred
years ago by Bhim Sen, that prime minister so hungry for
immortality. The road was deplorable, the car lurched and
twisted through dust, over potholes, past portly Nepalese carried in reed baskets on the backs of porters, until we began
to come upon Bhadgaon stealthily, through outlying pickets
of houses, and back gardens bright with flowers and vegetables.

Bhadgaon is shaped like the conch shell of Vishnu. It is
clean, its streets wide, and it is as it was three hundred years
ago, because its people wisely surrendered to Prithwi Narain
without a fight. The houses in its squares, the temple eaves,
flame with all the colors of mellow wood. They crowd upon
each other with mounting galleries, windows shrouded by
shutters carved into representations of great peacock fans. In
the central Durbar Square there seemed to me to be a hundred gilded roofs, a score of colonnades with each column
supporting the *lingam* and *yoni*. Green monsters, designed by
a transported imagination, challenged me at temple doors, and
the glare of gold was so strong that I instinctively closed my
eyes against it.

In the center of the square is a great bell of bronze, hung
between granite columns and mounted on a huge square of
stone. Falling across it is the shadow of a tall pillar on which,
beneath a lotus canopy, sits the figure of Raja Bhupatindra
Mall, the greatest of Bhadgaon's rulers, dead for two centuries

and a half, yet still very much alive. For when I stood upon the plinth a Nepalese came to me, old and gentle, bowing politely and saying, "Madam, please do not stand there. You are standing on His Majesty."

In Bhadgaon the Hindu temples have almost driven out the Buddhist, but the metaphorical symbols of the two religions are intertwined on the golden and copper door of the splendid Durbar Hall, the all-seeing eye of Buddha, the trident of Vishnu, dragons, lions, lizards, multiarmed gods and goddesses in a riot of frenzied movement.

All day I would walk in Bhadgaon, while the sadhus watched me unblinking, their scrawny arms extended, until the shadows dropped and I left.

Westward from Katmandu, past fields of young maize and mustard, I found Swayambhunath, and even my bored chauffeur and bodyguard stirred a little with anticipation. Just as, I suppose, no Christian can have the knowledge that he is about to enter St. Peter's without some strange movement in his heart.

For Swayambhunath is where the lotus flower settled once the waters of the Tank of Serpents were drained by Manjusuri. The flower lay on the wet earth, watched by the Lord Buddha. The earth dried, and the flower grew into a tall hill three hundred feet high. Upon this hill was built the greatest and holiest of Buddhist temples. Its golden spire can be seen from any point in the valley, for it is one hundred and fifty feet higher yet from the hill that was once a white flower.

Six hundred steps lead from the road to the summit of the hill, and I climbed them all in the heat of one afternoon, leaving Ghorki and Peepchen at the foot. The steps were wide and shallow to begin with, but became steeper as I climbed. On either side of me, dappled by the leaves of tall trees, stood high and serene images, Buddha the Merciful, Buddha of Infinite Compassion, Buddha Calling the Earth to Witness, all with eyes heavy-lidded, and with limbs in gentle repose.

Before me and behind me climbed or descended groups of monks in saffron robes, pilgrims with backs bent and eyes lifted to the summit.

The temple at the top was vast and ranging, its center a vast white bowl upended, as Asoka's stupas must once have been, so white and so brilliant that its outline began to shudder in the sun when I stared at it. Upon its center stood a square base, on each of the four sides being painted the crimson, white, blue and black eyes of Buddha, staring in eternal understanding to the north, south, east and west. Above this base tapered the spire, thirteen golden discs of narrowing diameter, representing the thirteen heavens, the Pure Lands of Buddhist belief. From the top floated long, colored ribbons, twisting and turning, and embroidered with golden characters.

Before the entrance to the temple, and lying on its side, was the scepterlike *vajra,* the thunderbolt which the Lord Buddha took from the Hindu god Indra after a great contest of body and spirit. I turned from this to look out across the bright grass and dark trees of the valley, to the rivers scything down from the mountains to the great Bhagmati. The summit of the hill was crowded with monks and pilgrims, pushing their way to the scores of tiny temples at the foot of the great stupa. The noise was tremendous, its fundamental wave the sibilant murmuring at the shrines, "*Om mane patme hum!* Oh, jewel in the lotus flower!" But on top of this was the crying of children, the sounding of gongs, the ringing of harsh bells, the maniacal chattering of the rhesus monkeys in the trees.

Whole families, from great-grandparents to children who could scarcely walk, circumnavigated the great stupa, twirling their prayer wheels cheerfully—"*Om mane patme hum!*"

—and finally coming to their knees before a brilliantly blue image of the Lord Buddha.

There is another sacred hill in the Tank of Serpents, and the memory of it moves me far more than the thought of Swayambhunath, for it was later to be so terribly linked with King Tribhuvana. This is Pashupattinath, northward from Katmandu, in a gorge, in a forest from which palm trees stand up unexpectedly like feather dusters. There I found a jewel box of Hindu temples, horrible and beautiful, spilling down the slopes to the yellow Bhagmati and the burning ghats.

It is a place built for death, shrines fixed in the cliff walls, wide terraces of white stone rising up to the great temple. Roofs scarlet with tiles, held aloft by timbers carved into writhing images of procreation, birth and death, glowing with vermilion, yellow, blue and white. Carved stone gods, frozen in the middle of some terrible assault, belligerent or priapic. Sex in Pashupattinath is open, blunt, and unremarkable. Brown children play happily on great stone *lingams*, with both innocence and an awareness of their meaning. These children I watched with a surge of pleasure, but when I saw the fakirs crouching in their caves by the river, old, diseased, crippled and wild-eyed, I wanted to run from Pashupattinath.

The temple's spires and towers gleam with gold above the trees, Shiva's triumphant phallic symbol predominating, and the golden prongs of his trident reach forty feet toward the sky. For this is his temple and it commemorates the day when, alone on the earth without his trident, he took the form of a gazelle to escape the fiends that pursued him and at last found refuge in the forest at this spot.

I found Buddhist shrines there too, but it is predominantly a holy center to the Hindu. This is where his dead body is burned, this is where he washes his sins away, where I saw women dipping their bodies again and again in the water until it dripped from the great coins of gold that distended the lobes of their ears.

I knew that the temples were forbidden to Westerners, but as I walked back to my car that day I had forgotten this fact, for I was exhilarated by the atmosphere and absorbed by it. I saw the golden gates of a little temple and hurried to them, instinctively wishing to pass through, and before the waving arms of a gatekeeper took me, and forced me away, I saw a wondrous image of silver beyond the gates, burning coldly in the darkness, its feet vividly scattered with marigolds. Not only was the gatekeeper angry with me, but a crowd gathered, men with faces distorted with hate and anger, gentle Nepalese people whom I had loved suddenly turned fierce and murderous. They surrounded me, shouting, and only because Ghorki Ram took my arm and forced a passage for me to the car, did I escape injury.

That was not the end of it. Bijaya called me to Singha Durbar the next day and looked at me gravely across his big desk, warning me never to attempt such a foolish thing again, for at the moment I arrived at the gates a goat had just been sacrificed, and its entrails were being washed in the water of the Bhagmati. Bijaya told me this with an odd mixture of apology and indignation.

I went again to Pashupattinath after that, and this time I was careful to ask the gatekeepers where I might go and where I might not. Once, refused entry to a courtyard (although Ghorki and Peepchen were allowed to pass through) I saw the vast hindquarters of a golden bull, immense in flank, belly and virility, standing on a carpet of flowers. I watched Ghorki and Peepchen disappear into the crowds about this image of the sacred Nandi, and I turned away. There were bulls enough along the terraces of Pashupattinath, real bulls, white and humped, walking where they would,

with the devout following them, kissing their tails and sometimes drinking their urine.

The monkeys were thick on the temple steps, red-eyed and
quarrelsome, leaping from the images, gibbering at the pilgrims, vicious, dangerous animals, but unmolested. They
stared malevolently at Peepchen, who kept close to my heels.

When I told the King that I had been to Pashupattinath
he at first laughed at my pronunciation of the name, correct-
ing it mockingly. But when I told him how terribly moved I
had been by the sight of the burning ghats, and the funeral
pyres smoking there, an expression of great melancholy came
over his face. Six years later he and Pashupattinath were to
become so linked in my mind that I cannot, even now, think
of it without sadness.

TO SAY that I ever completely understood this king
would be an overstatement. Deliberately he chose to
be an enigma. Understanding was something he seemed to
fear and was consequently something he avoided. His bitter
endurance of imprisonment by the Ranarchy developed in
him a pride that made it impossible for him to show that he
was in any way hurt by it. He protected himself by the consciously created mystery of his palace, by the silence he imposed upon himself and his family, by locked doors and
golden keys, by the wing of black hair that shadowed his
thoughts. Behind all this, too, I am sure, was an intellectual
conflict between his acceptance of himself as the incarnation
of Narain, and his boyishly enthusiastic interest in all the
material innovations of the West, be they neckties or photo-
raphic enlargers.

He was an instinctively proud man. He was proud of the
potentialities of his position rather than its realities. He was
proud of being a Rajput, a warrior Kashatria, a god-king.

Every movement in his face, each instinctive and graceful positioning of his limbs, confirmed this. What blackness was at the back of his mind, what inherited or inculcated pictures of his family's bloody history, I never knew. I would have understood had his ambition been to be a despot like his ancestor Prithwi Narain. Instead he saw himself as a constitutional monarch some day, a projection of George VI in the mountains of Nepal, an ambition inspired by those books he had brought back from Calcutta in his trunks.

Sensitive to an extreme degree, he resented any foreign picture of him as an ignorant and feudal prince. This explained his passion for things Western, a passion that existed coincidentally with his contempt for much of Western morals. He was a master photographer who was not only an artist but who was superb in the laboratory as well. With cars he was mechanic as well as driver. He filled the Happy Cottage with electrical appliances, ordering Sardar Pushparaj to buy still more and more, lamps, heaters, hair driers, clocks, in good taste and deplorable taste. They were not ornaments to him; he was forever taking them apart and reassembling them.

His wardrobe, too, was inexhaustible. He had a Western suit for every possible occasion, and he changed his clothes three or four times a day, and every time he changed he also bathed. His clothes were made for him far beyond Nepal, from materials ordered in Calcutta, London, or Paris and tailored to the most meticulous measurements, which he had himself taken. In the same way he ordered the materials and the clothes made for his queens and daughters. There was not a jewel, a sandal or a sari worn by them that he had not chosen and ordered. With few exceptions, his taste was impeccable, and one of these exceptions was so bizarre that I am sure he intended it as a sad little joke. He came into the cocktail room once wearing a Western lounge suit and a garish American tie, hand-painted with a seminude blonde. I put my hands over my eyes and shuddered.

"No?" he said, and watched me for a moment with the gentlest smile. "Then we will change it." He went away, and when he returned he had changed everything, suit, shirt, tie, shoes, socks, and watch.

I do not believe there was anything he had not ordered from those mail-order catalogues. A broken nail on my finger would bring, the next day, the present of an elaborate manicure set. I exclaimed once, "Your Majesty, should I ask you for a flea circus I believe you would produce it." He nodded gravely, and I almost expected to receive one the following evening.

Where most Indians are outwardly emotional, laughing, crying without reserve, these royal Nepalese kept a tight control on themselves. Smile they might, a hesitant curling of the lips coming so slowly, but laugh, never. Nor would they cry. Sadness was always in their eyes, and once only did I think it about to break into tears, and I was the cause. But this was much, much later.

The King drew his sad amusement from the unexpected, from intentional surprises, from the inconsequential, a characteristic which, I think, was influenced more by his circumstances than his nature. He would come, perhaps, to the garden when I sat with the princesses, and he would say, "Now what shall we do this evening, Erika? Shall we sit in the garden?"

"Yes, if it pleases Your Majesty."

"Then we shall dance instead."

He was still slow to trust me, and sometimes I would catch his eyes watching me intently and doubtfully, but these occasions grew fewer and fewer. Now we were alone together often, for hours in the garden after we had danced, walking there among the flowers, his hand holding mine. When he came, the queens and princesses, if they were with me, would withdraw with such gentle tact and understanding of his wishes that I wanted to embrace them. I began to see a side of his simple but deep spiritual existence. One evening we walked where we had never been before, beyond the lake and the pale lotus, to a pathway that ran beside a distant wall. There we passed an opening in the wall, a niche with an encircling plot of flowers, and in it a smooth, egg-shaped stone, perhaps two feet high. As we passed, the King, scarcely pausing in conversation, put his hands together and *namash-kared* the stone humbly. So moving was the gesture that I repeated it, and we had passed this stone and greeted it three times before I said, "Why do we *namashkar?*"

He said, "It is the *Kumari,* the maiden, the virginal origin of existence." His mind leaped half a world, and he added with a half-smile, "The Virgin Mother, if you wish."

He was a devout Hindu, yet progressive. Years later, when his body was sick and his heart low, he welcomed the comfort given him by the Buddhist Bikku Amritananda. His people's beliefs, however, were his. No snake may be killed in the Valley of Katmandu, but when one day I found a cobra among the roses and the carnations of the Happy Cottage, I felt sure he would destroy it. The princesses and I were together, and we came upon the snake suddenly, as it curled its great length from the flowers. The princesses ran toward the palace, screaming, fear making them forget their father's orders. The King, when he was told, would not have the cobra found and destroyed. Instead he had all his shrubs and flowers in that part of the garden cut down to the earth, so that there might be no shelter for the snake and it could depart unmolested. And he told me, with no expression on his face to say whether or not he shared the belief, that to kill a snake was a sin bringing its punishment in childlessness or leprosy. For days I walked cautiously in the gardens.

When we talked of such things his mood was always melancholy. There were other times when his spirit was lighter, when he held his cigarette tight between his second and third fingers, inhaling deeply through the clenched fist. Sometimes, when he had lit the cigarette, he would calmly pass it for me to smoke, and when he had done this several times I began to light his cigarettes in the same manner. He would accept them humbly. Only if one appreciates the orthodox Hindu's horror of defilement by human saliva is the deep intimacy of this action understood.

Any conversation about his imprisonment, his life under the Ranas, was always begun by him, never by me. He would end such conversations abruptly, as if doubt had come into his mind, and he would take my hand, in the middle of a sentence almost, and say, "May we dance, please?" Dancing brought his body alive from its graceful lethargy. He was a quick and apt pupil. I could not, however, teach him the samba, and that made him petulant, angry at failure where his self-respect needed success. I scarcely knew the samba myself and again and again I asked him to lend me the instruction book by Victor Sylvester so that I might learn the steps in the morning and afternoon before we met. For some incomprehensible reason he refused to let me take it. We almost quarreled about it one evening, and although, so far as I knew, the dispute was mentioned to nobody and overheard by nobody, it was Dreamy who came to me the next day and apologized. That evening, without reference to his earlier refusals, the King gave me the book to take home with me.

If he loved ballroom dancing, he hated ballet. He had never seen a Western ballet in his life, yet one day when I mentioned my own love of it, his eyebrow lifted, his head half turned to one of the queens. She went away and came back with a great book of superb ballet pictures. I was enthusiastic about them, pointing to what I believe to be the most incredibly beautiful posture in ballet, when the leg is outstretched, thigh and calf rounded, the instep arching and body bowing. I looked up from it to see the King's face masked with disgust. He said, "It makes me feel sick!"

I thought of the beautiful caged birds outside his bedroom window, the angelfish in their tanks, the great white dahlia called "the King of Nepal" that bloomed in his garden, and I wondered at his blindness to this beauty. But in his dislikes he was almost fanatical. His passion for cleanliness was feverish. He plucked his own eyebrows, manicured his own fingernails, and bathed with a regularity unusual even in the East. His dual vision of the West, alternating between his adulation of its material achievements and his distaste for its habits, was obvious in his bathrooms. There, on shelves, were little colored regiments of toothbrushes, shining armories of the latest dental instruments. He used them daily.

"I will not," he said, "have teeth like an Englishman."

Except for dancing, he had no liking for Western music, and though we played those records again and again I never once heard him hum their melodies. In the sunlit patches of happiness that occasionally broke through his clouded melancholy, no more explained than the sadness itself, he would suddenly break away from me as we walked in the garden, and begin to hum a *rag*. A *rag* is simply a theme in Indian music, and to be appreciated it must be considered in relation to the Indians' attitude toward music. We Europeans, they say, are nervous, hysterical people because we play and listen to the wrong kind of music at the wrong time of the day or year. We will listen, they say, to a brass band early in the morning. The *rags* of Indian music are all composed for a fixed time of the day and for a mood suitable to that time, and no Indian would play or listen to a morning *rag* in the evening, a winter *rag* in the summer. Emotionally it is the most civilized approach to music that I have experienced.

Much of the King's admiration for Western products was centered on things German. I do not believe he had ever met a German, and he certainly could not speak the language. He knew nothing of Goethe and Heine, and he would undoubtedly have considered a Beethoven piano concerto a less adequate accompaniment to his mood than one of his own subtle *rags*. He respected Germany for what he believed to be its industrial efficiency, particularly in its photographic equipment, of which he had a great deal.

He also liked German dogs, particularly Alsatians. Though there were only yellow *pi*-dogs outside the palace in Katmandu, inside there were purebreds with fine pedigrees. They were not, however, as free. The King imposed his own imprisonment upon them and harshly demanded obedience from them. They were not allowed to wander in the gardens but were kept leashed to their kennels, and so they quickly wasted and died. When dead they were buried in the garden, beneath the trees or among the rose beds, each grave with its tiny headstone lovingly inscribed. With the death of one highborn animal another was bought, just as noble in lineage, and dispatched to Nepal from Germany, from England or America. This, too, soon joined its predecessors in the garden graveyard.

The queens and princesses all owned snub-nosed and moistly sad Pekingese, with English names like William, and Moon, and Diamond. Trapped in the hot, airless rooms of the palace, unable to scamper in the garden, they were killed by kindness and regretfully buried. The King's favorite among his dogs while I was there was not one of his great Alsatians, but an ugly affectionate little mongrel he called Lucky. It wore about its neck a golden chain bearing the *Nay Ratna*, the nine lucky gems of Hindu belief—diamond, pearl, emerald, ruby, sapphire, topaz, agate, lapis lazuli, and coral. Despite this protection I do not think poor Lucky lived long either.

May came, and the scent of yellow and white jasmine pervaded the garden. The crimson roses hung in the dusk like tiny lanterns, and the King and I began to spend more time alone together. Sometimes he would sit by me silently on the swing-hammock, holding my hand and watching me. He still marveled at my presence there, the fact that the Ranas permitted it. He liked me to talk about Europe, and when I told him of the Indian princes I had seen on the Riviera he ordered an atlas to be brought and opened it upon our knees, his finger following mine along the Mediterranean coastline from Rapallo to Cannes. He repeated each name after me, wistfully, until I caught his fingers suddenly in mine and exclaimed, "One day we'll go there!"

"One day," he said, "when I am free . . ."

It was the first time we had spoken of freedom. We were very close to each other that day, sharing many thoughts and many emotions unexpressed. Yet he was then and continued to be the enigma, wonderful, beautiful, sad, his breath perfumed, as always, by the fragrant *supari* he kept on his tongue. He was the Maharajadhiraja, King of Kings. The aura about him was almost tangible, a vibration in the atmosphere that seemed to precede him and announce his coming before he could be seen or heard. To me it was not always a pleasant feeling, a tightening of apprehensive muscle and bone in the back, a tension that remained with me all the time I was in his presence and relaxed hours later only, when I had returned to Tripureswar and was alone. And then I would be flooded by a great and peaceful happiness.

I think he was aware of this effect on me and consciously encouraged it, not in an appreciation of its theatrical aspect but in respectful observation of his position as the god-king.

One evening I waited long for him in the garden, queens and princesses long since gone, and the darkness moving in shadows beyond the hanging lamps. When the King came he came slowly, from far off, walking down the avenue of the trees, in that rhythmic stride, tall and slender in white Nepalese shirt and jodhpurs, a dark Astrakhan cap over his brows. As he came closer I saw, in the center of his forehead, a large biscuit-colored wafer. I stared at it as he stood silently before me. He smiled. "You wonder what it is? I have been to say my *pujas*, and the Brahmin placed it there."

"It looks like a pancake," I said foolishly.

"Then let us wash off the pancake and dance," he said, suddenly boyish.

Other incidents brought us closer together and demonstrated our intimacy far more graphically than words could do. As I sat in the garden one day with the princesses a scorpion walked jerkily from the flower bed, its tail held over its head like an umbrella. The princesses ran from it in a quick rustle of silk, but I took off my high-heeled shoe and pursued the insect into a drain, killing it there. I was trying to replace the shoe, standing on one leg and staggering a little, when the King came. He said nothing, but he knelt on the flagstones beside me, took my foot in one hand and put my shoe on it. This would be a natural action in a Westerner, and for that unremarkable. But the King was a Kashatria, the second-highest caste of Hindus. The earth and feet were the defiling province of the sweeper caste.

For a long time I had wished to repay him for the golden bracelet, and I decided on the writing of a story only after consideration of many other things. I wanted to give him not something I had bought, but something that sprang instinctively from my loyalty and devotion. I wanted him to know of my desire to help him. What I could possibly do to

help I did not know, but it seemed important to me that he
should know of the wish. With the cinnamon paper folded
in my bag I took it to the palace.

I gave him treatment in his emerald-green bathroom on the
ground floor of the Happy Cottage, close to the hall where
the hatstand stood with its caps and raincoats. It was a beautiful room, cool and perfumed by great vases of flowers. The
King sat on the divan in his bottle-green dressing gown, his
eyes half closed, inhaling from the cigarette in his clenched
fist, and deeply content.

"I have brought you a present, Your Majesty."

He looked up in pleasure. "What is it?"

I said that first I must prepare the room. I turned off all
the lamps except that by the divan, and this I darkened by
throwing my scarf across it. I opened the window and saw,
beyond it, the blue shadows of the garden and the high sky.
The night was very quiet. When all was ready I began the
story.

"It is called *The Young King and the Golden Bracelet*.
. . . Once, in a far, far mountain country called Lapen,
there was a beautiful king, the handsome warrior Anavuh-
birt. For all his life he had been imprisoned in his palace by
a great serpent, and his heart was heavy. To him one day
came a woman from across the mountains, and her name was
Akire. . . ."

And so the story went on—not, perhaps, a good story, but
it told of our lives, and it promised that one day, though all
seemed desperately dark, the king would be freed from the
serpent and would be renowned in the world. It was a fairy
story and I had composed it, yet I believed it would come
true.

Soon after I gave the King this story I made my first
positive attempt to help him. It was an ineffectual try and

hopeless from the beginning, I suppose. It presumed too much on the credulity of "Goebbels."

I knew now that in India there were forces in opposition to the Ranarchy—the Nepalese Congress Party, disaffected C Ranas and so on. I suspected, rightly as it was later proved, that the Indian Government would give no active sympathy or support to these forces unless it were convinced that within Nepal itself there was a center of opposition to the Prime Minister, a potential alternative to the Ranarchy. The King, as a constitutional monarch, was the only alternative, but undoubtedly the Indian Government, seeing only the picture of the King as presented to its ambassadors by the Ranas, would not consider him. He was the debauchee and lecher of Rana propaganda. It seemed to me that if someone could get to India and talk of the King's ambitions and hopes to the government in Delhi, this at least might be the greatest thing that had ever happened to Tribhuvana.

One morning, it was, as I sat at my bedroom window, watching the sun creeping across my flowers, that I realized I was perhaps the one person who might effect this. It was so terribly simple in design that I wondered why I had not thought of it before. My next *Strictly Confidential* report on the Senior Queen's treatment was now due, and in it I inserted this one paragraph:

> As the height of Her Majesty's blood pressure is not quite satisfactory I had a consultation with Doctor Siddhimani to help get it down more quickly. I had to point out that my treatment is in no way connected with blood pressure, and so I asked the Doctor Sahib to take some medical steps to bring it down. I think the easiest way of settling the matter would be if the patient could be sent down from the height of 4,500 feet to a place of sea level—*not* India, as it is too hot.

Not India, certainly, and indeed my thought was that Birdy might get away to Europe. But no one could leave Nepal except by way of India, and the Senior Queen of Nepal could scarcely pass through India without being officially received by the Indian Government. Thus she could carry a message, by letter or by word of mouth, from the King to Pandit Nehru.

As I look back on it now it was a childish plan. I doubt whether Bijaya, or his father, gave the suggestion one serious thought, dismissing it as interference from a busybodying European. Perhaps Doctor Siddhimani suspected something more than this, and perhaps he was alarmed at being involved in it. He was very angry with me when I showed him the report and became desperately worried when I refused to strike out the paragraph. I think he scotched the idea when my report reached Singha Durbar.

Singha Durbar, in any case, did nothing more than acknowledge the receipt of the report, and there the matter ended. I took a copy to the Happy Cottage and showed it to the King and told him what I had hoped from it. He smiled, and he embraced me, and for a moment I thought he would weep.

Two days later he recalled the report, and he said, "I have something for you." He placed in my hands another of his sad visiting cards, but this time it was not just a golden *mohur*. It was a golden brooch designed by himself, a flower of metal so malleable that it could be bent and turned like paper. The blossom itself was a golden coin about the size of a quarter, and on it the resounding syllables of the King's magnificent name, *Svasti Shri Girirajachara Chudmani Nara-Narayanetyad* . . .

I valued this gift for the reason behind it, but my heart was still more moved by something that happened later that evening. Without explanation the King led me into the garden, walking silently beyond the pool to where a little veranda stood in the shadows. As we approached a figure stepped out of the darkness, bowing low before the King. Tribhuvana stepped forward and, in great and obvious emotion, placed both hands on the bent head. He turned to me and with great pride said:

"This is my Crown Prince, this is my son Mahendra!"

Mahendra was a young man with none of his father's beauty. He was small and slender, with great reflective eyes, and he was dressed simply in Nepalese clothes of homespun. He looked at me for a moment, put his hands together as I namashkared him, and then turned his eyes back to his father's face.

Tribhuvana put one arm about his son's shoulders and one about mine and tightened them affectionately.

"And this," he said, "is my clever Erika who is trying to help us."

I do not think any more than those few words were said. Mahendra left almost immediately, a slight figure slipping away into the trees, as the King and I walked silently back to the palace. But I knew why the meeting had been arranged, and my heart was full of love.

I had been accepted.

SARDAR NARENDRAMANI DIXIT was a member of the Prime Minister's staff, a personal private secretary. He worked in the Foreign Office, which stood on the edge of the maidan close to Singha Durbar. It was a two-story building, whitewashed, red-tiled and ugly. A pathway led to it across a lawn. In the bare anteroom a row of clerks sat at long tables, their white legs crossed, their pens scribbling rustily on great sheets of cinammon paper. The floor was earth, studded with smooth cobbles. On benches facing

these industrious clerks waited those who desired the permits
and the chits without which it seemed impossible to move in
Nepal—Gurkhas, Sherpas, Newars, Hindus, and often Tibetan pilgrims, their smooth, stroke-eyed faces bland above
their magenta robes.

Beyond the anteroom was a veranda overlooking an im-
poverished garden, and a flight of steps went upward to
another gallery off which Sardar Dixit had his office, a large,
plain room, barred with dusty sunlight from its one, closed
window. There the Sardar sat daily at his huge desk. He was
a thin, ascetic man who invariably wore Nepalese clothes.
Yet, even in these, his smooth features, his diffident manners
and precise speech made him seem very much like an English
civil servant. I believe he himself was aware of the likeness
and subtly encouraged it.

I went to see him, I suppose, about once every fortnight,
sometimes on business, but more often because I enjoyed his
company. He was a man of wide culture and he had spent
some time in England and America. He fitted this experience
into his knowledge of his own country's affairs with a
shoulder-shrugging cynicism. We talked of the things that
mutually interested us, music, painting, literature. He seemed
to like me, but it was obvious that, politically, he considered
me a naïve and innocent child. When men underestimate a
woman's intelligence they promptly make fools of themselves, and the Sardar was no exception. I knew that he must
be submitting reports of our conversations to the Maharaja,
so I saw to it that the general impression of me at Singha
Durbar was maintained. I would call on him, sit in the chair
before his desk, and cry, "Sardar Sahib, for heaven's sake
talk to me! I get so bored in that stifling place." And he
would smile knowingly, his hands gently rearranging the
papers on his desk.

I was talking to him one day and moved from my chair

to his desk, to stub out a cigarette. There was a letter lying before him, embossed with a great coat of arms. My eye fell on it casually, but he caught the glance and picked up the letter. With an impulsive burst of confidence he said, "Do you see this, Miss Erika? This is a letter to the King from abroad. He'll never see it." He let it fall to the desk and smiled at it.

"Why on earth not?" I asked, ever the simple one.

He shook his head slowly. "No letters go to the King. They come to my office, and they go on to His Highness the Prime Minister." Then suddenly he seemed aware of what he had said, and he looked at me sharply. "Repeat that to no one, Miss Erika."

I shrugged my shoulders. But that evening when I went to the palace I told the story indignantly to the King.

"So?" he said, without emotion, and then patted my hand. "What did you expect, Erika?"

"That a king should read his own letters."

"Yes," he said, his expression suddenly defenseless. Then his mood brightened. "Tomorrow I have something new for you. We shall go to the cinema."

His only entertainment within Naran Hity Durbar was his cinema. Perhaps it was not only entertainment to him but was, like his mail-order catalogues, a window on the world outside, however distorted its view. The cinema stood outside the walls of the Happy Cottage, a square, white, columned entrance, a clean pediment holding a golden sun, neatly tailored shrubs growing on the lawn before it.

When I came the next evening I found that all the sentries who normally stood at the gates were now drawn up outside the cinema, and on the steps the King was waiting. He came down to greet me, smiling, with both hands outstretched, and he seized mine, making it impossible for me to *namashkar*. He linked his arm through mine and led me quickly toward the cinema. He was as excited as a boy, and he touched his tie, a beige one which I asked Mother to send me from Simla after I saw that painted American horror. "You see," he said, "this is a special occasion and I am wearing your tie, and I matched my suit to it."

The foyer blazed with rich, perfumed flowers. Otherwise it was as neat and as impersonal as any Western cinema. The queens and princesses were like flowers themselves, in brilliant saris, their ears and hair glittering with diamonds. We waited there for the King's sons, and they came at last with their Rana wives, beautiful women, pale faces still paler with powder, their saris shimmering with gold and silver thread and with winking sequins, their hair rich and lustrous. Mahendra came first, still in simple homespun, bowing low before his father, his hands together, thumbs touching his lips. As he had done before, the King placed his hands gently on the young man's head, with an expression of sad affection.

When Mahendra arose he smiled at me, and in the smile alone, fresh and sincere, was an acknowledgment that we had met before and that he remembered the meeting with pleasure.

The other two princes, Himalaya and Bashundera, wore European clothes. They were bright, high-spirited young men in their early twenties. Himalaya, brother of Vijaya and Bharati, was a child of the Senior Queen, a slender and handsome boy, with his father's good looks but none of Tribhuvana's ethereal quality. He was as short as a jockey and had a smile that broke with a dazzle of white teeth. Bashundera, youngest of all, was like Nalini and had her resemblance to their mother, the Junior Queen. He was slim, soberly dressed and slow to smile, but when he did smile the smile seemed to mean more than a courtesy. His high cheekbones gave the looks he inherited from his mother a hard, masculine quality.

He spoke to me, I remember, only of dogs, of Alsatians, for which he had more than his father's love.

The greetings over, we went into the cinema. It was not large, but it was luxurious, with deep armchairs spaced in tiers and divided by a central aisle. Lights played gently on the ceiling from concealed settings, changing color rhythmically. A great curtain of brilliant golden brocade hung over the screen. The King led me to the center seats and placed me by his chair, on the left. I shook my head, I said that one of the queens must sit there, but they pressed me into it with their gentle hands, smiling. Ladies in waiting rustled up and down the aisle, in saris as beautiful as the colored lights above us, offering us drinks and dishes of crystallized fruits. When the film began the King and I sat in the darkness like young people, his hand holding mine firmly, and I cannot, to this day, remember the name of the film we saw.

We went often to the cinema after that, as often as the King's whim took him, or as often as a new film came across the mountains on a coolie's back. When the film ended we stood in the foyer, drinking, eating, until the princes' cars came and took them and their silent, beautiful wives away to their own palaces. Then the queens and princesses disappeared through a passage to the Happy Cottage, and the King and I walked back alone by the gardens.

The monsoon season had begun, heavy, torrential downpours that filled the Bhagmati and swirled in yellow flood along the dirt roads. One evening I paused at the door of the cinema and watched the rain as it moved in thick, waving curtains across the roadway and the trees. I shook my head when the King suggested that we begin our walk back through the gardens, and he smiled and brought from his pocket a gray plastic mackintosh, fastening it about me, pressing the clip-studs and then gripping my shoulders briefly in impulsive pleasure.

He held an umbrella above us as we walked. When we reached the Happy Cottage he would not go inside. We walked for an hour in the rain until his light suit was black with it and it ran from his hair. His hand held mine, and I do not think we spoke.

The King's appearance publicly was sometimes essential. When a new French ambassador came to Katmandu, although his business would be conducted with the Ranas his credentials had to be presented to the King. So there was an official reception in the old Durbar Hall of Katmandu, by the Hanuman Gate.

I went in clothes that it had been possible for me to adapt from those I had brought to Nepal. I had no court dress, no hat, no gloves. The queens gave me beautiful gloves of their own, and I bound about my short hair a silver scarf. When I arrived at the Durbar Hall, instead of being taken upstairs to the guest gallery, as I had expected, and where the women of the British, French and Italian embassies sat, I was shown into the body of the great hall itself. I was given a chair in the middle of a row of stony-faced Rana generals in khaki and scarlet tunics. I heard the creak of polished leather, the tinkle of medals, and the throttled sound of breathing throughout the whole ceremony.

The room glowed with color and brilliance. The great glitter of chandeliers above, the velvet and gold capes of Brahmins, the saffron of Buddhist robes, the scarlet, purple, ivory, yellow, green and blue of saris. The Most Refulgent Order of the Star of Nepal glittering on khaki chests. The distant Winterhalter portrait of the Prince Consort looking down somewhat indulgently from the wall. And before me, the King.

King Tribhuvana in his coronation robes

The swimming pool in the innermost part of the royal palace in Nepal

The first meeting between King Tribhuvana and his Prime Minister the Maharaja Mohun Shamsher Yung Bahadur Rana at the royal palace at Katmandu

King Tribhuvana as a "prisoner" sitting between his
Commander in Chief and Prime Minister

King Tribhuvana in his Durbar Hall of the ancient palace Hanuman
Dhoka standing on his golden throne and presenting *pan* and scent to
the French Ambassador, M. Lévy, who had just presented his credentials to the King

At the "Shirt Ceremony" at Patan near Katmandu, Nepal. From left to right; Maharaja Mohun Shamsher Yung Bahadur Rana, Prime Minister of Nepal; King Tribhuvana of Nepal; a Nepal high-ranking officer; Bijaya Shamsher Yung Bahadur Rana, son of the Prime Minister.

The Buddhist temple (stupa) of Bodhnath near Katmandu, Nepal. The all-watching and all-knowing eyes of Lord Buddha are painted on all four sides

The Maharaja Mohun Shamsher Yung Bahadur Rana, Prime Minister of Nepal, in ceremonial robes. (Notice the resemblance between his robes and the King's coronation robes.)

The Bura-Nilkanta (the blue-necked Lord Vishnu) in the floating bed of snakes where Erika's picnic with the Indian Ambassador took place

King Tribhuvana of Nepal on his golden throne listening to the Indian Ambassador, who is delivering his credential speech

At the wedding of Princess Bharati of Nepal. Erika sits on the King's right, behind the Queens of Nepal

A dream has come true!
King Tribhuvana (in
Nepali outfit) with
Pandit Nehru who had
been his personal guest

The cremation of King Tribhuvana of Nepal at the foot of the holy
river Bhagmati at Pashupattinath, near Katmandu

Erika today: gazing at a statuette of the Maha Vishnu of which King Tribhuvana was the reincarnation, presented to her by Ram Gopal

He sat alone on a wide throne of red velvet, its arms two golden serpents rising upward to strike. He was a lonely and sad figure in a white sharkskin uniform, a jewel-hilted sword aslant between his legs, a simple black cap on his hair. He was watched by his own melancholy reflection, an enormous portrait of himself that hung on the wall behind him, next to another Winterhalter, this of Queen Victoria.

There was much coming and going before him of Brahmins in their skullcaps, and to this he seemed to pay no attention, but looked beyond them to the end of the hall, seeing nothing, or appearing to see nothing. Then he arose, retired to a screen behind his throne and presently emerged wearing a breath-taking crown. This was a skullcap of gold that covered all his splendid hair, encrusted with so many diamonds and emeralds that the gold itself was almost obscured. About its rim hung a fringe of more emeralds, great dewdrops of brilliant green the size of a man's thumb. In the center of the cap glowed a blood-red ruby. Rising from the top and sweeping backward in a perfect arc was the snow-white plume of a bird of paradise.

This was the great crown of the kings of Nepal, and apparently so that there might not be any misunderstanding the Prime Minister was wearing one exactly like it. He took his seat, brushed his hooped mustache, and the durbar began.

Monsieur Lévy, representative of the Republic of France, came to the steps of the throne, flanked by Brahmins and Rana generals, and the King descended a step or two to meet him. A handkerchief was handed to the King and he sprinkled it with *pan* to sweeten Monsieur Lévy's breath. The King spoke tonelessly in Nepali, and his words were translated. The Ambassador's courteous reply was translated into Nepali, he bowed and retired. The tradition that the King of Nepal should not be defiled by direct contact with a foreigner had been observed, and what the Ambassador thought of this sad, pale figure whom he had met for the first, and possibly the last, time I do not know.

Perhaps he had been told what others had been told before him, and what others went away to write in all good faith, that this King was a degenerate, that "the fairest, the softest, the most artful girls of Nepal were chosen to keep him contented; the sweetest opium of Mongolia was brought to him in jars of jade and its use encouraged alike by the paramours and the family physician. . . . To this end he had been enticed even before puberty with the dissipations which, in his twenties, left him vitiated of mind and body both." *

When the durbar was over, at four in the afternoon, the King left for Naran Hity, an escort of scarlet and green lancers clattering before and behind him, and I followed him rapidly in my car. I had begged him to stay in that white sharkskin uniform at least until I arrived, and when I reached the Happy Cottage he was waiting for me on his portico. He sat erect on his chair, smiling, his head firm above the stiff collar of the tunic, his hands loosely holding the golden sword. He looked magnificent.

He was relaxed now, after the tension and the mockery of the afternoon, listening tolerantly as I chattered. I reminded him of one woman in the French entourage who had come to the durbar as if to shop in the market, in a cotton afternoon frock, with no hat, no gloves and no stockings. I imitated her approach to the throne. "She bobbed up and down like a lamb!" I said.

"What can you expect?" He shrugged his shoulders. The shrug and the question summarized his opinion of Western women. His soft voice always hardened when he spoke of them, although he had met none of the British women in Katmandu and had no knowledge of them, except a suspicion that they must all have bad teeth.

* Hassoldt Davis, *Nepal, Land of Mystery*. London: Robert Hale Limited.

I asked him why he had not worn that incredible crown all through the ceremony. He said nothing. He half turned his head toward the door behind him, brought his hands together in a scarcely audible clap. There was the rustling movement of a sari, a bowing figure, and the gentlest of whispers from the King. The lady in waiting returned with a great wooden box like a bassoon case. He took from it that magnificent crown, and the sun struck it dazzlingly. The fringe of emeralds tinkled, and the ruby in the center seemed to burn. He passed his fingers softly through the white plume and then said, "Make your fist, Erika, so!" He held up his own hand before him, fist clenched.

I imitated it with my own hand, and he rested the crown upon it. The weight bore down my arm which, because of my work, is stronger than the average woman's, and the crown nearly rolled upon the floor. He caught it and returned it to its case. "You see?" he said, and he smiled that melancholy smile. "The crown of Nepal is not light after all."

"But why should Goebbels have one like it?"

"Could I have anything he may not have?" He stood up and put his hands together. "Now, may I take off this uniform?"

The two months which had been the contracted length of my stay in Katmandu were over, but the treatment I was giving Birdy was not finished. I wanted to stay, she wanted me to stay, and the King wanted me to stay, but his wish alone was not enough to give me permission. I wrote to Bijaya without much confidence, explaining that the treatment must be continued. Within a day or so his reply came, extending my stay for another three months, restating the terms of my employment, and, characteristically, demonstrating his pleasure with another gift of brandy and whisky.

The Prime Minister, too, sent a bearer with gifts, a basket of
oranges and mangoes.

Still, I was uneasy. Katmandu had little to occupy itself
with but gossip. If the Prime Minister was politically interested in my behavior, the interest of other Ranas was ma-
licious. The Rana princesses, locked in boredom behind their
high palace walls, talked, and their husbands talked. The
King had already warned me that my practice of allowing
Ghorki to sleep in a room at the guesthouse instead of in the
servants' quarters was causing sly gossip. I said that Ghorki
did this because I had promised Mother I would always keep
him near me. "Remember," he said bitterly, "they gossip."
I remembered. I remembered, too, what I had been told in
Simla, that in Nepal no woman should look at a man for
long. So when I drove by the *maidan,* or walked along it in
the morning, I did not look at the officers who stared at me
with their hands on their hips. I pulled up the window of
my car as I drove past, and I kept my eyes down. But still
they gossiped.

I had frequent visitors at Tripureswar now. I picked my
words with the care I would have shown in selecting jewels,
and the knowledge that what I said, how I behaved might be
retailed to the Maharaja created a bizarre atmosphere to our
conversation. Doctor Siddhimani came often, for a glass of
nimbu pani, a talk of Calcutta and India. "I have to look
after you, madam," he would say gravely, folding his brown
hands over his paunch.

Sometimes he called for no reason at all, and sometimes
to collect my medical report for Singha Durbar. One day he
did not come, and the report was overdue. I went to his home
with it, to the Dilly Bazaar. It was a poor home for a court
physician, and my heart was full of compassion for him. The
car drove through narrow streets where grass grew between
the stones, and cows and goats cropped at it, refusing to

move even at the most strident demand from the car's horn. I alighted at an alleyway and walked through this to a court-yard in the middle of a large tenement house, where chickens strutted and pecked at the gray flagstones. I climbed the wooden galleries to a room which even a poor Indian clerk would have despised, and there I found the Doctor Sahib, ill in bed, on his mattress on the floor, and struggling up to greet me. There were elderly women silent in the background, and Doctor Siddhimani sat amid his poverty with the nobility of a king. I respected him greatly, and even more when I found, outside his door, a group of Nepalese waiting for his advice and treatment.

Yet, even to Doctor Siddhimani, I kept up this pretense of being bored with the royal family and with life at Naran Hity Durbar. This pretense was a defense, against what I did not know, except that by now I had determined to do something to help the King even without knowing what.

My new contract with Bijaya gave me permission to treat other patients in Katmandu, and it was Doctor Siddhimani who brought me the Rajkumar, a young prince of the Ranas. The Doctor Sahib explained that the boy had grown too fat, that nothing had succeeded in altering this unhappy state, and that his parents hoped I might be able to help.

The boy was brought and sat in my living room. He was indeed fat, very fat. He sat in my one comfortable chair with the boredom of the overindulged and the overprivileged, his round, pampered face sulky beneath his Nepalese cap, and his servants standing deferentially behind him. Doctor Siddhimani, fussing nervously again like the White Rabbit, said that in his view there was something wrong with the young prince's feet, and perhaps I could examine them.

"Rajkumar Sahib," I said, "take off your shoes."

He raised his eyebrows at one of his servants.

"Oh, no, Rajkumar Sahib," I said. "You do it yourself."

He looked at me as if I were joking, and as if he did not consider this kind of humor in good taste. "I am not being funny, Rajkumar Sahib. You do that every day and you'll lose a little of your fat."

"I do not know how to," he said sullenly.

"Then I shall teach you." I showed him how to lace and unlace his shoes, and how to tie the knots. He soon learned and seemed pathetically happy at the achievement. He was with me for two hours. I gave him what treatment I could, but I told Doctor Siddhimani that all the boy needed was exercise, if such was not beyond the dignity of a Rana prince. Doctor Siddhimani, like Doctor Das Gupta, had already explained to me that one did not ask a Rana to pay for medical treatment, this being a privilege and honor. To me it was no honor, and I submitted an account. It was promptly paid, but the Rajkumar did not return. I hoped his parents considered the money well spent in teaching the boy to lace and tie his own shoes.

There were more durbars to attend, durbars for the King, for the Prime Minister. At one of Goebbels' durbars, while walking through the long, ranging corridors of his palace, I saw two huge portraits, one of Mussolini and another of Hitler. The sight of them was like touching something unpleasant in the dark. I was one of the world's refugees, I had left Germany because of Hitler, and this unexpected appearance of his face, staring down at me from paint and canvas in Nepal, was an experience from which I could not recover for some days.

I both hated and enjoyed those durbars, and some of my irritation I expended on my bodyguard. He was, at the best, a slovenly creature, with unironed uniform, unpolished belt and dirty brass. I felt that if the Ranas insisted on attaching a spy to me the least they could do was appoint one who had some self-respect. Before one durbar I said, "If you think you are accompanying me to a durbar like that, you are mistaken. Get your hair cut, clean your buttons and press your uniform!"

"Memsahib," he said unhappily, "no *pice*, no brass polish."

So I gave him his pennies, and for once his brass shone as a soldier's should, and I hoped the Ranas noticed the improvement in their creature.

It was after one of his durbars that the King was angry with me, for the first and only time, and even then it was an anger suppressed rather than demonstrated. This time I sat not in the great hall but in the guest gallery, and because Bijaya was beside me I spoke to him. When I went to the palace that evening the King's face was clouded, his voice thickened by distrust. "You were talking to Bijaya. What were you talking about? What were you telling him?"

I said, "Your Majesty, how could you possibly see what I was doing? You never once looked to the gallery."

"I know what you were doing. I know what jewels you wore, what clothes." And he told me. "Why were you talking to Bijaya?"

"It was nothing. It was just small talk."

It was a long time before I could convince him that my conversation with Bijaya had been harmless. The incident revealed to me, if I were not already aware of it, how close to the surface of his emotions was his doubt. For a day or so he spent less time with me, as if he were intentionally punishing me, and the hours I spent at the Happy Cottage were passed with Nalini and Vijaya and Bharati. We sang German *lieder*, we went through our German lessons. We played hide-and-seek and even this harmless, childish pastime had its own unhappy overtone. Vijaya and Bharati were waiting for me by the pool, without Nalini, and I suggested that we surprise her and hide from her in the bushes. We hid, and we watched her come out of the palace at last. She stood by the sundial, looking across the garden, and when she did not see us, as she expected, the smile died on her face, replaced by a frown that was at first puzzled and then strangely frightened. She called our names softly, and then loudly, and she began to run aimlessly. Her terror was so real, her belief that she had been deserted by her sisters so acute, that I never played the game again.

At last the King's doubt seemed stilled, and he was once more warm and gentle. As always after his spasms of melancholy, his spirits swung to a boyish extreme, and he indulged in his pleasure in surprising me. I told him of the durbars I had attended in Patiala, and how splendidly the Indian maharajas dressed—their brilliant turbans pulled gallantly over one ear, with great plumes rising from a central jewel. I described an Indian *achkan*, the knee-length coat of shimmering cloth with high collar and long sleeves, the gold-embroidered sash and diamond-encrusted dagger. I said chidingly, "How is it that the great King of Nepal has nothing in his wardrobe to equal magnificence like that?" He shook his head sadly, as if apologizing for being less grand than a Punjabi prince.

The next evening I was in the cocktail room with the queens and princesses. The King had not yet arrived. The door behind us was masked by a brocade screen of silver and green. I think I knew he was there some seconds before he pushed the screen aside with a dramatic sweep of his hand. He was dressed in turban, plume and *achkan*, and he was more splendid than any Indian raja I had ever seen.

"Do they wear something like this?" he asked humbly, and then, when he saw my face, he laughed, the soundless explosion of his lips that was laughter to him.

The evenings were now stiflingly hot, too hot for the Swedish drill which I had been teaching the princesses, and sometimes the King did not come to the cocktail room until late at night, when the air had cooled. One evening, as we waited for him, I could bear the heat no longer, and I suggested that we go down to the garden and sit by the lake. There we went, and we clustered in the swing-hammocks without the energy to speak. I looked at the water, the smooth, green-black darkness of it below the lotus flowers. The moon was high and full, reflected on the water in one perfect image below which the goldfish were motionless. On the far side of the water was the tiny rowboat in which the princesses and I sometimes amused ourselves, and this was poised on their upended reflection.

Suddenly I said, "I am going to swim!" Before queens or princesses could protest I had taken off my dress, my shoes and my stockings, and had dived into the lake in my underclothes. The dive broke the mirror-smooth water, rocked the boat, set the lotus leaves dancing and the goldfish arrowing away into the shadows. I drifted on my back, looking upward to the serene sky, while I heard the excited, chittering voices of the queens and princesses. They moved along the edge of the lake, calling to me in soft alarm, and then they began to run, actually run, to the palace. They returned soon with towels, with new stockings, with new underclothes, and looked so unhappy, standing there at the edge, that I swam to them and climbed out. They were shocked that I should think of plunging into such filthy water, though to me it looked as clean and pure as a crystal bowl.

The next evening the King silently handed me a present and watched me open it, his face bland and expressionless. It was a red and green bathing suit.

All of them, King, queens and princesses, seemed anxious to please me, with that moving intensity you sometimes see in children. In a corner of the royal gardens I once saw wild orchids growing like vines, the blossoms two great sprays of pink, white and mauve. I called to the King and to the queens to admire their beauty with me. The next evening each queen wore one of these orchids in her hair.

Their enthusiasm, however modest, could be fired by my most casual suggestion, and their excitement gave it a significance far beyond its importance. The making of an eggnog, for example, became the focal point of one whole evening. I had, in the middle of another conversation, mentioned the eggnog and asked the King if he had ever tasted it. He told me that he had not, and that the next time I came I must make one. They were all waiting for me the next evening, like children at a treat, in the garden by a table that was covered with a pure damask cloth and laden with a bowl of eggs, with glasses, a beater, and a bottle of brandy. Making that eggnog had all the solemnity of a deeply religious ceremony, with the King watching gravely, his handsome head held to one side, and queens and princesses in a silently attentive row.

I had told them of my love of picking and arranging flowers, and the King asked me to do this for him. Since nothing in the Happy Cottage was allowed to happen impulsively (except what the King chose to do himself as a surprise), since everything had to be fixed in day and hour inexorably, an evening was fixed for the arranging of flowers by Miss Erika. Upon my arrival I found a dozen vases, large and small, lined up along the stone parapet above the garden. With them was a pair of new gardening gloves and a selection of bright new secateurs. Each princess had a flower basket looped over one arm.

Together we went into the garden, clipping and plucking until the baskets were full. The garden contained every imaginable flower for the season, even rare pink and white camellias. I arranged them in vases, the princesses handing me each designated blossom and watching me with grave admiration. For the King's bedroom I prepared a great cut-glass vase of roses, a towering tree of color, twenty, thirty or forty roses, each of a gentle, differing shade. When he had seen it he came to me, put his hands together, and bent over them.

Now the King and I would be alone together for six or seven hours, and since time is not absolute but is shortened or lengthened by what one does with it, these hours passed like minutes. We walked in the gardens, hand in hand, and we sat alone in his tea pavilion. The nights were hot, the air still and the moonlight sometimes so bright that the flowers scarcely closed. Each evening the King chose some different route through the gardens, paths that twisted and idled among the trees, circling banks of milk-white camellias. Sometimes we sat together in one of the hammocks, silently, his hand holding mine, and we listened to the gentle rustle of a sari as a lady in waiting passed us unseeingly, or to the footfall of a sentry straying from his gate.

When we went to the pavilion he unlocked the door with his golden key, locking it again once we were inside. It was so beautiful there, the green moonlight coming through the windows. Before he would sit, the King stood by the door or by a window, silently for many seconds, his head inclined, listening. Then he turned and smiled and said, "Nobody knows we are here!" like a boy playing truant. We heard only the distant, tinkling movement of water, a bird rustling in the leaves of the bushes outside.

The King was very happy there, and we had much to talk about. Since the evening when I gave him the fairy story and my promise, I had again and again told him that I would think of some way of freeing him from the Ranas. I think he was moved, not because he believed there was really anything I could do, but because he was grateful for my desire to help him. I suppose even a drowning man might be grateful for the sympathy of the nonswimmers watching him.

I gave the King a handkerchief one day, a small linen square that had been mine since childhood, with my name embroidered in the corner. It was an impulse, and I said, "Please take it. If ever and whenever you need me, send it to me and I shall come. It doesn't matter where I am in the world, I shall come."

He said, "I'll keep it, but I could never send it to you. You know I shall be able to send you nothing once you leave Katmandu, for I can write no letters that the Ranas will not read. I shall keep the handkerchief, but there is nothing you can do for me."

At that time he was right, of course. I lived in a vacuum suspended above the earth. I was close to the King and his family, but to nothing else in Nepal. I knew nothing of the political undercurrents there or in India. I knew the King's bitterness and despair only. The more I thought of his sad position the more feverish my emotions became. In a desperation that was as angry as his was resigned, I began to ask questions wherever I went. I do not know why the Ranas did not hear of this or do anything about it if they did. I asked the Nepalese I knew, the postmaster, my gardener and my cook, the shopkeepers in the bazaar, the photographers in the Judha Road, Doctor Siddhimani and Doctor Das Gupta, I asked them all if they were happy under the Ranas, and I asked them what they thought of the King. They were all happy under the Ranas, of course, or said so, much too quickly for conviction. Ghorki Ram, astute little man, was more successful, and in the evening, when he took off my shoes, he would tell me that he had heard this and that, that this man or that had said that the King should be a real king.

I carried this news to the palace, but the King, instead of being pleased, as I had naïvely expected, looked alarmed. "Dearest Erika, do you really want to eat a poisoned cucumber?" Even this remark, with its casual reference to the Prime Minister's ultimate power, scarcely stopped me.

I transferred my inquiries to the British Embassy, hoping there to find some sympathy for the king who wished to be a constitutional monarch like George VI. The Embassy was a fine English country house in magnificent grounds. It lay back behind green lawns and slumbering shrubs over which, on Sunday afternoons, came the pleasant *plop* of tennis balls and the tinkle of teacups. The men and women there were pleasant and courteous, but they knew nothing of the King, nor did they seem to care. To the women the King was a handsome white figure at durbars who passed his time with an extensive harem. To the men of the British Embassy the realities of Nepalese politics were naturally more important than the hopes of the King. The Ranas ruled the country, the Ranas had come to the aid of the British Raj during the Great Mutiny, and so long as they remained friendly to Britain how they governed the country was unimportant. Or that is how it seemed to me.

I think I lost hope of ever enlisting any sympathy for the King among the British when I called, one day, and asked one of the embassy women if she would like to drive with me to Pashupattinath. I will admit that I wished her to come only so that I might talk to her about the King.

"Pashupattinath?" she said. "No, I don't think so, if you don't mind. Rather a smelly place, isn't it?"

My attempt to get the Senior Queen out of the country by a recommendation in my medical report to Singha Durbar had been a miserable little failure. I next proposed that when I returned to India I should myself approach Pandit Nehru and tell him of the King's ambitions and his imprisonment. The King received this suggestion indifferently. Perhaps the old doubts came back momentarily, or perhaps he saw, as I did not see in my enthusiasm then, that it was highly un-

likely than an insignificant physiotherapist from Simla would
ever reach the Pandit-ji or have her story believed by him
if she did. But the idea that I should myself take some positive action was a seed that began to germinate rapidly. When
it flowered it was into a proposal so obvious and so reasonable
that, for the first time, I saw hope in the King's face.

The idea came to me on the evening I dined at the Happy
Cottage. I had never, in all those weeks, eaten there before,
anything more than tea brought on the tea wagon by Sadface,
neat little sandwiches, and English cakes and cookies. Eating
or not eating did not worry me, but when the King discovered that I had never tasted Nepalese food he decided that
I should, and he began, with his quiet passion, to organize
the day and the time.

As requested in one of those brief little cinnamon notes
from Sardar Pushparaj, I arrived at the palace at half-past
six, dressed in a long sharkskin frock, wearing pearls and
sapphires. The garden was even more brilliantly lit that evening, colored lights hanging like stars among the sky of
leaves. There was a table set by the lake, and the light winked
on the cut glass and the filled decanters there. We drank
there and talked there softly, the King, the queens, the princesses, and I, and then, with grave ceremony, went upstairs
to the cocktail room. I saw now why that black glass table
was fastened by one end to the wall. It thus was left with
one head only, and this for the King. But he would not sit
there, guiding me instead to the place with a firm grip on my
elbow. "Royal *hokhum!*" he said. "It is my command, Erika."

The glass of the table was hidden beneath a cloth made of
fresh flowers, flowers of every imaginable color, petal upon
petal cunningly arranged. In the center rose a mountain of
fruit in a golden bowl.

At each place was set a golden dish in the shape of a V,
and there were seven dishes, for the King and his queens,

for the princesses, for Sala and for me. In her hair that night Sala, Sadface, again wore the diamond T.

The dinner was served by ladies in waiting, by Muffle and Ball and Whiney, their dark, round faces dimpling with pleasure as they moved swiftly and silently behind us. The curries were Nepalese, hotter than any I had ever eaten in India, and when they were finished *pan* was brought to cleanse our tongues and breath. I was familiar enough with *pan* in India, parings of lime and areca wrapped in a fragment of betel leaf. But this was *pan* I had never seen before, a green fresh leaf smeared with lime, folded into an envelope of the thinnest gold or silver leaf. A maharaja of India, I knew, took his *pan* wrapped in silver. The King of Nepal had his folded in gold, and it was golden *pan* I was given that night, and it was so thin that it dissolved fragrantly in my mouth.

We danced into the quiet, suspended hours of early morning, until the King put his hands gently together and said, "May I go now, please?" He walked down the staircase with me to the hall, something he did rarely, and when we were alone there for a moment I told him what I intended to do.

"I am going to ask Surjit Singh to help you."

Two

THE SHRINE OF THE BLUE-NECKED NARAIN

SARDAR SURJIT SINGH MAJITHIA was the Indian Ambassador to Nepal, a Sikh, a kinsman of the Maharaja of Patiala, and a member of a great and wealthy family. The Sikhs are the warriors and the rich-hearted troubadors of northern India, men of action, gallantry and courage to whom simple justice and honor are the basic essentials of human behavior. I have never met a Sikh whom I have not respected and admired, and of them all I have the greatest affection for Surjit.

I had met him at the Patiala palace in the months following the end of the war, but when I went to Katmandu I had no idea that he was ambassador there. Nor did I at first recognize him. I called at the Indian Embassy shortly after my arrival in Nepal, thinking it a courtesy to make myself known. In 1949 the Embassy lay southward of the city, a white house behind a screen of trees. It was a serene and friendly building with arching corridors, high windows, and cool rooms in which the ceiling fans whispered continuously. Surjit's office was on the first floor, green-shaded and with an enormous desk behind which he was sitting that day of my first call. He arose to greet me, and I saw only the turban and the curled beard of his face. I bowed.

"*Sat Shri Akal!* God alone is truth," I said in the traditional Sikh greeting.

He came from behind the desk, put his hands on his hips, and inclined his head quizzically. "Are you quite sure you're all there, Erika? Don't you recognize me?"

Now I saw who it was, and of course I remembered him, the warmth of his friendship in the days at the Maharaja's palace, the good humor of his plump and jolly wife.

"Your Excellency," I said, "please forgive me!"

He put both hands on my shoulders as if to shake me. "I'll forgive you if you'll drop this Excellency business. Sit down and tell me what you're doing here. I've known for days that you were in Katmandu, and we've been wondering why you didn't call on us."

I visited him and his family frequently after that, coming and going almost as I pleased in the mornings, and I do not know why I never thought of asking for his help long before I did. Surjit is one of the most handsome Sikhs I have seen, and all Sikhs are handsome. I have, still, a vivid picture of him as he was during those days in Nepal, noble head high on his neck, great almond eyes of compassionate intensity, his beard rolled and held tightly to his chin by a band that went over his head beneath his turban. Today that beard is gray, but then it was a shining blue-black. I have no doubt that he is still what he was then, a man's man, an airman who had been a fighter pilot during the war and who still flew his own plane, a sportsman who loved to hunt rhino and tiger, who could defeat most Englishmen at their own games. He liked to drive fast cars, to ride fast horses, to be, so far as the modern world permitted, the ideal Sikh of his ancestors.

He was, as the Germans say, a man "washed by all waters," and although he was knowledgeable in Western culture he was at the same time a strong nationalist. I never saw him wear anything but the dress of the Sikhs, white *khadi* jodhpurs, a white shirt also of *khadi* and buttoned to the neck, immaculately folded turbans in pastel colors for ordinary occasions, but dazzlingly white on ceremonial days. He had a natural animal grace that has been unequaled in any man I have met, except the King.

Children, Surjit's own or his nephews and nieces, seemed to fill the Embassy, with an *ayah* rustling after them chidingly, watched with smiling good humor by the Sardani Sahiba. They were refreshingly uninhibited little creatures, startlingly in contrast to the powdered young Ranas, to the porcelainlike Ketaki at the Happy Cottage. I would tell them stories and sing them songs that had been sung to me when I was a child. When one of them, a button-eyed little girl, refused to go to sleep as she had been told, I took her upon my knee and sang to her, *"Schlaf, Kindlein, schlaf!"* until she slept. This was in Surjit's office, and he watched me gravely from behind the desk, leaning his head on one beautiful hand, finger against his cheek. When the *ayah* had taken the child away, Surjit bent down to an open drawer, and suddenly I heard my own voice singing again. He had recorded it all on tape, and he clapped his hands when he saw my face, laughing without restraint.

He had a passionate interest in such electronic devices. He was a member of the Amateur Radio Club of India and had his own transmitting station in an upstairs room at the Embassy, with VU7AF as its call signal. He showed it to me one day with great pride, explaining it in great detail, knowing that I did not understand a word but enjoying himself just the same.

Proud of India's independence, of her emergence as a great nation, he entertained lavishly in Katmandu, holding splended *tamashas* on the lawns of the Embassy at night. For these he recruited Nepalese peasant dancers in grotesque masks and tiaras of flaming feathers, drums, tabors, cymbals and bagpipes. One of Surjit's *tamashas* would start before midnight and go on until almost dawn, until my ears were deafened by the brazen music, my eyes driven out of focus by the costumes of the dancers, the flags, the frenzied gyrations of arms and legs. It seemed to me that there were always too many clowns. Since to a Nepalese there is nothing funnier than a European hat, the performance of each clown consisted of little more than parading in as many Western hats as possible.

Now that I think of it, perhaps it was these *tamashas* that prevented me from appealing to Surjit earlier than I did. He invited the members of the British Embassy, of course, but his guests were principally Ranas and their wives. The Maharaja came too, sometimes, in his Prince Albert and white jodhpurs, his black hat with the diamond, his pince-nez and his hooped mustache. Surjit greeted all the Ranas with warm friendliness, and, although I admired and respected him, perhaps I thought of him as just another man who saw Nepal and the King through the highly particular lenses of the Prime Minister's pince-nez.

Of course Surjit knew nothing of the King, had probably seen no more of him than Tribhuvana's appearance at durbars, when Surjit received the *pan* and the perfumed handkerchief. Also, he was a diplomat, and a diplomat's duty is to treat with the powers that be, not those that might be, however estimable. These things I had considered before I ultimately decided to make my appeal.

I chose an afternoon when the Sardani Sahiba had asked me to take tea at the Embassy, and when Surjit and I were alone for a moment I said, "Surjit-ji, I have something terribly important to ask you in private."

He looked at me very carefully. "Are you in trouble?"

"No, it's not for myself."

He took my arm and led me into a little drawing room

next to his radio room. We sat together on a sofa, he at one
end, I at the other, and he leaned his tall body against the
cushions and extended one arm gracefully along the back of
the sofa. "We shan't be disturbed," he said. "What is it?"

"Surjit-ji, what do you think of the King?"

"The King?" He lifted his hand and let it fall. "What
should I think of him?"

"Don't you ever wonder about him?"

He smiled. "My dear Erika, you know this country now. I
have never spoken to him. Is it important?"

"I want you to help him, Surjit-ji."

He was silent for a moment, and then he said in an altogether different tone, "I think you'd better tell me what
all this is about, and ask me questions afterward."

Once I began I could not stop. How long I spoke to Surjit
without interruption I do not know. He watched me attentively, his head leaning on his hand, and the sunlight
falling on the wall behind him. I told him of the King's
despair and frustration. I said that the stories about his
lechery and debauchery were Rana lies, and that the King
wished to be free.

"He wishes to be free," repeated Surjit slowly. "Free to
be what, Erika?"

"To be a constitutional monarch," I said, and I told him
of the books the King had smuggled into the country. "I
admit there are things going on in this country that I know
nothing about, Surjit. But I do know about the King's unhappiness. He needs to feel that someone outside Nepal sym-
pathizes with his ambitions and will help him if necessary."

"And what do you want me to do?"

"I want you to write to Pandit Nehru, Surjit-ji, and tell
him what I have told you."

Surjit said nothing for some seconds. Then he raised his
hand from the back of the sofa and slowly lowered one

finger, as if marking the one thing that puzzled him. "Why should *you* do this for him?"

It was not easy to explain my emotional involvement in the King's affairs. It was so tenuous that it appeared absurd when I attempted to put it into words, but I had scarcely begun when Surjit put up his hand and smiled. "It's all right, Erika, you don't have to say any more, it's on your face." Then he frowned. "But you are asking me to involve my government in something very serious. I believe you, but I have only your word to give the Pandit-ji."

"Meet the King yourself, Surjit!" I said impulsively, and I began again to plead the King's cause. All the emotions, the desires, the tension I had felt in the Happy Cottage were released. "Surjit, you must meet him!"

I do not believe he was listening to me now—he was frowningly preoccupied with his own thoughts, tracing his finger along the back of the sofa. He was no fool. He probably knew more of the nature of the Ranarchy than I could ever learn, and, as the representative of India, he was more concerned with Nepal's political future than I imagined. But I had brought him an unfamiliar portrait of the King, and I believe that until then neither Surjit nor India had considered the King as a potential political force. I cared neither one way nor the other for the politics of Nepal. I wanted only the King's happiness.

He put his hands together at last and clenched them, looking up at me as if he had resolved the doubts in his mind.

"I must meet him," he echoed. "But how?"

"Surjit-ji, I will think of a way somehow. But will you promise to talk to him?"

"I promise, Erika, but I can promise only to meet him. I cannot promise to take any official steps."

When I took this news to the King he embraced me, holding me so tightly in his arms that I could hear his heartbeat. All the bitterness and frustration of his life seemed to explode in that one spasm of joy. That evening was one of the happiest we had ever spent together at the Happy Cottage, and it did not occur to us to answer one important question—how was Surjit to meet the King?

Now that I became a conspirator I discovered that the King had been one for years. Now there came a partial understanding of those unexplained absences, those evenings when he arrived two or three hours late for our appointment, or left after a few minutes with no more than a gentle "May I go now, please?" It became obvious that he was in some way in contact with the anti-Rana forces within Nepal, that his three sons were aware of this and helped him when they could. He never explained the nature of this contact, and I never asked for an explanation, but I believed that it was at its best only ineffectual. There was, also, a melodramatic flavor to his nightly excursions, and I believe that sad, bored side of his nature enjoyed the excitement of them, even when nothing came of them.

One evening we had been discussing how he might meet Surjit, and I said unhappily, "You can go nowhere without being recognized. There is only one man in the world with that face and those curls. You should disguise yourself, tuck that hair beneath some filthy cap."

He smiled at me, took my hand, and led me to a chest of drawers, pulling them out one by one like a boy showing his toys. They were full of disguises, wigs, false faces, false teeth, and I could not tell from his face whether they were actually disguises, or whether they were something more he had discovered, coveted and purchased from his mail-order catalogues. I was no wiser when he said, "In these I steal away at night."

Now I wanted to know how he stole away, how he got out of the grounds of Naran Hity Durbar without being detected, and I explained to him carefully why I wished to know, that I could not arrange a meeting with Surjit without such knowledge. The old doubts came back to him momentarily, and he would not answer me then, choosing his own time and his own methods. When he did tell me I could have shaken him for keeping it secret so long, throughout all those days of fruitless discussion since I had appealed for Surjit's help.

Although Crown Prince Mahendra's palace was inside the walls of Naran Hity Durbar, the two other princes, Himalaya and Bashundera, lived outside Katmandu toward the foothills. With the permission of the Prime Minister the King occasionally visited them, ostentatiously carrying his violin for an evening's entertainment. He would go in his Mercury, driving the car himself, with an armed Rana officer sitting beside him. At the Prince's palace the Rana would be left in an anteroom. The King entered his son's private chambers, changed into a disguise, passed through into the gardens, and there over a wall to make his assignations. He returned the same way, bathed and changed, collected his Rana escort and returned to Naran Hity. Even his daughters-in-law, Rana princesses, knew nothing of this.

"*Shabash!*" I cried, clapping my hands. "That is how we shall do it!"

The King, however, was nervous. "Erika, what have you told him about me?"

"That you wish to be a constitutional king, that your people would support you, and that you want India's sympathy and help. But you've got to talk to him about it all."

"It will work?"

"It *must* work!" I said. I went to Surjit the following morning. We sat again in the drawing room upstairs, and he smiled in gentle tolerance when I told him of the King's many disguises, and how he would slip away from his son's palace to meet the underground movement.

"You've been very clever, both of you," he said. "But when and where shall I meet him?"

I said that the King would ask for permission to visit one of his sons soon, and that the meeting must therefore take place near the Prince's palace. I suggested Bashundera. Surjit said that he knew the road to Bashundera's palace and suggested a grove of trees as a possible meeting place. "I shall wait there alone in my car," he said. "You tell me the day and the hour. But there is something you both must know."

"What is that?"

"The meeting must take place very soon. I have been recalled to India and another ambassador will take my place here."

I stared at him stupidly, and I wanted to cry. He took my hand. "Cheer up, Erika. I shall do what I can for your King."

I wanted to keep the news of Surjit's departure from the King, but I could not. He was too excited to be disappointed, however, and we spent the evening planning the meeting. So that I might be able to describe the place of the rendezvous to the King, I set out to find it the next morning, alone with Peepchen, while my bodyguard slept in the sun at his lodge. I walked for miles in the heat and the dust, stopping Nepalese and asking them in Nepali and Hindi where the Prince's palace was. They did not understand me, and when I at last found someone who did, it was by now too late, and I returned to Tripureswar, depressed and dispirited. "Why didn't you tell me you were going?" said the King that evening. "*I know* where the spot is."

The evening came at last. When I arrived at the Happy Cottage the King was waiting, his face tight with anxiety. He was simply dressed in white, and when I saw his empty hands I said, "There is a German proverb, *Kleine Geschenke erhalten die Freundschaft*—little presents keep friendship alive. Take Surjit a present."

He smiled and pointed to the violin case on the chair. "Open it," he said.

Inside there was no violin but a magnificent kukri, with a beautifully carved hilt of ivory and a jeweled scabbard inlaid with gold.

"That is my little present for Surjit," said the King.

Then he left. I went with him to the gate of the palace, carrying the violin case beneath my arm. His beige Mercury was waiting, and in the front seat was a young Rana officer, a shining revolver holster strapped to his belt. He alighted, saluted perfunctorily, and held open the door. I gave the case to the King, and he dropped it casually on the rear seat and drove away.

I went back to the palace. The queens, princesses and I sat in the cocktail room, scarcely able to talk. In less than two hours the King returned, coming upon us suddenly. He stood in the doorway, and his pale face was paler than ever I had seen it.

"He wasn't there!" he said.

Three days passed before I was able to call upon Surjit and ask why he had failed the King. During those three days the King did not once mention the evening, but his expression was ugly and bitter. I was angry with Surjit and I was also frightened. I was afraid that perhaps the Ranas had discovered the plot and that Surjit had cautiously withdrawn from it. I was afraid that he had given the whole affair a second thought and decided to have nothing to do with it. I was afraid of many things, and this fear and anger were mixed inside me when I finally went to the Embassy.

I had underestimated the good Surjit-ji. A servant led me

upstairs to the Ambassador's bedroom, and there he was, ill, his cheeks sunken, his eyes bright with fever. That he should permit me to see him in bed, without his turban, his hair in its knot, his beard untidy, that he should be willing for me to see him as no Sikh would wish to be seen, was an indication of his own concern. He had been ill for four days, and for the first two of them with so high a temperature and delirium that he had been unable to send word for me.

Ill though he still was, he insisted that I sit and talk with him. It may have been the fever, but he was more excited about the meeting with the King than he had been before. He insisted that we arrange another.

"But Surjit-ji, you are returning to India."

"There is still time."

He made me talk again about the King, testing me again and again with shrewd questions to determine whether this man was real, or merely a picture in my emotions. He began to talk of the airstrip that was being built outside Katmandu at Gaochar. I had heard of it, but I had not known until then that Surjit was principally responsible for the proposal. He had flown the first plane into Katmandu, his own Dakota, I think, and now he began to talk of the plane and the airstrip.

"You know, Erika, your King should seek asylum in India. Supposing when I fly home, soon, I took him with me?"

"Surjit-ji, is it possible?"

"That's up to him, but first we'd better meet. You arrange another day."

So once more we planned it, and I took the day and the hour to Surjit. Then, two evenings before the night fixed, the King and I were sitting in the gardens, alone. He looked up suddenly to the sky and said, "The moon!"

It was pale and liquid, in its third quarter.

"You understand?" he said. "The moon will be almost full.

It will be like daylight and we shall be seen. You must postpone the meeting."

I argued with him desperately, I said that it was impossible, that Surjit was soon returning to India and there might not be another opportunity. But he shook his head obstinately and insisted. I went to Surjit, expecting him to be angry. He smiled, patted my shoulder, and said, "Don't worry, Erika. He's right, and we must fix another day."

So another week passed, and the moon waned. Once again we fixed an evening. Once again the King wore his simple white Nepalese clothes with the orchid I placed in his buttonhole. And once again I carried his violin case to the car.

This time it was some hours before he returned, and this time his face was radiant. He sat beside me, took both my hands between his, and told me what had happened.

At the door of his son's palace he had said *"Namashkar!"* politely to his Rana escort and gone inside to the private chambers. There, both Himalaya and Bashundera were waiting, alone. The King stripped off his clothes and dressed quickly in the dirty linen of a Nepalese peasant. With the kukri thrust through his sash, he slipped down the stairs to the gardens, climbed the wall and set out to walk alone to the grove of trees. The moon was no longer strong and was hidden for the most part by heavy banks of clouds, but when it broke through these the King dropped into the mud of the paddy field and lay there until there was darkness again, or crawled forward on his belly.

When he reached the grove he saw a car waiting, its lights out, and he was about to rise and run to it when the moon came out and shone on leather and bright buttons. The man in the car was not Surjit, but a Rana officer keeping tryst with a shadowy figure in a dark sari. The King lay for long minutes in the ditch, watching the car until it drove away.

Then he lay longer still until another car came and stopped beneath the trees, its lights dying.

This time the King saw Surjit's turban, the curled black beard along the line of his jaw. The King rose out of the ditch and ran toward the car. Surjit opened the door, grasped the King roughly by the shoulder, pulling him inside and thrusting him down to the floorboards. At the same time he started the car. He drove furiously. The King, himself a fast driver, said that Surjit drove like a devil, never once taking his eyes from the roadway to glance down at the crouching figure at his feet.

At the Indian Embassy Surjit turned into the great drive and pointed his car toward the open doors of the garage. Inside, he switched off the engine and the lights, closed the garage doors, and then returned to sit in the car with the King.

What these two men said to each other, what was proposed and agreed between them, I never discovered. Afterward, all Surjit would say was "He is a good man, your king, Erika." And, of Surjit, the King said only, "I like him," and this with his faint, mysterious smile. But I know that each must have searched for some reassurance from the other. Surjit was being asked a great deal, to decide, in the cramped darkness of the car, where neither could see the other's face, that this was not the debauched creature as painted by the Ranas but a man of conscience and integrity, a man worthy of his help and his government's. On the other hand, the King's hypersensitive nature must have suffered cruelly. For the first time he was speaking of his troubles and his ambitions to the representative of a foreign state, a stranger, a man whom he had seen but once before and that momentarily under the chandeliers of the Hanuman Palace.

When they had said all that could be said there, Surjit

gently advised the King that it was time for him to return.
Tribhuvana pulled the jeweled kukri from his sash and placed
it in the Ambassador's hands. And Surjit—Surjit's memory
was good, he remembered what I had told him of the King's
love of watches—now unstrapped his own magnificent golden
watch and gave it to the King.

Then the King was driven back to the grove of trees,
crouching on the floorboards again, the car rocking violently
at high speed on the broken road. Once there, he climbed out
silently, crawled across the paddy fields, and mounted the
wall into the garden of his son's palace. There he bathed,
changed, and, with the empty violin case under his arm,
joined his Rana escort and returned to the Happy Cottage.

The wild suggestion that the King should seek asylum in
the Indian Embassy, that Surjit should fly him out to India,
came to nothing. Perhaps it was discussed there in the garage,
I do not know. Certainly there was no time to arrange it, for
within a few days Surjit returned to India. A Dakota was
flown in from India, landing at Gaochar. It left one afternoon, and I stood in my garden at Tripureswar, watching it.
It rose, flew over Katmandu and three times encircled the
royal palace, and I knew that in this way Surjit was saying
farewell to the King and urging him not to lose hope.

That evening was the worst I had ever spent at the Happy
Cottage. The King was a caged tiger in despair. For a moment, for an hour or two, lying in the mud of the paddy
fields, crouching in the dark garage, it must have seemed that
the walls about him had been breached at last and he would
soon be free. Now Surjit was gone and all was as it had been
before.

The King told me that he and the queens, the princesses
and Sadface had stood by the lake that afternoon, watching
the Dakota as it circled the palace and flew southward toward

India. They watched the sky long after the sound of the engines was gone.

"Erika, my last hope went with it. I am in prison again, and I shall never escape!"

I bowed before him, with palms meeting, and I touched his feet.

THE new Indian Ambassador was Sir Chandreswar Prasad Narain Singh. I did not know him. The thought of going to a stranger, and once more pouring out my heart in a confusion of appeal and exhortation, depressed me. At the best I might be merely an annoyance to him, at the worst a joke worth telling the Ranas. Since Surjit's departure I had had uneasy reflections on the risks I was running, the extreme one being the poisoned cucumber the King had mentioned. I am not, by nature, a conspirator, having neither the patience nor the duplicity, and I felt sure that before long the Ranas would realize that this silly European was not as silly as had been first imagined. But I was most afraid for the King. By bringing him into contact with Surjit I had given him great hope. That had ended in nothing, in an airplane circling the palace, and in great despair. His feeling that he had been abandoned was evident in every word and action. If Sir Chandreswar refused to help I did not know what would happen to the King.

In the days immediately following Surjit's departure the atmosphere at the Happy Cottage was almost unbearable, and we found little pleasure in our dancing. The princesses, who knew, or did not know, what had happened, were none the less infected by their father's dark mood. Because there was sadness in his face they, too, were sad. Their soft whispering became inaudible. Their eyes, when we sat together in the

garden, were held to the terrace outside their father's bedroom. When he came they and their mothers watched him
with unhappy anxiety. Deeply disturbed by them, I tried to
reassure them in gentle ways.

One day Ghorki Ram brought me two beautiful magnolias
from my garden, waxen blossoms framed by dark leaves. I
told him that they were too beautiful to be given to me, that
I would take them to the palace as a present from him to the
queens. He smiled in happy agreement. I wrapped the flowers
in silver paper and laid them both in a cloud of tissue, and
Ghorki carried them gently in his hands as we drove to the
palace. I presented them to Birdy and to Dreamy, saying,
"These are from Ghorki Ram, my servant, who loves you as
I do."

Smiles of pleasure fluttered across their faces, and they held
the magnolias as if each were a jewel. The King, standing
behind them, smiled for the first time since Surjit's plane left.
Never could this royal family receive a present, the humble
little things from my own possessions, the soap I found in the
Katmandu bazaar, without genuine surprise and without giving in return. That night each queen gave me a two-hundred-
rupee note for Ghorki Ram.

As soon as I thought it politic after Sir Chandreswar's
arrival, and before the King had received him in official durbar, I called at the Indian Embassy and left my card. I wrote
to him the same day, welcoming him to Nepal, wishing him
success and happiness, and asking for an early opportunity of
meeting him to "discuss a matter of extreme importance." I
sent Ghorki with the letter, and with a sheaf of flowers from
my garden. I received a reply from Dr. Shantiswarup Gupta,
who had been Surjit's secretary and who was now secretary to
Sir Chandreswar. He thanked me on the Ambassador's behalf
for the flowers, and added, "His Excellency would be glad

if you could see him at ten o'clock on the morning of Thursday next . . ."

The King said nothing when I told him of this, but he smiled a little wistfully.

Sir Chandreswar was a dignified Hindu in his late forties. In his Gandhi cap and white *achkan* he was like a modest college don. He was not tall, and he had none of Surjit's distinct Sikh masculinity, but behind his little black mustache his round face was gentle and compassionate. As he rose from his desk, his hand outstretched, his faded eyes looked at me over the tops of his horn-rimmed spectacles in kindly but shrewd scrutiny.

Our conversation began with pleasantries. He was a cultured man, a Fellow of Patna University and its vice-chancellor since the war. He liked to paint and to play tennis, and I think we talked of these things, and of the beauties of Nepal. His mood was sympathetic, and his understanding generous, and instinctively I knew that I could trust him. My doubts, the fears I had had, evaporated. I knew that perhaps it was going to be easier to talk of the King to him than it had been with Surjit. Surjit had been in Nepal a long time before I came and had listened to the Ranas and had heard their stories of the King. Sir Chandreswar was a stranger to the country. There had as yet been no tennis parties for him, no baskets of mangoes and oranges, no jolly little hunting excursions to the Terai.

He ended our general conversation by saying, "You said, madam, that there was a matter of extreme importance . . . ?"

I do not remember what words I used to tell him the story, except that, toward the end, and almost in tears, I said, "Your Excellency, I am so worried, what will happen to the King now?"

He had been listening attentively, his body immobile, his hands flat on the desk before him. Now he rose from his chair, came round the desk to me, and placed a hand on my shoulder. "My dear child, don't worry. We shall think of a way to help him."

I asked him how, and he shook his head. "You must give me time to think about this. Ask the King what he wants from me, and then you and I must meet again. But not here. Supposing we arrange a little picnic in the country?"

He came down to the car with me, and once more he said, "Don't worry. We shall help him if we can."

I flew to the palace and told the King of this promise. "Your Majesty," I said, "smile again, please!"

Day after day I waited to hear from Sir Chandreswar, and day after day without word. He presented his credentials to the King in the Hanuman Palace, a simple, modest figure in Gandhi cap and *achkan* among all that glittering gold and scarlet. He bowed before the King, accepted the *pan* and the perfumed handkerchief, and neither his face nor the King's betrayed that there was anything between them but the ritual of this ceremony. But I was aware of an emotional under-current as if it were a vibration shaking the whole palace. When the Prime Minister glanced up to the gallery where I sat I thought there was mockery in his bland expression. Bijaya was sitting next to me, and I thought I detected irony in every word he said. But the Prime Minister probably did not see me, and Bijaya talked only of his son, the nine-year-old Pasputti Shamsher, whom he wished to place in the Bishop Cotton School at Simla, asking me to write to the headmaster on the boy's behalf.

Although I waited impatiently to hear from Sir Chandreswar, the King did not mention the Ambassador again. His absences from the palace at night, however, increased. Now he would be three and sometimes four hours late, arriving without explanation, with the faintest smile only on his lips. One evening I sat in the garden with the princesses, singing with them in German, wondering why he did not come. The shadow on the sundial moved round until dusk finally dissolved it. The lights came on among the trees, the rooks flew up harshly and wheeled toward the mountains. Yet even then, at this moment he often chose for his dramatic appearance, he did not come. The hours passed and I could talk no more. Always the burden of entertainment fell upon me when I was with the queens or the princesses, and, although I knew that they were content to sit in silence with hands folded, I felt compelled to challenge their gentle silence with noise and laughter.

Perhaps that particular evening I was overtired, or too worried that no word had yet come from Sir Chandreswar. I suddenly said to Nalini, "If *Bua-ji* does not come in ten minutes I shall leave." And to myself I added, *I only hope the chauffeur is waiting at the gate, otherwise I'll have to return.*

Queens and princesses looked at me in shocked silence.

The ten minutes passed, and the King did not come. I stood up. "*Namashkar,* Birdy and Dreamy! *Namashkar,* Nalini, Vijaya, and Bharati!" And I left them quickly, hurrying through the gardens, along the crazy paving, out of the white walls to where my car usually awaited me. It was there, but its chauffeur was not. I could not walk the long way to Tripureswar in the dark, after the curfew gun, and in stiletto heels that would have broken an ankle within two hundred yards. So I went back, feeling a little absurd.

There was the King. He stood by the steps of the portico, white hat pulled down over his black curls, one foot a little forward, one hand at the lapel of his jacket and the other holding a leather driving glove at his side.

I greeted him politely, but coldly, for I was still stupidly angry with him and with myself, but he did not chide me for running away. He took my hand and led me down into the garden to a swing-hammock where the queens were waiting.

On this we sat, Birdy on his left, I on his right, and Dreamy to the right of me.

The hammock moved gently for some minutes. He said nothing, staring into the shadows. Then he suddenly picked up my hand and held it so that the palm was upward and open. Into this he placed the driving glove, closing my fingers over it and holding all tightly in his grasp.

"Now, Erika-ji," he said very firmly, "will you please pass this to Dreamy?" And he moved my hand toward her.

The grip of his hand was fierce on mine, and mine on the glove. Within the leather, unmistakably, was a revolver.

"Now," he said, when Dreamy had taken the glove and covered it with her sari, "now you see why I am late." He gave me no further explanation, but that evening he was very happy as we danced.

Word came from Sir Chandreswar at last, asking if I would give him the pleasure of my company on a visit to Bura-Nilkanta. But on the morning of the day the meeting was to take place there came another note:

> I am very sorry, it has not been possible to make a program for Bura-Nilkanta this afternoon. I am hoping to arrange a trip Saturday next. Yours sincerely——C.P.N. SINGH.

Once more the King and I were depressed. We were, after all, like children, cautiously fumbling, and frightened that everything we did was or would be discovered by the Ranas. By the time Saturday came I had heard nothing from the Embassy and had almost decided that Sir Chandreswar had forgotten, when a Sikh messenger walked up my pathway and handed me a letter.

> Apropos of our conversation when you saw me last, this is to inquire if 5:15 this afternoon will suit your convenience for going to Bura-Nilkanta.——C.P.N. SINGH.

The King expected me at the palace at five o'clock that day, and there was no way of warning him, no letter that could be written, no messenger to be sent. My car was outside on the gray road, the chauffeur asleep in the back with the black peak of his cap pulled over his eyes. I did not call for Ghorki, or Peepchen, or my bodyguard, but ran down the pathway to the car, woke up the driver and told him to drive to Naran Hity Durbar as fast as he could. He did this with alacrity and pleasure. We went through the black and white gates of the palace grounds, down the tree-lined drive to the entrance to the Happy Cottage. There I greeted the sentries with a curt *Namashkar!*, waving my hand to stop them from informing the ladies in waiting that I had arrived, which was their usual custom. Surprisingly, they let me through into the gardens with no more than an amiable smile.

I passed through the little courtyard where the fountain was playing musically, into the gardens, and on until I was close to the lake, and suddenly I was shocked by what I had done. Never before had I been to the palace uninvited, and never before in the morning. I wanted to speak to the King, but I had refused to have myself announced, and I did not know how or where to find him.

The garden was very still, except for the trembling call of the pigeons. A goldfish broke the surface of the lake with a sudden noise that startled me. I walked on until, from the cover of the bushes, I could see the portico.

The King and Sardar Pushparaj were sitting there at a table covered with books and papers. The Sardar's dried-lemon face was bent over his scratching pen, but the King was sitting upright, staring away into the garden with an expression of bored melancholy. I tried to attract his attention, coughing gently, clearing my throat, but he did not hear me. I moved closer, to one side, and behind the Sardar's back, and there I hissed, *"Your Majesty!"* His sharp ears caught those words, and he looked over the Sardar's bowed head to where my hand was waving urgently from the bushes. He watched me for a few seconds only and then turned his eyes away casually. I waited, and at last he said something to Sardar Pushparaj, left the portico and entered the Happy Cottage. He reappeared behind me, almost instantly, emerging from the glass door, catching me by the wrist and pulling me quickly into the hall, and from there into his emerald-green bathroom. He locked the door behind us, stood for a moment listening, and then turned to face me.

"What is it, Erika?"

He was dressed as I had never seen him. Not as a Nepalese, nor yet as an Indian, but like a magnificent Malay. He wore a sarong of glistening ivory, tight at the hips and pleated in fine folds so that a wide panel of golden cloth fell from his waist to the ground. His feet were like lotus flowers, the toes grasping a single button of gold on each white sandal. His white silk shirt was buttoned with diamonds, and his firm neck rose from it like a stem supporting the flower of his head.

"Don't be angry with me for coming like this."

"I am not angry. You are worried. What is it?"

I told him of the appointment with Sir Chandreswar, and that it was set for the time he himself had asked me to come to the palace. He embraced me impulsively. "Erika-ji! You are my clever Erika! You've got things moving again. You go to Bura-Nilkanta with His Excellency, and come back here when it is over. Don't announce yourself, come directly."

He showed me to the T door again, watching me smilingly as I crept past the portico where Sardar Pushparaj's head was still bent in silent contemplation of his papers.

That afternoon Sir Chandreswar, Dr. Shantiswarup Gupta and I drove out to Bura-Nilkanta in the embassy station wagon. It was a happy thought that Bura-Nilkanta should

have been chosen as the site of our "picnic," and I do not
know whether it had been Sir Chandreswar or I who decided
upon it. It lies ten miles to the north of Katmandu, down a
gray dusty road, past fields that were as bright and glistening
that Saturday afternoon as a pointillist landscape. It is a great
shrine of Vishnu, Nilkanta the blue-necked one, the "soul of
the universe with a thousand eyes, omniscient, floating on
primordial waters, lying on a snake with a thousand hoods."

To me it had a poignant association with the King. If
imprisonment by the Ranas kept him from visiting much of
his country, he could never visit Bura-Nilkanta even if he did
achieve the liberty he so passionately desired. Himself the
incarnation of Vishnu, he was not permitted to approach a
temple or holy shrine of Narain, for the Nepalese believed
that if this happened then great calamities would overtake
him and them. But because it was also believed that no man
should be robbed of the beauty of Bura-Nilkanta, a replica
of it was built for each god-king to see in the Balaju Gardens
outside Katmandu, where huge Asiatic carp rise to eat the
grain that is scattered on the lake, where a score of black and
crimson elephant trunks break from a white wall to fill the
tank with green water, and where a white horse, which is to
be the Lord Vishnu's final incarnation, peacefully crops the
grass beneath the trees.

If the setting for the Balaju Nilkanta is as beautiful as this,
the great blue-necked one to which Sir Chandreswar and I
went, and which the King might never see, is moving in the
extreme, an enormous image lying on a tank of serene black
water, twenty feet long and incredibly lovely. Seventeen
hundred years ago a farmer, turning the black earth of his
land in this valley, struck something with the fire-hardened
point of his wooden share. He was amazed to see, at the spot
where his plow had been halted, a stream of pure milk flowing. He called the village priest, and together they dug away

the earth from beneath the plow. At last they uncovered this image. The plow had struck one of the hands, and it was there that the milk was flowing. Because of this miracle it was known that the image was made potent by Vishnu's actual presence, and it was removed and placed in the tank where it lies today. It is watched by Garuda and by Hanuman, bird-god and monkey-god, and by Lakshmi, the round-limbed beautiful consort of Vishnu.

The image lies with legs crossed at the ankles, arms relaxed by the side with palms upward. Its head rests on a pillow made by the white distended hoods of many cobras, or perhaps the many heads of one great serpent—Anata the Infinite. The blue coils of the serpent's body twist and turn to form a braided bed on which Narain lies in eternal sleep, awaiting the next creation. Neck and limbs are of gentle blue stone. The cobra hoods, in scabbards of white, gold and silver, throw shadows across a face infinitely disturbing in its serenity.

Why this should be known as the Blue-Necked One, apart from the color of its stone, I was never sure. There is a legend that Narain once drank poisoned water and was given a thirst so great that he climbed to the peaks of the Himalayas for relief, shattering the stone with his trident and releasing three streams that gathered in a lake that was blue with the poison that had tortured him. But this is a legend closely resembling the draining of the valley by Manjusuri, and it was not important to me. The beauty of Bura-Nilkanta was enough in itself.

Sir Chandreswar and I walked silently from the car to the tank. Flowers lay among the cobra heads and across the blue stone face. Scarlet, pink and yellow petals drifted on the water. Worshipers walked out along the little quay to the feet of the great image, knelt there, touched the sacred stone, scattered their oblations of flowers and devoutly retired. In the shadows of the wall beyond the tank a single Brahmin, his neck hung with long rosaries made from shells, sat immobile.

At the edge of the tank Sir Chandreswar bent down, unlaced his European shoes and walked barefoot along the stones to the image. Barefoot, too, I joined him, and we paused there, with little brown Nepalese children at our feet, marigold flowers dribbling from their hands to fall on the water and scarcely disturb its surface with a ripple. Sir Chandreswar solemnly scattered a handful of coins, each falling with a precise, sharp sound on the stone, and then we went back to the bank and put on our shoes.

Dr. Shantiswarup stayed by the car, but the Ambassador and I walked across the grass to a dark grove of trees. He posed good-humoredly while I took his photograph, and then he took my arm and we walked on, deeper into the trees where no one could see us or hear us.

"Now, Miss Leuchtag, let us talk about your King. Tell me again what he wants."

"To be the constitutional monarch of a democracy."

Sir Chandreswar smiled at this, but not intolerantly. "Let us sit down. This is a great ambition for a man and needs thought."

We sat beneath the trees, and it seemed to be very dark there, although beyond the grove the sun was brilliant on the grass and on the light saris of the peasant women about the great image. I told him that Surjit had met the King, and that he had promised to help, even by flying the King out of Nepal to asylum in India, but this had come to nothing with Surjit's recall.

"I think," he said, "that I should meet your King, also, although I cannot promise to fly him out of the country. But first tell me what it is he wants from India."

"Your Excellency, I could not be sure. I think it is sympathy. I think he wants to be sure of a friend outside his own country, someone who might help him if ever he tries to overthrow the Ranas. He knows that nobody in the world thinks of him. He knows what the Ranas say about him."

Sir Chandreswar looked at me closely. "Is he going to overthrow the Ranas?"

"I don't know. All I know is his unhappiness, and his longing for India's help. I think he would like Pandit Nehru to know what he is really like."

Sir Chandreswar put his hands on his knees and looked down at the Bura-Nilkanta for a long time in silence. At last he said, "I shall be going to India soon." He saw the sudden despair in my face. "Don't be alarmed, it will be for a visit only, to attend the funeral of a relative. Perhaps I could talk to Pandit-ji, and perhaps bring a letter back for your King. I say perhaps, you understand, Miss Leuchtag. I can promise nothing."

"Could you take a letter from the King to Nehru?" I asked suddenly.

"I could," he said. "Would he write one?"

"I don't know," I said, and I truly did not. "And if you brought a letter for the King, how would you meet him?"

He smiled at me. "Now, you are a clever woman, you can think of a way."

It did not seem to me that Sir Chandreswar was the type of man for the sort of rendezvous that had so much appealed to Surjit's nature. Then the idea came to me slowly. "Your Excellency, when I told you about the beautiful gardens at Naran Hity Durbar, you said how much you would like to see them."

He looked at me shrewdly. "I could ask the Prime Minister for permission to visit them . . ."

"And meet the King there by accident, and give him the letter?"

"Would that do?" he asked.

"No," I said unhappily. "You would not be allowed to visit the gardens alone. You wouldn't be allowed to talk to the King without a Rana officer being present. He is not allowed to talk to foreigners at all."

"But it is an idea," he said, and he stood up. "We will deal with first things first. You must ask him to write to me, and I will ask Pandit Nehru to write to him. Now we must go back."

When the car left me at Tripureswar he pressed my hand gently. "Don't worry, my dear child, we shall manage it somehow."

It was dusk when I reached the Happy Cottage that evening, and the King was waiting. He took my hand quickly and led me across the lawn, across paving stones that had been laid in the shape of hearts and diamonds, clubs and spades. As we walked softly through the trees there was a rustling on our left, a harsh cry, and I looked toward it. There was a great peacock slowly opening the wondrous beauty of its tail. In the light of the lamps I saw the electric blue of the feathers on the bird's throat and breast, the black and golden eyes on its fan. When we had passed, as if it had made its *namashkar* to the King the peacock closed its tail and let it fall to the grass.

We came to the little veranda beyond the tea pavilion, where I had met the Crown Prince Mahendra, and as we approached three figures rose to their feet. They were the King's sons, the Yuvraj Sahib Mahendra in his plain Nepalese dress, the young Himalaya and Bashundera in thin European suits, and all had their heads bowed, the palms of their hands together, thumbs touching their lips.

We sat together at a little table in the darkness, our faces momentarily revealed by the glow of our cigarettes, and I heard the peacock crying harshly as it stalked below the trees.

The King sat by my side, holding my hand in his, as I told them of my meeting with Sir Chandreswar, of his promise to bring a letter from Pandit Nehru should it be possible. The princes said nothing, but I saw the dim movement of their heads as they turned their faces to their father, and the emotion that passed among them all was almost tangible.

The King made me repeat again and again the story of the meeting at Bura-Nilkanta. His voice was full of hope and joy. He lifted my hand and said to his sons, "She is my clever Erika, she will help us all!"

I BELIEVED that the King would write the letter to Sir Chandreswar immediately, but he did not. Day after day he avoided it, and day after day I pleaded with him despairingly. In that despair, perhaps, I did not fully realize what was being asked of him. For all the years of his life he had disciplined himself to betray nothing of his fears, his hopes, or his ambitions. Now he was expected to put them on paper, to entrust that letter first to me and then to a stranger, and finally to believe that it would be treated seriously by the Prime Minister of India. Now I know what doubts he had first to overcome, but in those days I thought only of the unnecessary delay and the fact that Sir Chandreswar would soon be leaving for Delhi.

The King's birthday was approaching, and in thinking of it I forgot some of my anxiety. It was to be his forty-third birthday and by the Western calendar it fell on the thirtieth day of June; but astrology plays a large part in Hindu life, and the court astrologer, a Brahmin of inferior grade, was instructed to study the King's horoscope and find an auspicious day for the celebrations. The King had a firm faith in such things, and I suspect that the astrologer had also been instructed to find a favorable day for the King's meeting with

Surjit, without being told the reason for it. In this instance the Brahmin worked for a week before submitting his advice to the palace. The King smilingly refused to say which date had been chosen. He wished it to be one of his surprises, and only reluctantly told me at last that it was July the fourth.

My problem then was what to give him as a present. I remembered the ring, the silver band I wore, with the elephants on it, and I remembered how it had pleased him when first he saw it. I went to the Middle Bazaar and found a goldsmith, a berry-skinned old man sitting cross-legged in the shadows of his shop, his bald head shining above his white shirt and black waistcoat. Fortunately he spoke Hindi, and Ghorki interpreted for me as I held up the ring. "Madam would like this copied in gold, and soon. Can it be done, master?"

The smith took the ring, turned it in his fingers, photographed it in his mind, and handed it back to me. It could be done, he said.

I went every morning to watch the ring being made, sitting cross-legged as the smith sat, with Peepchen beside me and Ghorki behind, and sometimes the smith asked to see my silver ring again, holding it beside the one he was making. They were very pleasant, those mornings, the cool shadows of the shop, the brilliant sun on the square outside, the tinkling of cycle bells, the lowing of the wandering cows, the noise and color of the bazaar.

One evening, when the golden ring was still unfinished, I was sitting in the palace gardens below the portico, with Nalini, Vijaya and Bharati on the swing-hammock, singing *lieder* with them. At a table on the portico the King sat with Sardar Pushparaj, papers before them. A lady in waiting came to us suddenly, whispering, "Madam, His Majesty would like to see your ring with the elephants."

I believed that he had suddenly remembered it, and that

he desired Sardar Pushparaj to order him one like it. I said,
"Please give His Majesty my humble *namashkars*, but I cannot give him the ring."

She came back. "His Majesty asks madam for the ring."
Again I refused. She came a third time. "Madam, it is a royal
hokhum, an order from His Majesty."

So I handed her the ring and sadly watched it taken to the
King, thinking this to be the end of my birthday present. But
he merely held it up before Sardar Pushparaj, pointing to the
elephants, and then casually returned it to the lady in waiting. Something he had remembered about the ring, something
that had come into his conversation with the secretary, that
was all it had been, no more.

As July the fourth approached I said to the princesses,
"What have you prepared for your *Bua-ji?*" and of course got
only a gently whispered "I don't know." So I said that whatever it was they were accustomed to give him on his birthday,
this year there would be something different. They would
each make him a handkerchief, and I would show them how.
From the King's bottomless treasure chest we secured Irish
linen and little raffia sewing baskets. We sat among the flowers with industrious needles, making handkerchiefs, each embroidered with the letter T.

On the morning of the official birthday the King held a
durbar, this time at Nevan Hity sitting on the red velvet
throne, the snake-headed arms curling upward beside him,
and the golden skullcap with its pendant emeralds on his
head. Dark-suited Brahmins attended him, and beyond sat
the Prime Minister, legs straddled, curved saber aslant, and
on his head, too, a golden crown and fountain plume of
feathers.

Beginning with the Maharaja, the Rana nobles came before
the throne to pay their empty and ironic respects to the King.
They came with hands outstretched, palms down, and on top

of each hand was a coin which the King touched gently with his fingers. This was the ceremony of *damrakhnu,* the salutation of loyalty and respect, and although the cynicism of it, so far as the Ranas were concerned, made me bitter, it was deeply impressive.

That afternoon I prepared my presents. I had collected the ring from the bazaar, and it was beautifully made in warm, soft gold. I had made a little bag from some chamois leather I had brought from Simla, neatly stitching it with thread of green, his favorite color. In this I placed the ring. I had ordered, from India, a large studio portrait of myself, and through the cover of this I passed a beautiful feather that I had found one day in my garden.

For Ghorki's loyal *damrakhnu* I prepared a silver rupee, mounting it on multicolored crepe paper, attaching to it a message of greeting in Hindi written by Ghorki. Peepchen's present was a silver candlestick.

I was to be at the palace by eight o'clock, and when the car came for me I was ready in a white sharkskin evening gown and white sandals. I had found an old, chipped tray in the guesthouse, and this I covered with an Irish linen cloth, placing our presents on top. Holding this in both hands, the folds of the cloth falling over my arms, I walked to the car. Still holding it, and with Peepchen sitting obediently beside me, I was taken to the palace. The sentries at the gate of Naran Hity stood away from the walls and stared in astonishment.

The garden of the Happy Cottage that night was more beautiful than it had ever been. A fountain was playing in the center of the lake, its clear water rising in an unbroken fan, colored by lamps hidden among the lotus leaves. Floodlights were also concealed in the trees and shrubs, and the tea pavilion glowed like a mauve lantern once more.

I waited, alone, below the portico, the tray heavy now in

my hands, until the queens and princesses came out of the glass door. They rustled toward me, smiling happily. For the first time they were not wearing saris, but the *khemeeze* and *salwar*, the elegant, trousered costume that was once worn by Moslem women only but is now worn by all women in the Punjab. Their *salwars*, wide trousers pleated and pleated again at the front, were in brilliant colors. Over the long-sleeved *khemeeze* they wore the *dopatta*, the filmy, gold-bordered veil framing the back of their hair and necks. Diamonds glittered at their ears and in their hair. They moved like flowers across the lawn.

Still the King did not come, the tray became heavier, and I began to feel ridiculous. When he did come it was unannounced, of course. Suddenly and silently he appeared from the glass door, tall and immaculate in evening dress, a blue sash bending across his chest and knotted in a rosette at the hip. There was a sparkle of jeweled orders on his breast.

"*Namashkar*, Your Majesty," I said. "But if I am to touch your feet in birthday greetings, you must take this tray." And I thrust it gratefully into his hands.

We did not dine until midnight, and before that the King's sons came with their wives. Sadface was there too, in the background, wearing Punjabi dress with the diamond T in her hair, her thoughts withdrawn behind her beautiful eyes as she changed the records to which we all danced. There was an atmosphere of gently restrained gaiety that changed subtly as we sat down to dine. There were then no smiles and scarcely any conversation. The menu, paradoxically, was Western, and it seemed odd to me that on his birthday, on a day chosen only after much study by the court astrologer, this royal incarnation of Vishnu should dine from roast saddle of mutton and strawberry ices.

The King sat at the head of the table, and no one at its

foot. I sat on his right, the queens on his left, and nothing was said as we ate. All that morning and afternoon I had composed and memorized a little speech in the King's honor. Yet so solemn were these unhappy people, and so silent, that I had not the courage to ask permission to deliver it. I was depressed (as perhaps they were too) by the realization that nowhere else in Nepal but here was the King's birthday being celebrated.

When dinner was over we sat in the cocktail room, and there the King and I danced, while his sons and daughters and wives sat on chairs and on the floor, playing children's games —ludo, and snakes and ladders, and tiddly-winks—until it was three in the morning, and the King lifted the needle from the last record. "May I go now, please?" he said.

In the morning Ghorki Ram brought me a note that had been left at Tripureswar. This was not from Sardar Push-paraj, but had been written in the King's hand. "Everybody is terribly tired. Please do not come to the palace today. Go also to bed early. T."

A week after his birthday party, as we sat alone together in the tea pavilion, the King silently handed me his letter for Sir Chandreswar. I took it to the Embassy early next morning, with a covering letter of my own, and with a flaming torch of flowers from my garden. The Ambassador was not there, and, none too happily, I handed the letter to Shanti-swarup Gupta, with instructions that it be placed in Sir Chandreswar's hands only. That afternoon I received a diplomatic reply:

> How delightful it is to find a present from you as the first thing this morning! Please communicate my heartfelt thanks for this thoughtful act. I greatly appreciate the gesture.——C.P.N. SINGH.

SIR CHANDRESWAR went to Delhi and returned to Katmandu within a few days, bringing with him Nehru's letter to the King. I did not suggest, nor was it suggested to me by either, that I should deliver this letter. It was imperative that they should meet. The simple plan which, in loyalty and devotion to one man, I had put in motion, had now moved on to clandestine negotiations involving the Prime Minister of India. Surjit's boyish enthusiasm and adventurous nature had given the affair the color of an escapade, and I had been in emotional sympathy with it. Sir Chandreswar cloaked it with the mystery of high diplomacy, and there was no place for me in this. I did not ask him what Nehru had said, and he did not tell me. He smiled at me reassuringly and said that he hoped to see the King as soon as it could be arranged.

And there was the difficulty. He made his diffident request to see the gardens at Naram Hity, and the Ranas brushed this aside with a yes, a no, a perhaps-sometime. I was depressed when Sir Chandreswar told me of this failure. "My dear Miss Erika," he said, "did you think it was going to be easy? The King has waited a long time, he will understand that such things need patience."

Whatever Sir Chandreswar may have thought of the King's patience, Tribhuvana himself was near despair and was beginning to think that he was going to be no more successful with Sir Chandreswar than he had been with Surjit. Soon, too, it would be time for me to leave Nepal. The extra weeks granted me by the Ranas were ending. I could stay no longer, and it would not be easy for me to go knowing that the King was still a prisoner, that the letter from Nehru remained undelivered.

We had found no answer to the problem of how the letter could be passed to the King even should the Ambassador visit the royal gardens. In those days of waiting my mind was full of fantastic proposals. I told the King that I would hide in the palace overnight, and when the Ambassador came I would come out of hiding, attract the attention of his Rana escort, and thus leave him free to talk to the King.

He smiled at me. "You little optimist, Erika! Do you think that Goebbels wouldn't know you hadn't slept at the guest-house? Are you determined to eat that poisoned cucumber?"

So nothing was decided, no plan of mine was feasible. This was a conspiracy, and yet it was not, because nothing was being conspired. I would wake in the morning and tell myself that today the Ranas would give Sir Chandreswar permission to visit the gardens. Before I had breakfasted I would know that it was impossible, because the Ambassador had not yet asked for permission again, believing that to do so too soon would only arouse suspicion. Sadly I began to prepare for my departure. At the Foreign Office, Bijaya told me that I could not take my luggage with me across the mountains in this monsoon weather. He was having wooden crates made for me, he said, and these would be swung over the mountains by rope railway from Katmandu to Bhimpedi. He seemed genuinely sorry that I was going, and for my part I was sorry that he was a Rana.

He told me, also, that I would receive letters of warrant, entitling me to declare that I had given treatment to the Royal Family of Nepal. When the document came I showed it to the King, proudly indicating the crest at the top of the paper. He passed his finger gently across the gold and blue arms, the crossed kukri, the footprints of Buddha, the sun of Shiva.

"*I* have no crest," he said.

I went to see Sir Chandreswar as often as I could. Although he was not much older than I, his fatherly manner was comforting. He told me again and again not to worry, that the

King would be in his care when I left, and that what could
be done would be done. Every evening now, the King and I
sat alone in the gardens, or in the dusky tea pavilion, hour
after hour, listening to the eternal movement of the streams
that flowed through the trees. Sometimes we sat together for
seven hours, and the time did not seem long. Now it was that
the King told me so much of his life, of how in his youth he
had determined to make his body and spirit strong, so that
the Ranarchy could not debauch him as it had done his father
and grandfather. He told me how each morning he had
wrestled with his Japanese instructor, and how in the afternoons he had ridden two horses at great speed, a foot on the
saddle of each. He put his body to great tests of endurance,
and he paid a high price for this desperate attempt to be a
whole man. Twice, before my coming, he had suffered from
serious heart attacks.

Such confidences indicated the change in him since the first
days I knew him, or at least the change in his attitude toward me. His boyish liking for surprises, however, had not
changed. One evening—it was a Thursday, the day of his
regular visit to the Prime Minister at Singha Durbar—he said,
"Tomorrow is a great occasion. This morning Goebbels asked
me about my dancing lessons, and he wants to see what prog-
ress I have made. Tomorrow you put on your nicest cocktail
dress, and your best shoes, and we shall give him a performance."

Dutifully I arrived at the palace the next evening, in a
cornflower-blue dress with tight bodice and flared skirt, high-
heeled shoes and my jewels. The Maharaja, brushing his mustache, would see that this silly European woman was behaving
just as he imagined. But the Prime Minister did not come.
At the hour he was expected, the King silently left the cocktail room, and he returned a few minutes later carrying his
driving gloves. He picked up my hand and led me through

the inner gardens to the entrance to the great part of Naran
Hity. There his car was waiting, the sentries backing away
from it, beckoning with their hands in the humblest *namashkar*. The King slipped into the driving seat and opened the
door for me, his hand out to take mine.

"But the Maharaja . . . ?" I said.

"Oh, *him!*" And he laughed.

I asked no more questions, but let him play out his surprise.
We drove alone, no Rana escort with us, and I knew that
wherever we were going it would be within the grounds of
Naran Hity. He turned off the main drive to the left onto
an old road, one that was strange to me, where the trees
crowded in upon us and whispered sharply as we sped past. We
passed the broken walls of an old palace, and the King flicked
his hand toward it. "That was my father's private palace," he
said, and he added sardonically, "—where he kept his five
hundred wives."

We stopped at a corner of the old official palace. There were
sentries at the doors, not standing, not even alert, but lying
on the ground asleep, with their backs propped against the
wall and their rifles across their legs. The King looked at them
and smiled. He put a finger to his lips and tiptoed gently past
the soldiers, into the palace, up a wide staircase, at the top
of which waited the Yuvraj Sahib Mahendra and his princess,
bowing low in *namashkar*.

"You see?" said the King, as if he had explained all this
before and I had been too obtuse to understand. "My son
wishes to give you a party."

Mahendra was a shy young man, and it was difficult to get
him to talk. He had none of his father's clouded emotions,
only a diffident serenity. He and his wife showed me their
palace with the pride a Western couple might take in showing their home. I was taken to each room, even to the bedroom with its huge Chippendale bed. Their children came

tumbling after us, little girls with powdered faces and jewels in their ears, little boys with the King's sad eyes, and when they had all studied me long enough, and decided that I was no monster, they climbed into my arms, chattering like monkeys.

As we drove back that night, to where my car was waiting, the King hummed to himself happily, a *rag* for the evening when the heart is content.

He said to me one day, "Erika, I have a surprise for you."

"Your Majesty, *that* will be something quite new."

"I am building something for you, here in the gardens. It will be yours alone."

"*Namashkar*, Your Majesty, but you can give me nothing I need."

"You shall see," he said.

Now and then in the days that followed I heard a hammering and a banging from beyond the palace, from the other side of the Happy Cottage. The King did not mention the matter again, but when the noise grew unusually loud he would listen to it and would look at me with suppressed amusement. Then one day the noise stopped, and I heard no more noises for two days. On the evening of the third the King took my hand and said, "Tonight we shall not dance upstairs. Come with me."

He took my hand, the queens and the princesses following with little smiles of excitement on their lips. We walked around the portico, along the pathway by the lawn, and we turned at last into a courtyard enclosed on three sides by the Happy Cottage. A fountain was playing in the middle of the flagstones, and dark green shrubs crouched close to the earth. It was dark there, and the moon scarcely touched the stone, although it shone brilliantly on the roofs above us.

The King looked at Dreamy and she gave him a key which

he placed in my hand. It was stamped with rich yellow gold, and engraved upon it was the letter E. He pointed to a building at the far side of the courtyard. "It is yours, Erika," he said. "Put on the light above the door and you will see."

I switched on the light, and it glowed on a plate that said ERIKA DANCE HALL. I put the key in the lock and opened the door, King, queens and princesses crowding about me to see the delight in my face and clapping happily. The door opened onto a long, rectangular room where light glimmered on salmon and silver walls. The rich curtains that hung across the windows were salmon and silver too, and the floor was smooth and shining in parquet blocks. There was the radio-phonograph, and a grand piano with my birthday portrait framed upon it. There were flowers everywhere and a heavy, pervading perfume. I walked alone into the room, opened the piano, and softly touched a key. The sound did not break the spell.

"Come," said the King, "now we shall dance in your own dance hall."

I wanted to cry.

He said to me, "Erika, I wish to honor you in a very special way."

"There has been too much, Your Majesty," I said.

"But this is different. I want you to dine with us in the Holy Rice Hall at Naran Hity."

There were ten days only before I left Katmandu. July was two-thirds over, and the crates which Bijaya had sent me were almost packed. Sir Chandreswar was preparing safe-conduct through India for me, promising that a Sikh police-man would escort me from the border to Simla, and doing all he could to soften the realization that I was to leave Nepal before he and the King met, and before Nehru's letter was delivered.

A great comfort to me in those last days was the knowledge that whatever doubt the King had had in the early days was now gone, that he now trusted me entirely. I could never blame him for that doubt, and in everything I did and said I tried to convince him of my loyalty and devotion. This invitation to the Rice Hall was one of the many professions of his faith in me which he made during my last week. His trust suddenly flowered like a lotus, petals opening, concealing nothing.

I had been in the East long enough to appreciate the sacred significance of a grain of rice. Mr. Kathait had warned me that in Nepal rice was even more sacred than in India. In walking about the bazaar I had taken great care to keep a respectful distance between myself and the saffron mounds of rice outside the shops. I was careful not to approach any food sold in the markets. Once only did I make a mistake. Attracted by the blue, vermilion and orange sweets offered in a little store, I went inside to buy some and was driven from it with loud cries of anger and indignation.

Thus the King's invitation to the Rice Hall moved me deeply. He was not asking me to dine with him, but to share with him part of his spiritual existence. The Rice Hall at the palace of Naran Hity is perhaps as holy as Pashupattinath. I had heard of it, I had never seen it.

That evening it was very hot, no moon, and the sky a great indigo bowl of stars. We walked slowly through the gardens, the King and I first, hand in hand, the queens and the princesses following, magnificently dressed. We walked through the magnolia bushes to the official palace, and through its doors to the foot of a broad staircase. As we climbed I heard only the gentle whisper of feet on the steps, the tap of my high heels echoing away down empty corridors.

We paused at the top of the staircase, before two great doors of gold, scarlet and ivory, and there were hand basins with hot and cold water, soft fleecy towels. We washed our hands and we cleansed our mouths, and, instinctively, I removed my shoes. The King opened the doors and we walked into a long, high hall of white and black marble, tall French windows along one wall. I do not remember that there were lamps there, but there was light, an amber glow that melted on the white walls and gathered itself in tiny sparks on the gold. This, said the King in a scarcely audible whisper, was the Rice Hall where he ate the life-sustaining grain in ceremonial dinners with his Brahmin priests.

At the far end, on a shallow dais, were seven low tables and seven low stools, placed in two rows, of four and three, and facing each other. Each table was covered by a white cloth brought forward at the front into a starched and pleated fan for use as a napkin. The King took me to my table, softly explaining that when he dined here with the Brahmins he ate from golden *thal,* and they from dishes of silver. There was a golden *thal* on each table this evening, piled with yellow rice, and about it were little dishes of silver and gold containing meat, fish, vegetables, chutney and chupatties.

The King did not dine with us, but stood apart, watching silently. We, too, did not speak as we ate, leaving the left hand unused in our laps, breaking a piece of chupatty with the right hand and picking up the rice with it. When we had finished I looked up to the King and said, "Have I made any mistakes, Your Majesty?"

He shook his head gravely. "No. *Bohut acha,* Erika. You have been very good."

And, silently, we left the Rice Hall.

The following evening we returned to the official palace, the King and I, and alone. He did not take me to the Rice Hall, but to another, almost as large. There, in the empty silence and the glitter of gold, silver and cut glass, were long

tables laid with rice, with meat and with fish. The only light
was that which came through the French windows from the
night outside, strangely disturbing.

"What is it for?" I asked.

"For my grandson tomorrow morning," he said wistfully.
"*Annaprasan*, the ceremonial rice feeding. When a Hindu boy
is six months old he is given a few grains of consecrated rice,
and the men of his caste eat with him, and so he is initiated."

For a long time, and without speaking again, he stared at
the silent room, and I loved him for wanting to show me this.

I had often said, as the time for leaving came closer, "I
cannot go back to India and not hear from you. I must write
to you, and you must write to me, and I shall tell you what
I am doing in India to help you."

He shook his head. "It's impossible. I cannot send a letter,
and I cannot receive one that the Ranas will not see."

"There must be someone here we could trust, someone who
could deliver my letters to you."

He shook his head again. "There is no one to trust."

"I shall find someone, and you must find someone. Between us we shall make it possible."

And we did. It was, perhaps, inevitable that I should think
of Doctor Das Gupta. I had grown very fond of him and
frequently called on him. Sometimes I went early in the
morning, for I rise early and occasionally forget that others
do not. I would go into his garden where the grazing cow
lifted its head to stare at me, and the Doctor Sahib's china-
doll children tumbled out, calling "Erika-*ji!*"

Then the good Bengali would come, called from his morning meal, dressed in *dhoti* and *khemeeze*, bowing, and saying
again and again, "*Buon giorno, Signorina!*"

The appearance of the doctor's home always moved me,
its shabbiness, its reflection of his own tired and overworked

body, his inner longing for the good days in Rome. He would take me through to his sitting room, past the anteroom where his poor patients were already waiting. The furniture was sparse—a sofa, two chairs, a table, and the pictures of Italy on the wall. There the Doctor Sahib would sit and talk to me, a middle-sized ordinary man, his hair brushed back from his big head, and his expression very gentle.

When I was with him I had always been aware of the fact that his attachment to me went beyond our common love of Italy, and it was this awareness that convinced me I could trust him. I knew that he could not be bribed, nor could any correspondence depend on the danger of bribed men. Certainly if any man in Nepal needed money, it was the Doctor Sahib. He had no car in a country where transport was essential. I would see him wobbling off in the mornings by bicycle, on his way to treat a Rana patient for nothing. Money would have bought him a car. Money would have enabled him to buy the cigarettes he craved and which his good wife Mara forbade him.

But, just the same, I knew that I could not buy Doctor Das Gupta's help with money.

I had already, weeks before, asked him what he thought of the King. "He keeps me waiting when I go to the palace," he said unhappily. "Sometimes for an hour, sometimes for two."

I could not explain to him that this was all the power the King had, to keep a man waiting.

"Always," said the doctor, "they keep me waiting. The Ranas too."

I did not know where his loyalty might lie, to a sense of justice, or to the Ranas on whom his living and his life depended, but I had to take the risk. I remembered how he had treated me for dysentery, and how, when I asked for his account, he looked at me in sorrow and said only, "*Signorina!*"

I called upon him a week or so before my departure, and he came into the garden to greet me, in his *dhoti* and sandals, his hands together in *namashkar*. I said, "Doctor Sahib, I must talk to you, but not here. Somewhere where we can be alone."

"*Signorina*, when I go out I am always watched. It is known where I go, whom I speak to. Is it important?"

"It is very important, Doctor Sahib. And no one must hear what we say."

"Very well," he said, after much thought, "let us go for a walk."

We went along the road to the river, down a dark lane walled by trees, to a rope suspension bridge spanning the river. On this we stood, alone, unheard from either bank, and I told him as much as I could—that I was trying to help the King, that he wished to reign over a free people, and that when I returned to India I wished to write to him. Would the doctor see that my letters reached the King?

He looked gravely at the yellow water below us. "How can I do that, *Signorina?*"

I said, "Doctor Sahib, I don't know. Perhaps when you go to treat the King, or his sons."

"We are never alone together."

"Doctor Sahib, *please* . . ."

"I will try," he said at last. "Tell His Majesty that I will try."

But one man alone would not be enough. The King knew this, and I knew it. So many letters arriving from me for Doctor Das Gupta would, in time, make the Ranas curious, curious enough to open them. One evening the King said to me, "There is another man to whom you may write, and who may send my letters to you. He has come here to meet you."

We were standing by the lake and, as the King raised his hand, a tall Nepalese came down from the shadows of the portico. He had a fine head, with gray hair beneath his cap.

He greeted the King devoutly, and spoke to me too, in Nepali that I could not understand.

"This is Sardar Krishnalal, who will help us." The King put his hand on mine and added, "This is my dear friend, Erika." He said a few more words in Nepali, and Sardar Krishnalal smiled gently and *namashkared*.

He was, I discovered, everything that the King could not trust Sardar Pushparaj to be, secretary, confidant, emissary. He helped the King in the little things that were the only things permitted him, the ordering of his garden, the designing of his jewels, and now, it would seem, the planning of his liberty. He spoke no English, but I saw in his eyes, as he looked at the King, the same loyalty and devotion I felt myself.

I had, finally, to assure myself that my letters would reach Doctor Das Gupta. I had no high opinion of the Nepalese Post Office and I knew also that the Ranas operated a semicensorship of all mail that passed through it. If I addressed my letters directly to the Doctor Sahib they would be handled and delivered by the Nepalese. I thought of this problem for some time before I reached a solution which was, as is so often the case, very simple and very obvious. I decided that if the head of the Indian Post Office in Katmandu agreed I could forward the letters to his care and ask him to pass them on to Doctor Das Gupta.

The day I decided upon this I went to the Indian Post Office. I could not go during the hours it was open, for then Sher Bahadur Gurung, the Postmaster, sat in public behind his counter, and what was said to him or by him could be heard by all. I went early in the morning, when the office was closed and silent. I knew that he lived behind the Post Office, and I found a door in the garden wall at which I knocked for a long time before it was opened by the Postmaster. I had disturbed him at his meal, and beyond him I

saw the beautiful little courtyard of his home, with its fountain and quiet flowers.

I said, "Master-ji, forgive me, but I urgently need stamps
to write to my mother in Simla."

He opened the door to let me into the courtyard, and I
closed it behind me securely.

"Madam, the Post Office is closed."

I said, "It doesn't matter about the stamps, I wanted to
talk to you. I am going home to India soon. If I dispatch
some letters to you from Simla, in your care, will you promise
that you will place them in Doctor Das Gupta's hands?"

I had expected some argument, or at least a request for
an explanation, but he looked at me very closely and said:
"Of course, madam. You may trust me."

It was that simple.

The King was still not satisfied. He decided that there
must be a code which we could use in our letters should the
situation need it. The devising of such a code gave him the
same pleasure which it would have given a schoolboy, and
when he had finished it he handed me a copy with a slight
flourish of pride. He had typed it himself on two sheets of
blue stippled writing paper, on the second of which he had
affixed his seal, red wax with the letter T impressed.

He told me that his letters would be signed "H. Lall," and
that when this was written in red ink then the letter would
contain a message in code. If it became necessary to avoid
using my name I would be addressed as "Lakshmi," and in
my heart I thanked him for this. The code itself consisted
of alternative words for forty-five people and things. Thus
Pandit Nehru was referred to as "Doctor," and the Governor-
General of India, Chakravarti Rajagopalacharia, as "Veteri-
nary Surgeon." I had told the King that, on my return to
India, one of the many people to whom I would appeal for
help on his behalf would be my dear friend B. P. L. Bedi, the

nationalist leader. For Bedi, too, the King found a code name, and it was one with subtle allusions. Remembering that Boris who had once befriended him, he called Bedi "Hotel Manager." The rest of the code ran thus:

Ghorki	Surjit Singh
Friend from Patiala	The Maharaja of Patiala
Friend from Simal Hill	A Nepalese
Serpent	A Rana
Big Snake	The Prime Minister
Bird	Ambassador (Sir Chandreswar)
Pigeon	Doctor Das Gupta
Moor	The King
Big Moor	The Senior Queen
Small Moor	The Junior Queen
Goldfish	Prince
Small Goldfish	Princess
Weather	Situation
Flower	Letter
Like	Watch
Call	Write
Walk	Safe
Tired	Danger
Play	Come
Crawl	Know
Fin	Lock
Indian Sweet	Help
Well	Happy
Hankie	Wire or Cable
Doll	Man
House	Palace
Stable	Singha Durbar
Boot	The Public
Rain	Burn
Coin	Free
Pencil	Power

Button	Money
Tie	Bribe
Cigarettes	Army
North British Golf Ball	Rifle
Kro-Flite Golf Ball	Machine Gun, Bren or Tommy
Silver King Golf Ball	Colt Revolver
Tee	Bullet or Cartridge
Safety Match	Hand Grenade
Lighter	Dynamite
Kite	Airplane
Storm	Invasion

NUMBERS:

Quarter-dozen	5,000
Half-dozen	10,000
Three-quarter dozen	20,000
One dozen	40,000

The last names in the code, with their direct references to arms and ammunition, showed how wide the King's ambitions were ranging, but I do not think their significance struck me at the time. We were sitting in my dance hall when he gave me the code, on one of my last evenings at the palace, and from then until I passed through the Terai into India, it burned a hole wherever I placed it. I hid it in a different place every day, and several times a day. It was in my pocket the day I went to Singha Durbar to say official farewell to the Prime Minister, and, for the first time, I did not consider the risk of a poisoned cucumber a melodramatic overstatement.

Some days earlier I had written to him, telling him that I would soon be leaving Nepal, thanking him for his presents and his hospitality. I told him that I had seen much of

Katmandu on my morning walks and that I had grown very attached to it. I then added a paragraph which, I hoped, would prove that I had turned out to be just as silly and naïve as he had expected.

> Otherwise I kept myself almost completely aloof; and I must say I enjoy my loneliness, as I feel it is a good thing to be a guest of one's own. It was Goethe, the great German poet, who said, "I feel lonely only in a crowd."

The Prime Minister promptly replied through his private secretary, Sardar Dixit.

> I write to inform you that His Highness the Maharaja will receive you for leave-taking on Wednesday next at four o'clock in the afternoon. I have to request you to attend Singha Durbar at the time stated.

I scarcely remember the details of that "leave-taking." The code was in my handbag in my lap, my mind and heart were full of sadness at what seemed to be my desertion of the King. My efforts to help him had come to nothing, or so it seemed. He had not met Sir Chandreswar, and Pandit Nehru's letter was still undelivered. I remember only the picture of the Prime Minister's face as he sat on the couch with me, a pale, bland moon, a hand rhythmically brushing that hooped mustache.

What he said was only polite and bored small talk, and he seemed to have forgotten that five months ago, in this same room, he had told Bijaya that he wished to meet me again. In a few minutes he rose, shook my hand, and departed through the far doors, surrounded by his escort of officers.

He sent me one final present before I left, a portrait of himself in his ceremonial robes, his golden crown and bird-of-paradise plume. It was framed in turquoise and coral.

THE King would not speak of my going, as if it were not to happen, and it was I who had to bring the fact into the open between us. I had fixed my departure for the last day of July, when the monsoon rains would be slackening. I said to the King, "I cannot bear to say good-bye to you, any of you. I shall leave the palace one evening, just as usual, and never come back."

He said, "You cannot do that, Erika, we love you too much. Such things must be done properly. You must tell us the day you are going, and you must take leave of us."

I refused to tell him, but he was not a fool. He discovered the day somehow, from Sardar Pushparaj or Sardar Krishnalal, and during the brief time left to us he made his feelings manifest in a dozen ways, the opening of the lotus petals that had enclosed his emotions for so long. Thus it was that he gave me my dance hall, took me to dine with his Yuvraj Sahib, invited me to share the holiness of the Rice Hall, and showed me the preparations for the *annaprasan* of his grandson. Long, long hours we sat together in the garden, in the tea pavilion, or walked hand in hand past the *kumari* stone, and as the time grew shorter I appealed to him, "Do not despair. I shall do all I can in India to help you, I promise you. And Sir Chandreswar will not forget you."

I had often asked him to show me the private rooms of the Happy Cottage, pestering him, I suppose, and he had always answered, "Yes, sometime. Sometime, perhaps." Now, in his final demonstration of trust, he showed me all. He made the occasion a ceremony, of course. We went in a little procession—first the King and myself, then the queens and princesses in a rustling stream of colored saris.

I was first shown the bedrooms of the two queens. But for their color, powder blue for the Senior Queen and dusty pink for Dreamy, they were identical, Western in style. In each the floors were covered with thick, white fur rugs. The large bed in each room stood obliquely in the center, away from the wall, and in each room, too, was a strangely old-fashioned washstand and hand basin. The windows were closed tight, and the atmosphere was drenched in perfume. There were sitting rooms with tables, chairs and sofas, brocaded furnishings, a radio, and a riotous fall of rich flowers from every cupboard and shelf. In her sitting room Birdy had a little vitrine full of glasses, bottles of spirits and liqueurs, although she rarely drank anything but a little brandy, and certainly not in her bedroom. There, too, in the vitrine, I saw the silver vases I had brought her from India, next to my own framed portrait.

The King walked happily about these rooms, pulling out drawers, opening the doors of cupboards to show me saris, salwars, cholis, underwear, stockings, furs and sandals, spreading the long waves of the saris across the room until my head became unsteady from the insane whirl of color. Queens and princesses stood with their hands clasped loosely, and on each face was a smile of pride, pleasure and approval.

From the bedrooms we went downstairs to the palace kitchens, their equipment white, red and shining, and as magnificent as the most ambitious of the American advertisements where the King had no doubt first seen them. He gravely drew my attention to the electric ovens, the enormous refrigerator, the ranging cupboards of stainless steel, the white tiles and glistening chromium. On from this unexpected miracle we went to the King's special pride, a suite of rooms unequaled by any photographer in Bond Street—reception room, studio, darkroom, workroom and storeroom.

"My reception room," said the King, "but whom do I receive?"

On its walls were pictures he had taken, portraits of his

family, of his dogs, views of the gardens at Naran Hity. The shelves of the storeroom were stocked with films, plates, chemicals, cameras, tripods and enlargers, enough to equip a sizable shop. While I stared in amazement the King moved about the rooms, touching his possessions in gentle affection.

Holding my hand now, with the queens and princesses following, he took me to his study, a dusky brown room with bookshelves from floor to ceiling. The shelves were full, mostly with English books, and when I asked if some of these were the treasures he had brought back from India in those trunks, he smiled and inclined his head. By the closed window was a giant globe, and I walked across to it and spun it, and when it finally halted I traced the Mediterranean coastline with my finger, saying, "There! That's where you'll go one day, and there, and there!"

He played this game with me, sadly, asking me to describe each cove and bay, until he turned from me and opened a drawer of his great writing desk. He spilled across its surface sheaf after sheaf of writing paper, green, blue and pink, each with an initial in the top right-hand corner, his own initial or the queens'. "You see?" he said. "We may not write letters, but we have our own writing paper."

We left the queens and the princesses in the cocktail room and passed from it into a little anteroom, and beyond that to his own bedroom. The bed was wide and set square in the center of the room. The sheets were white silk, and the coverlet was white and gold brocade. The air was full of the scent of sandalwood and roses. In one of the locked windows was a central disc of thick glass, and the King tapped it with his finger, smiling. It was, he said, his "spy hole," and he invited me to stand close and look through it. The disc was a telescope, bringing the distance closer, the far gateway to Naran Hity Durbar, the entrance to the Happy Cottage. He said, "I always knew when you came, before they told me."

On the terrace outside the window the sun shone on his aquaria, beautiful fish moving silently in their own green and yellow worlds. Exotic birds, with fabulous feathers, preened themselves in cages of gold.

He took me from the bedroom to a little writing room where was his small desk and a small corner library. Beneath the glass top of the desk I saw the visiting card I had given him, and the handkerchief which I had asked him to send me should he ever need my help. He opened a door from here to his yellow bathroom and then turned to me, arms outstretched, palms open, as if he were saying, "You see, I have kept nothing from you. Now you know all there is to know about me, and I am in your hands."

I was due to leave Katmandu on July 31. Everything was prepared, the eight wooden crates which Bijaya had sent me were filled. Bijaya himself had said good-bye to me with obvious regret, though not without asking me to submit my final medical report on the Senior Queen. To Sir Chandreswar, also, had I said good-bye, imploring him not to forget the King, and once more he had patted my hand and told me not to worry, the King was in his care. There had been other farewells, to Sardar Dixit, to Doctor Siddhimani, to Doctor Das Gupta, and promises to them all to send news of my safe arrival in Simla.

Now there remained only my leave-taking from the royal family. I decided that I would go to the Happy Cottage for the last time on the twenty-ninth and leave them all without saying good-bye, for I was afraid that I would not be able to endure the emotional climax should they realize it was my last evening with them.

I went to the palace hoping that my face was not betraying my feelings. The princesses were waiting for me in the gardens, and we sat together, saying little, watching the lake, the tortoises sleeping in the falling sun, the flowers closing, and darkness coming. When the lights came on and the rooks flew up, and I knew that this was the last time I would see and hear this, I stood up and ran across to the portico, standing beneath the windows of the King's bedroom. I began to sing to him, the first few bars of "Santa Lucia." He came out immediately onto the terrace and stood by the caged birds, smiling at me.

When, at last, he came down to the garden with the queens, he was not smiling. He took my hand between both of his. "This is your last evening with us."

"It's my last evening with you," I said.

"Then we shall dance, all of us, just as usual." He led me to my dance hall, asking for my key when we reached it. When he had opened the door he stood back, and I heard a rustle of excitement among the queens and the princesses.

There was scarcely an inch of the room that was not covered with presents. They spilled onto the floor from the chairs, the tables, the radio-phonograph and the piano, a rainbow of colored paper and ribbons. Queens and princesses knelt among them, bringing a present to me held in open hands. This time their presents came not from Narain, but from themselves, the nicknames I had given them written on pasteboard cards. Clothes, jewelry, ornaments—diamond earrings in the shape of flowers from the King, a watch in a ruby-encrusted horseshoe of gold from Dreamy, a golden compact from Birdy. And more, and more they brought me.

I could say nothing. Love and gratitude, loyalty and pity overwhelmed me. I sat down and put my hands over my face. The King took them away gently.

"Erika, *maffi do,* forgive me! I am only a poor Nepalese and know no better. If we have offended you by something, forgive us."

Dreamy came to me. "Erika, *maffi do!*" And Birdy too. "Erika, *maffi do!*" They all sat with me on the sofa, the presents at my feet and on my lap, and again and again they whispered, "Erika, *maffi do!*" I bent before the King and touched his feet.

"Your Majesty, I meant this to be my last evening, but I must come again now. May I come tomorrow for the last time?"

They were happy again then, and the King said, "You will come, I knew you would come."

So, the next evening I came again, no longer in a cocktail dress, but in my traveling suit, for everything else had been packed. The queens and the princesses were waiting in a little group by the lake, and the sudden appearance of them shocked me. All were dressed in black saris, black the color of mourning, of grief for my departure. Their faces were very pale, and their eyes on the edge of tears. I was crying before I reached them, and I took both queens in my arms, holding them about the waist, while they whispered to me. "Erika, come back!" they said, not in appeal but in reassurance.

When the King came, for the last time as the rooks left for the mountains and the pigeons were silent, he was dressed wholly in white, white cap, shirt, waistcoat, jacket and jodhpurs. The dark wing of his hair over his melancholy eyes seemed blacker than ever. His face was sad, but he smiled when he saw my bush jacket, insisting that I turn before him so that he might admire it. Then he said, "May I go, please? I must go to Singha Durbar to see Goebbels. But I shall be back soon, I promise you."

And he was back soon, taking my arm and saying lightly, "Now, let's dance!" Once more I was led to my dance hall, and once more it was filled with presents, gold, silver, silk and ivory, and a prosaic zip-fastener bag to hold them all. The King gave me two presents, the first a simple handkerchief of no value, with "Remember me" embroidered in one corner. He then said, "Erika, will you always wear the key to your dance hall?"

I took it from my throat, about which it hung by a cord. He removed this and broke it. "Gold needs gold," he said, and from his pocket he pulled a thin golden chain, threading it through the key and fastening it about my neck. His fingers tightened about my throat momentarily, and he turned away.

No one could dance, and we scarcely spoke. We ate a little, and we drank a little champagne, and the queens and the princesses sat sadly in their black saris, diamonds shining in their hair and tears in their eyes. When I could stand no more, I stood up. "Your Majesty, may I go please?"

He arose, and the women of his family gathered behind him, Birdy, Dreamy and Sadface, Nalini, Vijaya, and Bharati, a cloud of black. Rain was falling outside, staining the walls and the flagstones of the courtyard. Suddenly they all had black umbrellas in their hands, crowding close to shelter me. The noise of the rain, striking the leaves of the trees and the taut skin of the umbrellas, became louder and louder as we walked. When we reached the little veranda, where the King and I had once sat with his sons, I stopped. I bent before Tribhuvana. "*Namashkar*, Your Majesty!" I said, and to the queens and princesses also.

I ran from them quickly, without looking back, through the door in the wall, through the courtyard, through to the great sweep of steps that led down to my car. Awaiting me there, each beneath an umbrella, were all the ladies in waiting from the Happy Cottage, little presents in their hands, tears mixing with the rain on their cheeks.

It was still raining when I left Tripureswar early next morning for the mountain pathway to India. The old cook from my guesthouse accompanied me all the way to Chandra-giri, and he cried bitterly when we parted.

Three

"THE FLOWER IS SWEET AND BEAUTIFUL"

THEN there began fourteen bad months. I had been so transported by the time I spent in Katmandu that anything following should have been an anticlimax. Instead, I seemed to exchange one state of emotional tension for another. I returned to Simla, my beloved Simla, feeling curiously ineffectual. Had I felt sure that Nehru's letter would soon be delivered to the King, then I would have had a sense of fulfillment, a certain peace in my mind. But I had no such feeling. Time and distance separated me from Nepal. In Simla no one knew, no one cared, just as six months earlier I had not known and had not cared about the King.

At night I looked from my window as I had always done, but now the blue hill slope of the bazaar, and the red and yellow lights winking there, gave me no pleasure. Every day at sunset I looked eastward to Nepal, beyond the rosy snow peaks, and every day I wrote to the King. I put the letter in an envelope addressed "To Our Friend" or "To H. Lall," and this envelope I placed in another addressed to Doctor Das Gupta, care of Postmaster Sher Bahadur Gurung. I registered it, and because a registered envelope must carry the name and address of the sender I was suddenly faced with a problem that had not occurred to me when I planned all this. Letters arriving regularly in Katmandu with my name on the back would soon arouse as much suspicion as if I had boldly addressed them all to the King. So I went to my friends, asking them if I might put their names on the back of letters I was sending to Nepal. Most of them agreed without question, and with those who looked as if they wished to ask why all this was necessary I did not press the point. Then I took the letters to other friends who were journeying down to Kalka, or Delhi, or Lucknow, and I asked them to post the letters there.

It was long afterward that I discovered how these letters finally reached the King. Doctor Das Gupta would keep them, none too happily I imagine, until he was called to Naran Hity Durbar or to the palaces of the princes. He was called to the latter more frequently than to the Happy Cottage. There was always a Rana present when he treated the royal grandchildren. Because the princes' wives were Ranas, too, he dared not hand over my letters to the princes in their presence. He waited, for days sometimes, until he had that second's opportunity to thrust my letters into the hand of Mahendra, or Himalaya, or Bashundera.

The letters I wrote were full of advice and encouragement, silly, foolish and hopeful, and in each of them I appealed to the King not to despair. I worked hard during those fourteen months, at my work, and in the service of the King. Whether it would be of any value to this cause, I did not know, but I knew that I had to catch the lapel of this man and that, talk to anybody who was anybody, saying again and again that here was a king who wished to be a real king and who was in need of help.

The first letter from the King arrived within a week of my arrival in Simla. In one way it set the tone for all of his letters which were to follow. It read as though all the old fears and doubts had come back as soon as he picked up the pen to write. In that first letter he called me Kate, which is indeed my name, but one he had never used before.

MY DEAR KATE——We all hope that you must have reached Simla safely and comfortably. Nothing of interest to write about in this place till now, only we all feel sorry and alone without you, and we all hope that you still remember us. Excuse me, I will write more in next letter. ——Your Grateful Friend.

It was signed "H. Lall" in blue ink. So his letters came, slowly in the beginning, and then more frequently as his confidence and courage returned a little. With each letter I hoped to hear that Sir Chandreswar had at last visited him and delivered Nehru's letter, but the news did not come. Boyishly, realizing that I was in Simla with the riches of the world at my feet (or so it seemed to him) he showered me with requests and orders, for catalogues, for photographic and electrical equipment, for patterns of cloth, for news of fashions, all of which I was to send to Sardar Krishnalal.

A month after my return to Simla a letter arrived (addressed this time to "Dear Miss Kate") telling me that Dreamy was ill with heart trouble, and that a specialist from Calcutta was coming to see her. He thanked me for some suit materials which I had obtained from Lila Ram's store in the Simla bazaar and excitedly explained that Sardar Krishnalal was going to order bolts of the material.

Dreamy is under Doctor Das Gupta's treatment, and she is improving. You can imagine how this matter upsets me. This is the cause I could not write prompt answers to your letters. We all hope that you are keeping well there. Except Dreamy we are all well here. This is now our great hope—that you still REMEMBER us, but our remembrance is so much that it could not be described in this small letter. We have not yet practiced dancing. After Dreamy's recovery we will practice, but without our beloved teacher . . .

I wrote again and again, asking the one question I wanted answered, whether Sir Chandreswar had brought the letter.

Up to this day the bird is not permitted to visit my
garden. The Big Snake is trying his best to avoid it. Please
do not FORGET us!

There was, however, unpleasant news. The Ranas, gossip-
ing behind their high walls, remembered how Ghorki Ram
had lived in the guesthouse and not in the servants' quarters
at Tripureswar. The King wrote angrily:

Now here the serpents comment shameful remarks on
Ghorki Ram . . .

He told me that Sher Bahadur Gurung had gone on leave
to India and advised me to send letters care of the Postmaster's deputy, but I was not happy about it until Gurung returned to Katmandu. From day to day I was never at ease,
always waiting for news that my last letter had reached the
King safely, and when I heard this there was still the next
letter to worry about, and the next, and so on.

I had written to Sir Chandreswar as soon as I arrived in
Simla, reminding him of his promise. He replied almost immediately.

We often talk about you. Your absence from Nepal
has indeed created a void which is difficult to fill. No
longer do I get any messages, nor can I send any. We
miss you a lot.

I wrote also to his secretary, Shantiswarup Gupta, who
knew something of what was going on, asking him for news
of the King, and his reply, too, was of little comfort.

K, so far as I know, is quite well. One could write
volumes about him, and yet the tragedy is that, the circumstances being what they are, there is so little one *can*
write about him.

The King was ill and told me nothing about it, except that
this was another reason why he had been unable to dance since

my departure. I knew that perhaps his heart was troubling him, but he would not admit this. The bird had not come to his garden with the flower, he said, and if his heart was sick at all, it was because of this.

> We still hope that Simla has not changed your mind toward us. If you forget us we will be very unhappy. Please remember this . . .

Dreamy's health improved, and the King wrote to say that she would be well enough to celebrate the festival of Durga Puja toward the end of September. Because I wished to share the occasion with them, if only in imagination, I asked my Indian friends to tell me about Durga. She was, they told me, a beautiful maiden who took shape from the flames that sprang from the mouths of the gods, a radiantly beautiful girl with ten slender arms. They moved about her head and shoulders like wings, bearing Brahma's sacred roll, Vishnu's discus, Siva's trident, Varuna's conch shell, and Indra's great thunderbolt. Armed with these, and astride a lion from the Himalayas, a circlet of snakes about her neck, she slew the buffalo demon Mahishashur after a contest that lasted many days. Her festival is celebrated by three days of great happiness, for which houses are cleaned and decorated, and men and women fill their hearts with love and joy only.

I wrote to the King to take heart from the story of Durga and to believe that in time he, too, would triumph over all evil. I counseled him to be wise and circumspect in his behavior, and he replied in such a way that I could see the gentle smile that must have been on his lips as he wrote.

> DEAR MISS LAKSHMI——I thank you for your advice— be still more grave. I will try very much to be grave. The photo of Lakshmi is in my portico, the reflection is in my heart. Do not forget us. . . .

The weeks passed on into October, and he told me that Nepal had celebrated the five-day festival of Diwala, and that this year all the windows of Katmandu had been lit with electric lights, instead of the little oil lamps which were traditional. Then, suddenly, there came a letter signed in red ink. In the middle of chatty, conversational paragraphs was the news I thought would never come.

> The bird came to my garden and gave me the Doctor's flower, but you are the person who sowed the seed and took care of the plant. The flower is very sweet and beautiful. What more? Not only I, but all my party offer you our heartfelt thanks for the trouble you have taken to plant and make it free from pest.

My heart was full of joy, and I had to talk to someone about this great news. Fortunately Surjit was nearby, staying in his great house at Chota Simla. He frequently came to see me without warning, "popping in" he called it, and Ghorki, delighted to see the great man, would come running, crying that Surjit Sahib was here! Surjit had already done much on the King's behalf, contacting the Nepalese Congress Party in India, particularly the Koirala brothers, who were among its principal leaders. Now I took him the King's letter, with its news that he had at last met Sir Chandreswar. Surjit smiled tolerantly at the code. "An amateurish hand at this, your King, Erika."

"Surjit, will the King be free soon, now that Nehru has written to him?"

"Be patient, Erika. Nepal will be free in time. Five years, ten years, perhaps more. Think how long it took us in India."

He could not tell me what Nehru might have written in the letter, or what promises India had made to the King. From what he said I got the impression that the Indian Government might be prepared to let the Nepalese liberate them-

selves in their own way and their own time, giving them sympathy and support afterward. When he saw the disappointment in my face, he patted my shoulder. "Cheer up, Erika,
our friend will be all right, you'll see."

I was always happy to see Surjit, a tall, striking man, coming to my rooms at the Metropole in his turban, *achkan,* and
khadi jodhpurs. He was no longer in the government service
but was campaigning for a seat in Parliament, and soon he
was absent from Simla for long periods. I missed him, and I
wrote to him, asking whether his kinsman, the Maharaja of
Patiala would help the King. Surjit replied:

> I am trying to persuade His Highness to go to Kat-
> mandu. You might be aware of the betrothal of the
> Yuvraj of Kashmir to the daughter of Sarda, the eldest
> son of the present Prime Minister. You know how
> friendly Patiala and Kashmir are. So let's see if this works.
> I will also try and see if I can persuade Her Highness as
> well.

I decided to see the Maharaja of Patiala, if it was possible,
so that if he should go to Katmandu and meet the King it
would be with my story in his mind. I had already told the
Maharani about the King, and I had often spoken of her to
him. He mentioned her frequently in his letters, referring to
her as *"Die Kleine,"* the Little One, a name her friends had
given her. Her emotional and romantic nature responded instinctively when I told her Tribhuvana's story; and when I
asked that she obtain for me an interview with the Maharaja,
so that I might tell him also, she said impulsively, "Of course,
Erika, of course you must meet him!"

Patiala was a tall, noble Sikh, with great almond eyes like
Surjit's, a neatly coiled fringe of black beard, magnificent in
colored turban and *achkan.* He listened to me politely, head
bent slightly. I told him of the King's political ambitions, of
his imprisonment by the Ranas, of his passionate desire for

freedom. When there were no more words left in me, he said, "Thank you, Erika. I shall think about it. Leave it with me."

What he thought about it, and what he did as a result, I do not know. It was enough to me that I had told him about the King. I wanted the great and powerful to know, whoever they were and wherever they were. One day in Simla, where or how I do not now recall, I met a tall Indian with a surprisingly young face beneath his white hair. I saw him across a room, and he was so striking in appearance that I asked who he was. I was told that he was a Kashmiri, which was obvious in his grace and carriage, and that his brother was the chief of police in New Delhi. I asked him if he would call on me at the Metropole the next day, because there was something I wished to discuss with him. He came, out of curiosity, no doubt, and listened without comment when I told him the King's story. He then asked me why I thought he could be of any help.

I said, "I need the help of your brother. I want him to put my card in Pandit Nehru's hand and tell him what I have just told you."

Surjit shook his head when I told him what I was doing. "Be careful, Erika, or you will ruin everything."

But I was ready to ask for help from everyone I could, not only great men like Surjit, Patiala, and the police chief at New Delhi, but others like Amrit Ralia Ram, a Christian businessman of Delhi. Like Sita Ram Suri, a journalist friend, he gave me advice and information where I most needed it, on the political situation in India, the strength and purpose of the Nepalese Congress Party. All that they told me I retold to the King in my letters. My dear friend Sherene Rustimjee combed the Indian press for me, making clippings of all references to Nepal, to the Ranas, to the King and to the Nepalese Congress Party, and sending them to me. To this day she still does so.

It was Bedi to whom I turned most hopefully, B. P. L. Bedi, Doctor Honoris Causa of Oxford, one of the greatest men produced by the struggle for Indian independence and certainly the best-loved man in northwestern India. He is a descendant of Guru Nanak, founder of the Sikh religion, yet he is himself neither Sikh nor Hindu, but a Communist of sorts, that peculiarly distinct type of Communist thrown up by the nationalist movement. He is married to an Englishwoman, and his attitude toward the English is a mixture of admiration and distaste, an attitude not unlike the King's.

I wrote to him immediately I reached Simla, asking him to visit me when he could. He had been a patient of mine, and we had become dear friends. He came to Simla almost at once.

My heart moves with affection every time I think of him. A great man of learning and letters, he is also a man whose compassionate understanding embraces the spirit of a sweeper. In appearance he is like a rock, tall and of immense breadth at the shoulders, a broad nose, slanting deep-set eyes, and thick black hair. He wears rough cotton robes like a toga, a saffron *khemeeze* with mother-of-pearl buttons, and his great toes burst like roots through his crude leather sandals. Always he looks as if he has just come from a successful battle or is about to engage in one he has no doubt he will win. But his voice is gentle and soothing, his manner as humble as Gandhi's.

He lives simply. He has one chipped mug that serves him for drinking, shaving, and for use when he bathes. To walk with Bedi in Simla was, for me, to walk with a nation's heart. Slowly, pace by pace, we would go through the bazaar, while men, women and children crowded close to us, bowing, touching his feet, calling "Bedi Sahib!" It was not possible to talk to him as we walked. There was always someone pulling at his robe, so many asking for his attention that he could not possibly have introduced me to them. When he could not remember a name he would never ask, but would slyly say, "And how's the old trouble?" and before long they had themselves told him who they were, and he was comforting, encouraging and inspiring them.

It did not seem strange to me that I should ask help for the King from this man who was a Marxist, who believed that so long as there was one poor man in the world he himself should live no better. I approached Bedi because of his great heart, and because of his responsive sympathy for those in trouble. I knew also that what would most interest Bedi's shrewd mind was perhaps the poverty and the oppression of the ordinary people of Nepal.

When I had told him about the King, he asked me what I wished him to do. I said that, politically, he would do what he felt best, and I would not advise him, but I had frequently spoken of him to the King, and the King had come to think of him as a friend. I asked him to write a letter of encouragement to Tribhuvana. He wrote the letter immediately, his muscular arms sweeping back his rough woolen shawl.

DEAR H. LALL——I had at last the pleasure of meeting Lakshmi. It delighted me indeed to know that lights burn bright where the world knows only pitch dark exists. Her explanation was very touching and found no difficulty in making another heart beat in unison with sympathy and understanding. For, to those in whom much is given, from them much is demanded, and to give all help generously and determinedly to the plan I have given her my promise.

This business demands all success and will get it. With God's will and men's purpose, both combined, it yields a force which no barrier can resist. The necessary conditions now she knows which are essential for a start. In wishing you well I call myself——HOTEL MANAGER.

The "necessary conditions" were patience. Bedi urged me to implore the King to be patient, and to wait. I know that he pleaded and intrigued for the King's cause in India, although I did not ask him to tell me what he was doing. It was enough for me to know that Bedi was working for us.

The King's letters still came from Katmandu. Sometimes they contained nothing but sad gossip, revealing plainly to me at this distance the pathetic uselessness of the life he was forced to lead. He had received a new police dog from Germany. He had ordered new camera equipment and was anxiously awaiting its delivery. Little Ketaki remembered me and asked for me each time she came to the Happy Cottage. In the middle of such letters would be a single sentence that revealed all his longing and his isolation.

> In this God's wide earth we can get everything, but it is hard to get a reliable person.

We had little alarms which time and distance exaggerated into terrors. Bijaya's wife, he said, was visiting India, and I was suddenly afraid that she might meet the Maharani of Patiala who, by an unsuspecting word, might betray us. He reassured me.

> Madame B. Serpent will not go to any party, or visit any club, so I am sure she will not visit Little One in Bombay.

When Christmas approached he had his sudden fears. We had discussed our method of correspondence and the need for caution so thoroughly before I left Katmandu that it did not seem to me that we had left anything to chance. But when I told him that I would be sending him a Christmas parcel, he thought of something.

> You know our correspondence is secret. Except for Birdy, Dreamy, Sadface and a few goldfishes, no one

knows. So do not send any Christmas gifts or cards for Ball, Whiney and Muffle, because I will not give it to them. . . . The Christmas parcel will be opened in the Customs Office before I open it. Except letters, everything is opened here by the Customs officers. You yourself know the rules and manners of this place, so what more should I put down on this matter . . .

One day I received a short and blunt letter, signed in red ink, and disclosing alarm about something much more serious. It was headed "MOST IMPORTANT."

(1) The barometer of this place forecasts STORM.
(2) Destroy all my flowers. If you can keep secret let the blue flowers remain with you. If you cannot, destroy them also. Remember, if anyone discovers my flower from your place it will do harm to both, but I do not mind for me, I do not want to hurt you from my cause. PRAY FOR THE SUCCESS!

There was never any clear explanation of what lay behind this letter. "Storm" in the King's code meant invasion. That he should ask me to destroy his letters and "pray for the success" would indicate that the events of nine months later had been planned for an earlier date, and that the conspiracy had somehow failed. I waited for news, for a letter from him, for some indication in the Indian press of what was happening in Nepal. I waited until I could bear the silence no longer.

I sent him a letter, in care of Doctor Das Gupta, a letter in our code, containing what news I had and asking him for news of success or failure. I included a recent photograph of myself, for which he had repeatedly asked. While this letter was somewhere between Simla and Katmandu I received a shock.

It was at the beginning of February 1950, and I had gone down to Delhi to stay with friends. There I received a letter from him. It had been written at the Happy Cottage on

January 31, received in Simla on February 7, and forwarded to me in Delhi on the eighth.

> DEAR LAKSHMI——The pressure of work is so heavy nowadays that I could not write a single line to you, but I hope you will forgive me for not answering you promptly. As you know everything about my business, why should I write more about it. I will disclose only this much—that here everythings are going in our favour. I hope that in a few months everything will be alright, but the success and failure are in Almighty's hands.
>
> PLEASE REMEMBER after reaching this my letter to you do not send any letter or article until my next letter comes to you. THIS IS MOST IMPORTANT.
>
> . . . I am sure of it, we will meet very soon.

My joy at discovering that something tremendous was taking place in Nepal, that he could write confidently of meeting soon, was sobered by the realization that there was already a letter in the mail for him. I hoped that Doctor Das Gupta, to whom it had been addressed, knew enough of the situation to handle it with caution. While hoping this, I opened the next letter that had been forwarded to me. It was from the doctor.

> MY DEAR SIGNORINA——Hope this will find you in the best of health. I am leaving Nepal on the first week of February next, so you please don't write any letters. If you write any letter at all the letters will be redirected to you. I have got a son on the first of January. Both mother and her son are doing well.

I was happy for the doctor, his wife Mara, and their new child, but I could think only of my letter which must soon arrive in Katmandu. By one of those crazy accidents that always come to aggravate an already sore situation, I had put no sender's name or address on the back. Thus it would certainly be opened so that it might be redirected. If Sher

Bahadur Gurung opened it he might be relied upon to be discreet. If it were opened by anybody else I could rely on nothing. It is true that I had signed the letter "Lakshmi" only, but it contained my photograph.

I left my friends in Delhi abruptly, hurrying back to Simla by train and car, and taking one long, agonizing day on the journey. Arriving at Simla I went straight by rickshaw to the Post Office. The Postmaster was away, but behind the counter was an intelligent Anglo-Indian girl. I asked her to wire Katmandu immediately, asking for the return of my letter unopened. My excitement was by now edging on hysteria, but she made no comment. She sent the telegram and gave me a copy of it.

FROM THE DPM SIMLA TO THE POSTMASTER INDIAN EM-
BASSY NEPAL STOP SIR KINDLY LET ME KNOW BY RETURN
MAIL THE DISPOSAL OF SIMLA REGISTERED LETTER NUMBER
445 OF THE 2 2 50 ADDRESSED TO DOCTOR D DAS GUPTA
SURGEON SUPERINTENDENT OF THE BIR HOSPITAL STOP
IF THE LETTER NOT CALLED FOR KINDLY RETURN TO POST
OFFICE SIMLA

This telegram was sent on February 13, and for six days I waited for a reply. A week may pass quickly or slowly according to the amount of attention one gives to it, and to me that week was the passing of a lifetime. Daily, three or four times in the morning and afternoon, I called at the Post Office, asking for news, until, at last, on February 19, there came a reply from Postmaster Gurung.

REFERENCE YOURS BEG TO INTIMATE THAT THE REG-
ISTERED LETTER WAS DELIVERED ON 9 2 50 STOP ATTESTED
COPY OF THE ADDRESSEES RECEIPT IS ATTACHED HERE-
WITH.

Some good fortune that may not have seemed good to the doctor had delayed his departure from Katmandu, and he had received my letter. It was at such times during those fourteen months that I believed myself living in a madhouse.

After this the King's letters began to come again, with no explanation of the events which had momentarily disturbed our correspondence. Whatever had been planned had obviously not happened, yet because there was no word of disappointment, veiled or direct, in the King's letters, I sensed that failure had been a postponement only. Surjit still shook his head and warned me to expect the King's liberation to be a matter of years rather than months, but I was filled with a strange expectancy.

Things seemed to go on as before. There were changes. Little Nalini, the lovely one, married the Raja of Poonch and escaped from the imprisonment of Naran Hity. I was happy for her, but I still thought of her father, for whom release had not yet come. Letters passed between "H. Lall" and "Lakshmi" as if the world were not about to turn itself upside down.

> My tiny photo for your locket, and a snap of the Erika Dance Hall taken in haste, so it is very poor. Nowadays I am trying colour photography. If I can make any good pictures I will send picture to you. I am making a small dark-room outside my bedroom for developing cine colour films.

Yet there were some paragraphs in his letters, sandwiched between requests for catalogues, for electrical and photographic equipment, that showed the direction of the current newly flowing in the valley of Katmandu. Had I been more astute, or less locked within the cell of my own emotions, I might have read their meaning more clearly.

> Please do not forget us. We remember you twenty-four hours. This is not a lie. It is a fact. I will prove it in the future. I have very faint hope to see you soon.

The autumn of 1950 passed through October. I went walking alone, down toward Kalka, or westward toward the
mountains. Sometimes, in the blue evenings, I would see
sparks among the timber on the distant slopes, where peasants
had lit barriers to protect their homes from forest fires. All
night these fires burned, like a serpent, coiling, turning, glim-
mering in the dark. I went to stay a while with the Maharani
of Patiala. She looked from the windows one day and said,
"Erika, look, winter is coming. Can you see the snow line?"
It lay in a long bar of dull blue between the rim of the earth
and the sky. I wondered if there would be another year, and
yet another, whether it would be five or ten years as Surjit
had suggested, before the King would be free.

I stilled my troubled thoughts with letters, with presents
for the Happy Cottage. To send him something tangible,
something he could touch and know was from Lakshmi—this
was the only comfort I had. I sent little things, a scarf, a key
chain, cloths for their trays when they took tea, a book on
dancing, samples of material for the King's new *achkan*, new
shoes for which he had sent me measurements.

One morning, in the second week of November, I was
walking down the Mall. Snow had not yet fallen, but the air
was crisp and the earth hard with frost. As I walked, my arm
was caught by a friend.

"Erika, have you heard? Your King is in New Delhi!"

IT WAS, of course, Sir Chandreswar who made it
possible, the bird who brought the doctor's flower to
the garden and gave it to the Moor. The gentle, kindly
Ambassador kept his word. He had promised me that the
King would be in his care, and on Monday, November 6,
1950, this was literally true. The King and the royal family,

queens, princes and princesses, were safe inside the Indian Embassy at Katmandu, and the nation was in rebellion against the Ranas. As I slowly learned the news I realized that, from the day when the King and Sir Chandreswar at last met, the conspiracy must have gathered momentum until the King was ready to explode it into open revolt.

The Prime Minister can have had no suspicion of what was to happen. He gave the royal family permission to leave their palaces for a leopard hunt in the mountains. This seems to indicate his confidence that all was well, for it was a favor rarely granted. That Monday morning the royal family left Naran Hity in a convoy of five cars, led by the King's beige Mercury. King and princes drove the cars themselves, but in each was a Rana officer. The road to the northern mountains passed the entrance to the Indian Embassy, and the convoy went no farther than this. As he reached the driveway the King suddenly accelerated, swung the wheel to the left, and drove onto Indian soil, with the other cars quickly following.

A Sikh sentry opened the door of the Mercury and the King, in khaki jodhpurs and gray scarf, stepped out to shake hands with Colonel I. C. Katoch, the Indian military attaché, who invited him into the Embassy. There Sir Chandreswar was waiting, and to him the King made a formal request for asylum.

The Rana guards went quickly to Singha Durbar, and within an hour Bijaya had arrived with an armed escort. A revolver strapped to his belt, his soldiers all along the road outside the Embassy and in the fields surrounding it, he angrily demanded that Colonel Katoch bring the King to him. The Colonel carried the demand to the King, and I know what effect that must have had on Tribhuvana. For the first time in his life he was able to say no to a Rana.

Now Sir Chandreswar came to Bijaya and faced the angry

soldier calmly. "General Bijaya, will you please take off your revolver. While you are armed the King will never speak to you."

Bijaya unstrapped his pistol reluctantly and placed it on a table. He waited for the King, and waited, the first Rana ever to do so, and when Tribhuvana at last came what he said to Bijaya was short and abrupt. "I am the King. I am not satisfied with your treatment of my country or of me. You will tell that to His Highness the Maharaja."

Twice that day Goebbels sent messengers to the Indian Embassy, demanding that Prince Mahendra leave and take up residence at Naran Hity in the King's place. The King, confident of the loyalty of his sons, refused to discuss the demand. On Tuesday morning the Council of Leaders met at Singha Durbar, a puppet council with many Rana faces but one voice only, that of the Maharaja. This announced the deposition of King Tribhuvana and the enthronement of his grandson, age three, who had been left at Naran Hity in the care of an *ayah*. This was Gyanendra, Mahendra's second boy, and he had been deliberately left behind in the flight, the King refusing to abandon his country without a member of his family at its head. So the Ranas made a king out of the innocent, round-faced boy, although no one took the action seriously. The Prime Minister's appeal to the Indian Government for recognition of the child was bluntly rejected.

For four days the Indian Embassy was in a state of siege. A car was jammed across the roadway leading to it from the bazaar, and no supplies reached it. But Sir Chandreswar was not unprepared, he had stored adequate supplies of soap, cooking oils, rice and rations. There were candles should the electricity supply accidentally fail, and water in case the pipe suddenly burst. The royal family had brought some clothes in the four boxes that had ostensibly been their luggage for the hunting expedition. Sir Chandreswar supplied sheets, blankets and towels. Thus the royal family waited, the King, queens and Mahendra in the Embassy library, Himalaya, Bashundera and the princesses playing table tennis with the attachés.

At last they escaped. On November 10, under the protection of Indian officers, they were driven to the airstrip at Gaochar, and thence taken by plane to India. Pandit Nehru was the first man to welcome Tribhuvana.

With the King's arrival in India the "storm" he had mentioned in his letters to me some months before now broke out. An armed force of Nepalese Congress supporters invaded southern Nepal, occupied Birganj, captured the Rana governor and set up a provisional government. In the west peasant guerrillas went into action. An aircraft flown by Nepalese Congress supporters passed over Katmandu unmolested, and from its belly it dropped a cloud of leaflets appealing to government troops to support the rising against "the godless Ranas." In the valleys of the Himalayas, along the fringes of the green Terai, for three weeks there was rifle fire and sporadic fighting. Men who the King had sometimes believed cared nothing for him now fought the Rana troops to cries of *"Tribhuvana ki-jai!"*

But while men were killing and being killed in Nepal the real struggle against the Ranas went on in New Delhi. The King had landed there from his plane on November 11 and been taken to Hyderabad House. In sudden, boyish delight at his liberty, he asked to be taken to a night club and a cinema, but I doubt if he went to either. He was too busy, surrounded now by a regiment of politicians, Indian and Nepalese. He became, overnight, "The Hero of Nepal," and from the valleys where fighting was still going on the peasant rebels sent this message:

A great and unprecedented reception awaits His Majesty when he comes here from New Delhi as the beloved Sovereign who brought an end to our miseries.

It was Pandit Nehru who finally made clear India's standpoint when, in December, he reported to Parliament:

"We were anxious that there should be peace and stability in Nepal. At the same time we felt that the introduction of substantial political reforms was essential for this purpose. It was on this basis of respect for Nepal's independence, combined with an urgent interest in political reforms there, that we carried on our conversations with the representatives of the Government of Nepal who were recently in Delhi."

For the Prime Minister had sent a delegation to India in an effort to get the Government there to recognize a regency in favor of young Gyanendra. This India had rejected. Said Nehru:

"We have continued to recognize His Majesty, King Tribhuvana Bir Bikram Sah. We feel that in all the circumstances this is the right course, and any discontinuance of recognition would produce many complications and would come in the way of a peaceful settlement. Any other arrangement, such as the replacement of the constitutional head of the kingdom by a Council of Regency, appointed by the Prime Minister to act in the name of a child king, would make the introduction and smooth working of progressive constitutional changes more difficult."

A British delegation flew to Katmandu for a two-day study of the situation there. They were greeted at Gaochar by an enormous crowd of men and women who shouted, "We want King Tribhuvana!" even when the Rana police beat at their heads and shoulders with *lathis*. Crowds also gathered outside

the Indian Embassy in Katmandu daily, calling, "Tell
Pandit-ji we want our King!"

At the beginning of January the Prime Minister surrendered a little ground in the hope of holding the rest. His
representatives in Delhi agreed to the return of the King as
constitutional head of the country and to a Constituent
Assembly chosen by adult suffrage, to be convened not later
than 1952. An interim cabinet would be set up meanwhile,
consisting of seven Ranas (including the Prime Minister) and
seven representatives of the popular party. There was to be
an amnesty for all political prisoners.

I read of all these events as if in a dream. This was what the
King and I had longed for as we walked alone in the gardens
of the Happy Cottage. I remembered how often he had
despaired of ever being able to talk to his people of the mat-
ters close to his heart. Now I read the messages which he
sent to them.

> I hope soon to serve our dear and sacred land, and
> to do my utmost to make the new changes a success, so
> that they may do good to my people and advance them
> to the democratic goal they have in view.
>
> A great step forward has been taken and new re-
> sponsibilities have been cast on all of us. May we prove
> worthy! I shall do my part with a full sense of duty, and
> having the good of my people as my concern.

The Prime Minister, too, began to issue proclamations to
the people of Nepal, hanging onto the coattails of events in
a desperate attempt not to be left behind.

> I would like to assure you, dear brothers, that your
> welfare and benefit will always be foremost in our hearts
> as it has ever been. Even with the changes now envisaged
> in the administration of the country we shall stand loyally
> and steadfastly behind you, as you have always behind
> your Government and country.

And while he was issuing this statement the Maharaja and his adherents within his own family were reported to be busy emptying the treasuries of the country, turning their private palaces into forts, and making large deposits in Indian banks. The Maharaja was determined to remain within the reformed government if he could, but he was also determined to live well should exile become inevitable.

The fighting was over, and in the newspaper clippings that Sherene Rustimjee sent me I saw pictures of the good Doctor Das Gupta bandaging the wounded. More than two hundred men stepped from the cells in which the Ranas had held them for years, and three hundred more awaited release. From the gates of the jail to Singha Durbar a great red cloth was laid, and the prisoners walked along it, their necks hung with garlands, their feet treading flower petals. The crowd shouted their names in joy and cried, *"Tribhuvana ki-jai."* Before the white palace of Singha Durbar, once the heart of Ranarchy, the leaders of the released men held up their arms for silence, and when all was quiet one of them spoke with great feeling:

"We wish to pay homage to our beloved Panch Darkar, Maharajadhiraja Tribhuvana Bir Bikram Shah Deva, who has been the fountainhead of the revolution and whom we hope to welcome in our midst in the near future. We renew our pledge not to take rest until Ranarchy is torn, root and branch, from our land!"

So the year moved into February and at last the King was ready to go home. Some of the Ranas had made their peace with him, not the least being Bijaya. He and the King met in Kashmir. One evening they went alone onto a lake in a boat and sat there for a long time in the moonlight. When they came back to the shore Bijaya was a loyal King's man.

Fifty thousand people awaited the King's arrival by plane at Gaochar, calling his name, calling him as his ancestors had been called, "The Golden Basilisk!" He drove in triumph to the Happy Cottage.

Not once during the three months he was in India did I see him. Immediately I heard the news of his flight I sent a telegram to him.

> HIS MAJESTY THE KING OF NEPAL HYDERABAD HOUSE NEW DELHI STOP TO HIS MAJESTY KING TRIBHUVANA CONGRATULATIONS ON HIS MOST WONDERFUL SUCCESS STOP AWAIT HIS MAJESTY'S HOKHUM FOR ANY SERVICES REQUIRED——ERIKA

The telegram was acknowledged by a secretary. From the King himself I received no word and no letter. I waited to be called to him, and I was not called. For a while, and selfishly, I was hurt by this, but then I understood that there could be no place for me in his life at that moment. When he wished to see me, I would be ready.

I RETURNED to Katmandu in the autumn of 1951, two years after I had left it, and nine months after the King had himself returned in triumph. My visit had been planned for earlier that year. Soon after his return the King wrote to me, asking me to come, and the plans had been made. They were abandoned. After the King's escape, all the strain I had placed on my mind, my heart and my body during those fourteen months in Simla suddenly became impossible for me to bear any longer. I fell ill, and when I recovered, toward the end of the summer, the King wrote again, urging me to come, and to come before the middle of November because he would then be leaving Katmandu on a tour of his kingdom. "Please do come," he wrote. "We are all impatiently awaiting your arrival."

So I went, at the beginning of November. Once more the

shops in Simla Bazaar were closed for the winter, and there
was little I could buy to take the royal family. I collected the
best from my own treasures, an embroidered tablecloth and
a set of white Jena glass for the King and queens. As my loyal
damrakhnu, I took each member of the family, including
Sadface, a golden sovereign wrapped in a hand-rolled square
of scarlet silk. I flew to Katmandu this time. The old mountain pathway, which had once served the double purpose of
keeping foreigners without the country and Nepalese within,
was now obsolescent. The airstrip which Surjit had pioneered,
and which Sir Chandreswar had exploited, was now an airport. There was talk of breaching the mountains with a great
highway that would be known as King Tribhuvana Road.

So I flew, and I saw the Ganges below me like a silver
snake on the brown earth, the blue and white stairway of the
Himalayas. When I alighted at Gaochar I was in tears. This
was partly due to the fact that both take-off and landing in
a plane always affect me emotionally, but it was also because
I was greatly moved by my return. I had come alone, too. I
had been told, incorrectly as it proved, that I would not be
able to take Peepchen on the plane with me, so I had left her
behind. Because I could not leave her alone I had left Ghorki
behind also, and I missed them both.

I was met at Gaochar by a handsome Nepalese who greeted
me as a friend. I did not recognize his face, and perhaps I
answered his greeting a little icily, for he sat in the front of
the car and did not speak to me again as we drove toward
Tripureswar. We arrived there at noon, not at the same guesthouse, but another, close to Doctor Das Gupta's house. I saw
his brown cow in the garden, and I heard the bubbling cries
of his children at play. I was expected at the palace by three
that afternoon, but I was suddenly very, very tired and spiritually exhausted. I fell on my bed in my traveling clothes,
not a bed such as I had had before, but an assembly of hard

boards. None the less I fell asleep immediately, into that unconscious oblivion of the physically weary. I awoke reluctantly to the sound of excited voices, a chittering behind the darkness of eyes that would not open. I heard my name being called again and again, and when finally I opened my eyes I saw the shadowy white figure of a servant, *namashkar*-ing desperately and crying that the car had arrived to take me to Naran Hity Durbar.

Somehow, in minutes only, I made myself ready in a gray-checked dress and red hat. My box containing the presents was taken to the car which, this time, was a fine modern vehicle of brilliant scarlet. The driver had been exercising his impatience on the horn, a vulgar instrument that sang *ta-te-ta-tum*. The sound of it swung my mind sharply away from Nepal, across the world and back to my childhood in Germany, when the Kaiser had had such a horn on his car, and the people had said it played *"Für unser Geld!"*

To this abominable sound I was taken to the Happy Cottage. For a moment it was as it had always been. The deep green of the trees, the flowers, the sun's reflection on the lake broken into fragments by the movement of the goldfish, the great leathery leaves of the lotus. The queens awaited me, but of the princesses only Bharati was there. Nalini was away in India with her husband, and Vijaya was ill in New Delhi. The queens and I embraced, and I wept.

The King came as he had always come, suddenly appearing from the trees. He seemed more erect, but this must have been an illusion, for never had a man stood more upright than he. His face was as beautiful as ever, and even the events of the past year had not erased its wistful melancholy. I touched his feet, and he lifted me by the hands with great gentleness. For a while there was an odd, strained atmosphere between us all, as if there was too much to say and too much to feel.

It was I who broke this spell, asking for my box to be

brought and set on the flagstones outside my dance hall. There, with the pleasure of small children, we unwrapped my presents, spreading the straw and the paper about our feet. We danced that evening in my dance hall, which was full of autumn flowers, and the phonograph played the music it had played two years before.

"Erika," said the King, "*Maffi do*. Forgive me, we shall have little time together. I am not what I was. I must work. In a few days I must leave Katmandu."

But that evening we sat together on his portico, alone. We spoke little to each other. He held my hand and we watched the shadows gathering in the garden. As we sat there a letter was brought to him in a long envelope. He opened it, drew out the foolscap sheet and read it. He smiled and then passed it to me. It was the Prime Minister's resignation.

We said nothing to each other. There seemed to be nothing that could be said.

I stayed in Katmandu for three weeks. It had changed. It was not just that Singha Durbar, for example, was no longer the great palace of the Ranas but a humming government secretariat. The shell had been cracked and a new life had been born in the city. I felt it in people's voices and saw it in their faces. It reminded me vividly of the atmosphere of India in 1947.

The weather added to this sense of change. I had known Nepal in the spring and summer. Now the mornings were chill, and when I stepped out of my bedroom in the mornings I saw a white mist lying on the lawn, thick and fleecy, and dissolving slowly. The paddy fields were dry, the golden-headed rice long since harvested. In the bazaar men and women wore their beige scarves turned twice about their throats, and the snow line was low on the distant mountains.

There had been changes, too, in the life of Doctor Das

Gupta. I remembered him as a sad man, shabbily dressed, a man who had once attended one of Surjit's *tamashas* in a dinner jacket and polka-dot tie. Now a little affluence had come his way, rewarding him for his earlier hardships. Outside his home stood a car. Every day his consulting room was filled, and there were women and men who came to ask his advice, not only about the sickness of their bodies, but about the fine new social problems with which they had been faced by the revolution.

I went to the palace almost every day. The King was not always there, or if he was there it might often be for a few minutes only. His clothes had lost some of the neatness I remembered, and this was not, I believe, because he had become untidy in mind but because he was now a working king and believed that his people should see him as such. The red car, crowing *"Für unser Geld!"*, called for me more or less when I wished for it, but I had no regular chauffeur. Each night when I returned to Tripureswar I would order the car for a certain hour the next day, and I would pray that the chauffeur would convey the order correctly to his relief. He never did. The car would be fifteen minutes, half an hour, an hour late, and when it finally arrived the chauffeur would be grinning cheerfully, as if to inquire what liberation was worth if it did not include the freedom to be late.

There was no telephone in my guesthouse. A service had existed in Katmandu prior to the revolution, but it had been a toy of the Ranas. Now it was being extended, the new poles marching drunkenly down the roads, even linking Doctor Das Gupta's house within its circuit. When my car did not arrive I often walked over to the doctor's home and pleaded with him to telephone the royal garage and wake them up.

One evening, when the doctor was out, I used the telephone myself, asking the operator for the royal garage in Hindustani and my execrable Nepali. We spent some minutes at this before we both decided that all was understood. At last a voice answered me from what I believed to be the royal garage.

"This is Miss Erika," I said. "Will you please send the car at once? It's already an hour late."

The voice laughed. "This is not the royal garage, Erika, this is Prince Mahendra. But be patient with our wonderful telephone service and I will send the car to you."

Some evenings, even when my car arrived, I would be stepping into it, ready to depart, only to be stopped by a messenger from Naran Hity Durbar, carrying a note in the King's handwriting—"Erika, forgive us. I cannot see you tonight. I must work." So would I be abandoned, dressed and nowhere to go, the sun setting early, the air chilling, and the electric lights in the guesthouse scarcely enough to read by.

I hated that, but I knew that the King was truly busy. Every day on the *maidan* an army of workmen assembled more of the equipment needed for his grand tour of Nepal. In the center of the grass had been erected the enormous colored marquee in which he and his staff were to live. About it was a score of smaller tents, forming a little town. In the mornings Mohan Devi and I played among the canvas and the guy ropes with the children of Doctor Das Gupta.

Mohan Devi was the daughter of Sardar Krishnalal. A day or two after my arrival in Katmandu the King said, "You know you have offended Sardar Krishnalal by not speaking to him?"

"But I haven't seen him this time."

"You have. He welcomed you at the airport."

So the handsome man who had greeted me so amiably had been the Sardar, and I had not recognized him and had treated him diffidently as if he had been a stranger. I begged the King to send him to me as soon as possible so that I might apologize. He came the next morning, and because he could speak no English he brought his daughter to interpret for him. She was a bright little girl of perhaps fifteen or sixteen, with smiling eyes behind her huge horn-rimmed glasses. I asked her to tell her father how sorry I was not to have recognized him, and he shook his head gently and held my hand between both of his.

After that Mohan Devi came to my guesthouse every morning, to drive with me, to walk with me, her brilliant sari draped over her brown arms, a flower in her hair. She had seen little of her own country, and thus it was I who showed her, for the first time, the beauty of Pashupattinath, of Swayambhunath, of Bhadgaon and Patan. We went often to the Buddhist temple of Bodhnath, the holiest Tibetan sanctuary outside Tibet, a dazzling white stupa surmounted by a spire of thirteen golden discs that hold aloft the Parasol of Law. On the base of the spire, of course, are the enameled and unforgettably blue eyes of the Lord Buddha, unblinking beneath black brows, "the eyes of wisdom seeing through eternity the realms of light."

The stupa stands on a great star-shaped platform and is surrounded by a low wall hung with prayer wheels. In the blue dusk of the early evenings, I remember, this wall glimmered with the yellow flames of a thousand lamps, tiny wicks floating in clarified butter. The wind turned the prayer flags on top of the spire, and the pilgrims walked round and round the stupa in the clockwise direction that brings good luck. The air was always full of whispering when I was there, of prayers, of the hammer of metalworkers in the little huts about the base of the temple.

I think I loved Bodhnath for the legend of its origin. The Tibetans say that once a tear of pity fell from the eye of the Enlightened One, and from this tear sprang a beautiful maiden. When she weakened before temptation and stole the flowers of Paradise she was condemned to be born again as the daughter of a poor Nepalese swineherd. In time she married, grew rich by raising geese, and decided that the fortune she had so acquired should be devoted to the building of a great temple. She begged the king for no more land than might be covered by a sheepskin. When he agreed she cut the skin into thin strips and thus marked out a great area on which the white beauty began to arise, first under her direction and then under that of her sons. These men placed certain relics of the Buddha Kasyapa inside the stupa, and as a reward they were reborn again in Tibet. Finally, an elephant that had been used to carry materials to the temple was so angry at having been given no reward that it turned itself into a demon king and became the enemy of Buddhism. One of the goosegirl's sons had to kill it.

And it was possible for me to believe all the story true as I sat on the steps below the white stupa with Moham Devi. One day, as we sat there, she suddenly sprang up and ran down to greet a girl of her own age, a girl with a round yellow face, high cheekbones and braided hair. She was brought to me and Mohan Devi introduced her as the daughter of the Chini Lama, the head of the temple of Bodhnath. They had been at school together in Darjeeling.

This bright young girl asked me if I would like to meet her father, taking my hand boldly and leading me to a house opposite the stupa, and up the mellowed brown staircase to the first story. There sat a magnificent man in a robe of yellow satin, his legs crossed in gray flannel trousers, his arrow-browed eyes smiling behind huge spectacles. He greeted me politely, with that gentleness that springs instinctively from great learning and great humility. There, I was told, he sat all day long, ready to touch in benediction the pilgrims who came from all over the world just to brush the dust from his feet. His two wives were with him, and they welcomed me with hard-boiled eggs and sticky sweets.

He was a man of great knowledge and wisdom (his daughter told me that he spoke seven Oriental as well as several European languages). He was the spiritual head of all Buddhists in Nepal, he had studied at Lhasa, and he was called the Chini Lama because his grandfather had been born in China. Yet his daughter, Mohan Devi's friend, had been educated at an English convent school and played hockey with skill and enthusiasm.

He was one side of Nepal. I saw another side one evening at the Happy Cottage. When I arrived the King was standing on his portico with a tall, striking man in a snow-white gown that was flung across his shoulders like a toga. His hair was white, too, and his face marked with lines of great suffering. The King introduced him as Ganesh Man Singh, and such was the simple nobility of the man that I bowed very humbly. He was, said the King, one of the new ministers of government.

Ganesh Man Singh talked to me very gently about Nepal. Because I wanted to know, and because I believe that knowledge comes only to those who ask for it, I said, "Ganesh Man Singh, why do you wear white?"

He said, "Madam, for twenty years the Ranas kept me in jail, fastened by a chain to an iron ball. So that I may never forget those sorrows, and the sorrows of my country, I shall always be in mourning."

There were too many evenings during my brief second stay in Katmandu when the King was forced to break his appointment with me, sending his messenger even as I waited for the red car. "Erika, *maffi do,* but it is not possible for us to meet tonight. There is work that I must do."

He spoke always, during those days, of the work he was doing, the work there was to be done, and although much of the atmosphere of the Happy Cottage remained unchanged— the silence, the whispering, even the golden keys and locked doors—this one thing seemed to change everything. The King was now a king. Yet I should have remembered that even a revolution would not extinguish his boyish love of surprising me.

The other guesthouses in Tripureswar were full of visitors. The barriers were down, and there were businessmen from India in Katmandu. Mani Ram came to me one morning in distress. "Madam, would it be possible for you to let a gentleman from Calcutta share your guesthouse?"

I said, "Mani Ram, I have no objection, but you know what gossip is like in Katmandu."

He waved his hands unhappily. "I promise you, madam, we shall do it discreetly and delicately. His side of the house will be locked, and you will be quite separate."

I told him to do as he wished.

That evening I waited for the red car, and it was even later than usual. In anger I walked along to Doctor Das Gupta and asked him to telephone the royal garage for me. He did so, thoroughly enjoying the use of the instrument, and when he had finished he told me that the King had just canceled my visit. Very depressed, I went back to my guesthouse. When one is in such spirits bed is as consoling a place as anywhere else, so I went to bed. I put on a thick silk nightgown, wrapped one woolen shawl about my waist and another about my shoulders. Thus I nursed my discontent and tried to read.

An hour later there was a knock on my door, and I thought that at least someone had come to keep me company, Mohan Devi or Doctor Das Gupta. So I called for whoever it was to come in. There was a screen at the door, hiding it from the view of the bed. The door opened, closed, and a man cleared his throat uncertainly. He said, "Forgive me, madam, I am your neighbor, the gentleman from Calcutta. I've brought you the latest newspapers."

I called for him to come in. He was a tall Moslem of middle age, elegantly polite. His name, he said, was Khan, and he was a lumber merchant. I was so pleased to see somebody to whom I could talk that I forgot I was in bed. I clapped my hands for the bearer and ordered tea. It was placed on a low table, and Mr. Khan sat on the bed beside it, holding a teacup in one hand, and gesturing with the other as he told me the news from India.

Perhaps life at the Happy Cottage had made it seem so only, but I believe that in Nepal my ears were hypersensitive. In the middle of one of the lumber merchant's longer stories I suddenly said, "Forgive me, Mr. Khan, but don't you hear a noise in the garden?"

He listened politely. "I hear nothing, madam."

"Mr. Khan, there is somebody there. Please go and see."

He put his cup on the table and went out, and that was the last I ever saw of Mr. Khan.

I sat waiting for him to return, scarf about my waist, scarf about my shoulders, staring over the screen to the top of the door. At last it opened softly, and there on the far wall I saw a familiar shadow of the familiar profile.

"*Namashkar*, Erika," said the King, coming round the screen and smiling.

"*Namashkar*, Your Majesty," I repeated stupidly, thinking of myself wrapped up in bed like an old woman, thinking of the tray with its two teacups. He sat down on the edge of the bed and stared at them. Beyond, in my living room, I heard the movement of feet, a murmur of voices.

"With whom have you been having tea, Erika?"

"Your Majesty, I do not know. He said his name was Khan."

"And you are in bed, having tea with someone you do not know?"

"Yes, Your Majesty."

He looked at me with a shocked gravity that was too exaggerated to be real, and then he laughed, pleased that his surprise had been more successful than he intended. He put his arm about my shoulders and sat there with me happily for an hour or more. He talked, and his conversation was no longer what it once had been, words of hope or sad frustration, but of things he was going to do, of what he could do. He got up at last and walked about my room. "You are packing?"

"I am leaving soon."

He inspected every item of my luggage, asking what leather this was, what label that. He opened every bottle of scent on my dressing table, smelling them appreciatively. Then he said, "Come and pay your *namashkars* to the others."

In dressing gown and slippers, his arm about my shoulders, I went out to the living room. There was his entourage, his aides, his equerries, his secretaries, all making humble *namashkars* to me. I said, "Gentlemen, much of what I have is packed. Is there anything I can offer you?" Making it quite plain that it would help my embarrassment to see them leave. They shook their heads, and the King said, "Now I must go."

I walked with him to his car and there touched his feet. He got into the driving seat himself, his entourage climbing in behind him. He pulled on his driving gloves, smiled once at me in great happiness, and then drove away. The road outside Tripureswar was quite deserted, and I stood alone on it, in dressing gown and slippers.

That last evening in Katmandu I was alone with him in the gardens for a little while. He put the palms of his hands together and he said, "Erika, *maffi do*. I want you to stay, but you have seen how busy I am, and I must leave for the country tomorrow." He looked carefully at my face. "Don't be sad. I shall see you in the spring. Bharati is to be married in Calcutta, and then you will see us all again."

PRINCESS BHARATI was married to the Maharajkumar Tikait Bradeep Chandra Banj Deo of Mayarbanj. The ceremony, which lasted from January 31 to February 8, was held in Darbhanga House on the corner of Chowringhi Road in Calcutta. My invitation came first in the form of a telegram from Major General Nara Shamsher Jung Bahadur Rana, and it was followed by a long list of the ceremonies which, at this sad distance, have become fused into one great picture of color, light, happiness and sorrow.

I traveled from Simla at the end of January, by car to Kalka, by night express to Delhi, and by plane from there to Calcutta. At the airport a car was waiting, flying the two crossed kukri of Nepal, and it took me to the Great Eastern. A suite of rooms had been ordered for me and filled with flowers, with cigarettes and spirits, and therein I waited for word from the King. It came abruptly, and as if he were still in Katmandu dispatching messages from Naran Hity. A telegram to the manager of the Great Eastern said: "Please send Erika immediately to Darbhanga House."

And to Darbhanga House I went, immediately. It was brilliant with colored lights, shining from every window and upon every tree and shrub in the gardens. Across the façade, above the entrance, was an electric sign, several feet deep and saying "Welcome to Nepal!" There were Nepalese servants everywhere, shoulders bent, hands together, ushering me up the stairs, through doors, along corridors. I remember a white room on the first floor, splashes of color from turbans and saris, the swing of dark *achkans* about white jodhpurs, the glitter of diamonds, the rich perfume of sandalwood and attar of roses, the singing sound of Indian voices. The crowd parted to let the queens through, and when those two gentle women saw me they opened their arms. The King arrived and I touched his feet and arose to feel his arms about my shoulders also.

Already the wedding ceremonies had begun. Every evening, every morning had its own deeply significant ritual to be performed and observed, so many of them, using up the hours of day and night eventually, that one could never have attended them all. On my second night at Darbhanga House the rooms and the gardens were full of lights and color and music, flooding out into Chowringhi Road. Behind the house was a great lawn, its green grass now an electric blue. Men and women in fabulous clothes were moving and weaving across the lawn before a great *shamyana*, a tent with a trumpetlike spire in the center. Inside were chairs, tables, sofas, rich rugs. It was lit by hanging lamps that glittered on jeweled tiaras, necklaces and rings. Servants walked swiftly among us, turning and twirling trays on the palms of their right hands.

By the side of the lawn stood the King's Gurkha pipers in scarlet and green, their cheeks puffing out as they began to shred the air with their music. While they were still playing General Nara walked into the *shamyana*, indisputably a Rana by his carriage, although a King's man now, stout and erect in his scarlet tail coat and black trousers. Behind him came the queens and Sadface, and behind them the princesses. Bharati looked beautiful, her face pale, her long lashes lowered over her eyes, somehow pathetically strange in the glasses I

had never seen her wear before. She was swathed in an orange
and gold sari, a huge diamond tiara in her hair, and diamonds
hanging from her fragile ears.

She was led to a sofa and seated there, and to her was
brought her young Maharajkumar, a young man in a golden
turban, his face as pale, his eyes as melancholy as hers.

Now the entertainment started, singers, dancers, conjurers
whirling in and out between the tables, while the Gurkhas
piped on outside and the air within the *shamyana* grew hot
and heavy. Prince and Princess sat silently, an empty, symbolic space between. Not once did they look at each other,
nor once lift their eyes from an unhappy scrutiny of the rugs
at their feet. Behind them stood the King, as handsome as
he had always been, but with a new weariness in his face.
He wore a simple khaki tunic and belt, but on his left breast
there glowed the rays of a diamond star.

I leaned over the back of the sofa between the two young
people and said, "Maharajkumar Sahib, do you like American
cigarettes?"

He looked up in surprise. "Yes, madam, I do."

"So does your bride. Here are some, now you offer one
to her." And they turned and smiled at each other for the
first time.

The ceremonies went on day after day. Marriage is as
much a sacrament to a Hindu as it is to a Christian, but to
a Hindu woman it is the only sacrament. For a girl there are
no ceremonial inductions into the great mystery and mythology of Hindu religion, nothing corresponding to the *annaprasan*, the rice-eating ceremony. She attains her religious
rights upon marriage and retains them only while married.
In this way marriage becomes not only a social duty for
Hindus but a religious duty also, and the week-long ceremonies at Darbhanga House that February were a mixture
of the sacred and the plainly joyous.

Yet one thing I hoped to see I did not see; by some over-
sight on my part it escaped me. This is the core of the marriage ceremony, the moment of union. It took place early
one morning, long before the sun had risen, and it was a
simple and terrible ceremony in which the King washed the
feet of his daughter and she handed to him, and to her
mothers, little bowls of rice, symbolic repayment of what she
had received from them.

I came to Darbhanga House at ten o'clock that morning,
long after this was over, although Bharati and her Maharajkumar were still in the temple at *puja,* their wrists bound
together by a strip of sari.

Later she came to the *shamyana* alone, and I did not ask
her where her husband was. There were few people in the
tent and she sat on a chair, suddenly pale and lost. I brought
her tea, gave her a cigarette, and made her smile.

That evening she said good-bye to her parents. All the
wedding guests were once more at Darbhanga House. Some
intuitive understanding of the significance of this farewell
led me to put on a black cocktail dress, black gloves and
scarf, and very few jewels. When I arrived at the house,
there was no music, and those lights that were not out were
dimmed. All the guests were in black, black saris, black
achkans. I was filled with mixed emotions of dread and grief,
and these were not mine alone but seemed to emanate from
everyone there.

We waited outside the house and Bharati came at last,
her hand held by her Prince as she walked toward the car.
This was lit inside and filled with flowers, and Bharati crept
into it, crouching in a corner with a silken-haired Pekingese
on her lap. I slipped to the other side and tried to comfort
her through the window, but the car suddenly moved away,
and the light inside was extinguished.

I turned to the King. His face was convulsed by great emotion. He called for his own car, leaped into it, and followed his daughter.

The guests left, and I went back into the house, passing from room to room, looking for the queens. In the corridors the ladies in waiting from Naran Hity were gathered in little black groups, silently weeping. I found Dreamy, sitting alone and crying also, but I could not find Birdy, who was Bharati's mother. I went higher in the house until at last I found her, alone in a small room. I comforted her until the King returned from his last and private farewell to his daughter. We sat in silence and drank tea, and then I left them.

I saw the King again the next day, to say good-bye to him before returning to Simla. I had dressed carefully in a scarlet dress with white polka dots, a white turban on my cropped hair. He called for me at the Great Eastern in his car, and silently we drove back to Darbhanga House. He left me there, and I wandered through to the terrace overlooking the lawn at the back. The *shamyana* was empty, the air very still. I stood there, leaning on the terrace wall, until the King came quietly behind me, gripping my shoulders and turning me about.

He was wearing a light European suit, a fresh flower in its lapel. He looked so much older than when I had first seen him, two years before in the mauve light of the tea pavilion. His face was still sad, but no longer with introspective melancholy. His sorrow was wider, more compassionate, and perhaps I should have read the message of it.

We talked for a long while in the dusk, and although I would like to remember what we said I cannot. The memory of those moments which, in retrospect, always prove to be the most valuable, are often filled with emptiness. Yet I remember saying that I did not wish to return to Simla. He took my hand consolingly and said, "We shall see each other again, in March. You know that I have another daughter?"

I knew that he was not thinking of Nalini who was married, Vijaya who was sadly ill, or even Triloki. He meant the Rajkumari Bimla who was the daughter of neither Dreamy nor Birdy, but who was his daughter. I said that I knew.

"She is being married in March. We shall see each other then."

He repeated this when we said good-bye. But I never saw him again.

$\mathcal{J}our$

"A LIGHT SHINING FROM HIS FOREHEAD"

KING TRIBHUVANA of Nepal died at three o'clock in the afternoon of Sunday, March 13, 1955. On the same day of the month, on the same day of the week, six years before, he had given me the golden bracelet.

I was in England when he died. Simla had changed a great deal in the years following the granting of independence to India. By 1952 it had become an unimportant hill town, the Mall peopled by ghosts only. My personal life also underwent changes which, although deep and irreparable, are irrelevant here. India could still work wonders on my emotions and imagination, but it no longer gave me any peace. Peepchen died in the spring of 1952, and I grieved for her, and I had no work now to occupy my thoughts. I stayed at Rookwood, one of the Patialas' homes, and there I sat on the veranda for long, sunlit hours, cross-legged. The Maharani would ask me what I was doing there all day long, and I said, "Thinking."

I do not know whether the marriage of the Rajkumari Bimla took place, I received no invitation. I wrote regularly to the King and heard from him when he was able to write. The revolution, which had seemed to be the beginning of a new life, as all revolutions must seem, had now ground itself to a halt in the bickering of politicians. Some of this state of affairs was reflected in the King's letters.

My replies go very late to my dear Erika. You must not think in your mind that I hesitate to write a letter to you. You know how much busy I am these days, so I cannot send a prompt reply to each and every letter.

Yet he did write far more often than he should, and far more often than I perhaps deserved. He came to India again in the summer of that year, and for a while we both thought that we might meet. But while in India he fell ill. He was often ill, now, as if his body were at last revolting against the great demands he had placed upon it. Nor did the unhappy state of his country give his tired heart the peace it needed. King and people were discovering that democracy is not, after all, a present given or a reward taken.

There was some trouble here. You must have read those things in the papers. Ninety percent is settled down. Still there are some troubles. Pressure of work nowadays is so much that I could not give you a prompt reply. I am very busy, hardly I get time to any recreations or to write letters.

When his favorite German boxer dog, Arlo, died, his unhappiness was great, but in telling me of it he sent me also his sympathy for the loss of Peepchen. There seemed to be nothing for me in India, now, and I came to England in October, 1952, and the horizon of my world, which had once stretched along the Himalayas, contracted to the walls of a bed-sitting room in north London. I wrote to him still. I asked him to send me something, anything that carried his initial, and he sent me a golden pin with the letter T in diamonds. I remembered his longing to travel, his childish delight in the labels on my luggage, so by return I sent him a sheaf of labels, telling him to stick them on the fine pigskin cases that had been nowhere.

Letters passed between us irregularly, now, until in the

early spring of 1953 mine were no longer answered by him
but by Hans Man Singh, his secretary.

> As His Majesty is not keeping well His Majesty is ad-
> vised by the doctors to take a complete rest.

A month later there was more alarming news from Hans
Man Singh.

> MY DEAR MISS ERIKA——His Majesty's health is giving
> such serious concern to the doctors that he is to travel to
> Zurich for treatment.

He left India by boat that summer. I sent him a cable of
loyalty and devotion, addressing it to "Mr. Shah," and in the
newspapers I saw photographs of him landing at Naples,
strange muddy photographs of a man in a dark lounge suit,
supporting himself on two sticks. He was in Zurich for some
weeks, and then he went home to Nepal, and now he was able
to write to me himself.

> I am very, very sorry that I could not see you though
> I had been to Europe for a few months. I hope that some
> day we will meet again.

We began to turn that hope into a definite proposal, and
our letters planned the journey I was to make to Katmandu
later that year. It was his idea, after I wrote of my longing
to see the valley again.

> Can you come to Nepal as my guest for a week or so?
> If you feel only convenient, and it does not harm your
> practice.

Our letters were clouded by the sudden news of Bijaya's
death. The King had grown to admire him as much as I did.
The talk that these two men had had alone on a Kashmiri
lake had wiped from the King's mind the memory of the
fact that it had been Bijaya who had surrounded the Indian

Embassy with troops and angrily demanded his return to Naran Hity Durbar. Bijaya was electrocuted one morning in New Delhi, as he took a bath. He was the favorite son of the old Prime Minister, and even in the sorrow I felt at his death I thought also of the bitter justice there was in the bereavement brought upon the Maharaja. It was as if there were some providence that stopped a tree from growing too tall in its pride.

It was agreed between the King and me that I should fly to Nepal in October 1954. As is my way, I prepared early. I sent ahead a crate of presents weighing over 100 pounds, and including, among so many things, records of *The King and I,* which the King loved. There were woolen stoles for the queens and Sadface, a tartan plaid for the King, Irish linen and gold-plated combs, even a hot-water bottle. To each one of them I also sent a Coronation five-shilling piece, wrapped with gold and silver ribbon. Then, when these presents were somewhere between England and India, his letter came.

> I shall not be here. As advised by doctors I am going outside Katmandu in the near future for treatment and change. The duration of my stay will depend on the condition of my health.

My visit was once more canceled, but I asked him to accept my presents and begged him not to return them just because I would not be there to see them opened. He wrote:

> So sorry to receive the presents in your absence. As requested by you I accepted your presents, but I could not enjoy them as they were not offered personally. Very sorry I could not see you in Europe last time. I hope to meet you this time somewhere in Europe in case I should be there. But you know I have to travel as a patient and stay either in the clinic or the hospital. Will have to act up to the instructions of the doctor.

So he came to Europe again that November, and, long afterward, I read that he spoke to the crowds who gathered to see him leave Nepal, and he said, "I do not know if I ever shall see you again."

All through the winter of 1954–55 I heard nothing from the Zurich clinic where he was staying. I passed that terrible time by planning to meet him on the Riviera in the spring, when he would see the places which our fingers had once traced on the great globe in his study at the Happy Cottage.

That Sunday evening in March I was in the little flat which I had rented, glad to be free from the prison of a bed-sitting room. Mother was with me, and a friend. The radio was playing in my bedroom and I was scarcely listening to it. The music ended and a voice began to read the news, telling me that three hours before Tribhuvana had died. I stood quite still in the center of the room, with Mother staring at me in alarm, and my friend, who knew nothing of my life in Nepal, carelessly humming "Under the Bridges of Paris."

I do not like to remember the days that followed. One cannot recall the real pain of grief any more than one can wholly recapture the extreme emotion of happiness. A scar is left behind to remind one that there has been great anguish, but to describe the pain is impossible. I know that it was important for me to learn all that I could about the King's last days, to see it as if I had been there. I wrote to Professor Luffler, the director of the University Medical Clinic in Zurich. I told him that I had been a close friend of the Nepalese Royal Family, and that the King's death had been a great and terrible blow to me. I would be grateful, I said, if he could tell me the things I wished to know. He replied with understanding.

King Tribhuvana came to us first in November 1953. The journey from Nepal to Switzerland was difficult for him, even in those days, and because his heart failed him during the sea journey he had to make a stop at Naples.

We were able to help him, after great efforts, to the extent that he was remarkably better in a while, and physically able to return to Nepal. Home in his own country he felt well enough until, in June last year, complications set in that brought him close to death. Against all expectations, however, he recovered, and he declared that he would come to us again in November 1954. We were alarmed about his visit, for our information about him was very grave.

When he came his condition was indeed much worse than it had been the year before, although an improvement had been noticed in the summer. While he was with us this second time we thought him well enough to take a trip to Nice by plane, but another heart attack occurred on January 31. I saw His Majesty on February 2 and 3, and then regularly with Professor Parkinson from London and Professor Lauder from Vienna. After a satisfying recovery from this heart attack in Nice the King unfortunately contracted influenza, which of course was very dangerous for his heart. The planned return to Zurich had to be postponed.

We were able to bring him back here in a special train on Wednesday, March 9, and we were surprised by how well he managed this journey. He felt very well in the clinic, recovering remarkably well during the first few days, although our prognosis was unfavorable. His death was unexpected and took place on March 13 at three o'clock in the afternoon. The King did not suffer, but from his remarks we concluded that he was often thinking of death. Repeatedly he asked the sisters, "Am I to die tonight?"

His Majesty was very popular with us all and we were very sorry we could not do more for him. His death has touched us very deeply. His body was taken away from the clinic on Wednesday, March 16, at 7.15 A.M. It was covered with flowers and escorted by eight Swiss officers and two Nepalese generals, as well as our sisters, doctors, and civic officials of Zurich. It was taken to the airport and accorded full military honors by the Swiss Army. The Queens were not present at the time of death. I saw them once only, and they appeared to be greatly upset. They boarded the plane beforehand and took no part in the ceremonies.

Death did not change His Majesty.

In London I went everywhere for news of the King's death and his last departure for Nepal, and I discovered the instinctive kindness there is in all British people, their sympathy and understanding. When I approached the librarian of *The Times* he gave me clippings of all stories which the paper had published about the King's last days. In northwest London a newsreel company screened for me again and again its film of the scene at Zurich Airport. The BBC Television Service did the same for me. I obtained a copy of the film and sent it to Birdy and Dreamy, and then there was nothing more I could do for the King, except fulfill my promise and write about him.

The King was taken home to his country and to the burning ghats at Pashupattinath. The Indian Air Force plane that carried his body landed at Gaochar at twenty-five minutes past noon on March 17. Its propellers were still turning when the first of forty-nine guns sounded on the *maidan*. A great crowd of weeping men and women watched as the body was borne from the aircraft to the silver palanquin in which, as a child, he had ridden to his coronation. Two hundred thousand Nepalese lined the road from Goachar to the Bhagmati. I remember that road, and I can see it still. There are broad stones drifted with dust and leaves, and the rise and fall of hump-backed bridges of pink brick. A yellow road, threading through green fields.

All Nepal mourned the King. Men shaved their heads and wore no leather on their feet, dressing as I had seen Lala Ram dressed that day when he welcomed me to the guesthouse. For thirteen days no Nepalese took salt, ate more than one meal between dawn and dawn, or slept on anything but straw. Mahendra, the shy young man in sunglasses who was now king and incarnation of Vishnu, was, by tradition, exempted from *kriya*, this demonstration of mourning, but he voluntarily imposed it upon himself and grieved with his family.

The funeral ceremony at the burning ghats of Pashupattinath was moving and terrible. The terraced steps on either bank of the river were strewn with flowers, and the petals were crushed beneath the feet of thousands of mourners. The *sraddha*, the mystic rites of death, were performed within a black tent. There Tribhuvana lay on a stone carved with serpents, his feet toward the water so that his soul might pass thus to heaven. A Brahmin cut a piece of flesh the size of a small dove from about the King's navel. Weighted with golden coins this was buried on a small island in the center of the Bhagmati, and the lighted tapers above it fluttered in the breathing of those who silently watched.

A sliver of bone was next taken from the King's forehead and placed in a golden casket. Holding this in his hands a Brahmin set out to walk to Redi, eight days distant, where he would bury the casket in the middle of the sacred River Gandakh. In time the bone would turn to ammonite, the spiral markings of which resemble the discus of Vishnu.

As thirty-one guns began to fire their slow salute, the oil-anointed body of Tribhuvana was placed on its pyre and the wood ignited. Thus passed what was mortal of him.

Now the Mahabrahmin, the poor priest called Sri Krishna Bhatta who had performed the funeral ceremony, turned his thoughts toward India. He was no longer poor. For thirteen days he lived in the King's palace, sleeping in the King's bed, smoking the King's cigarettes, waited upon and taking what he wished of the King's possessions. The royal kitchens prepared what he desired, but the food was deliberately contaminated by a paste made from the bone of the King's forehead.

For his services he received gifts worth 200,000 rupees. He received 10,000 rupees in alms. He received two elephants and a richly caparisoned horse, as well as cooking utensils and bedding. These were his reward for taking upon his shoulders the demons released by the King's death, although I do not believe this burden can have been heavy.

He mounted one of his elephants and turned it toward exile in India. The people of Katmandu and Thankot lined the road to stone him and to jeer, calling, "He who rides an elephant steals its corn!"

When the Mahabrahmin had gone, over the mountain pathway to India, the people of Katmandu turned back to the city. There were many foreign journalists in Nepal who had come to see the funeral, and one of them stopped a poor Nepalese on the Thankot Road and asked him why he wept so for Tribhuvana.

The old man replied, "He was God. I have seen a light shining from his forehead."

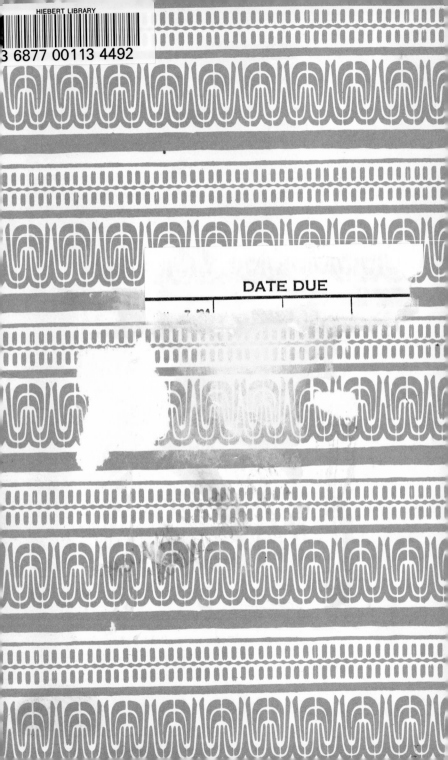

DATE DUE